TEACHER'S BOOK

CAROL NUTT

UPPER INTERMEDIATE
OUTCOMES

Eagle House, Lynchborough Road,
Passfield, Hampshire, GU30 7SB, UK
T +44(0) 1428751549
F +44(0) 1428751970
Email: enquiries@ejo.co.uk
Website: www.ejo.co.uk

EJO

HEINLE
CENGAGE Learning™

Australia • Brazil • Japan • Korea • Mexico • Singapore • Spain • United Kingdom • United States

HEINLE
CENGAGE Learning

Outcomes *Upper Intermediate Teacher's Book*
Carol Nuttall and David Evans

Publisher: Jason Mann

Commissioning Editor: John Waterman

Development Editor: Heidi North

Product Manager: Ruth McAleavey

Content Project Editor: Amy Smith

Production Controller: Paul Herbert

Cover and text designer: Studio April

Compositor: Q2AMedia

ISBN: 978-1-1110-3405-4

Heinle, Cengage Learning EMEA
Cheriton House, North Way, Andover, Hampshire
SP10 5BE United Kingdom

Cengage Learning is a leading provider of customised learning solutions with office locations around the globe, including Singapore, the United Kingdom, Australia, Mexico, Brazil and Japan. Locate our local office at **international.cengage.com/region**

Cengage Learning products are represented in Canada by Nelson Education Ltd.

Visit Heinle online at **elt.heinle.com**
Visit our corporate website at **cengage.com**

Printed in Singapore
1 2 3 4 5 6 7 8 9 10 – 14 13 12 11 10

CONTENTS

INTRODUCTION

WHAT'S IN *OUTCOMES* STUDENT'S BOOK?

16 units based round common topics Each unit has three interlinked 'lessons' of 50–90 minutes. The unit contents give clear practical outcomes. The first lesson teaches language leading to *Conversation Practice*. The second and third spreads develop reading or listening and teach more grammar and vocabulary connected with the topic.

8 writing units The two-page writing units on pp.120–135 teach different types of writing for everyday life and exams. Each has a model text, *Grammar* or *Vocabulary, Keywords for writing* and *Practice*.

4 Review units Each review has a learner training discussion, two pages of games, tasks and pronunciation exercises to revise language and then a two-page test including a listening exercise.

Grammar Thirty-two points of grammar are covered. Each *Grammar* section links to the previous text. An explanation or guided questions teach meaning. Exercises give controlled and freer practice. There's a link to the Grammar reference if you need extra help.

Grammar reference This is on pp. 136–155 at the back of the book. Each section has an expanded explanation, further natural examples of usage and extra controlled practice exercises with a glossary.

Language patterns This is a short translation exercise into students' own language and back into English. It draws attention to other aspects of syntax and grammar based on a pattern seen in a text.

Vocabulary Vocabulary is carefully chosen to enable students to talk about the topic in the context of English as a lingua franca. Tasks generally move from meaning, to contextualised usage to personalised practice. Other sections focus on word-building.

***Outcomes* Vocabulary Builder** The separate booklet allows students to look up meaning of new language which is key to learn, offers several examples of collocations and usage plus a page of revision practice.

Native speaker English Draws attention to common words or phrases that fluent speakers use, which students may hear or want to learn.

Keywords Most writing units have a focus on linking words and patterns, which help develop fluent, coherent writing.

There's a link to the text, a short explanation and practice exercises.

Developing conversations The sections teach typical questions, responses and patterns common to conversation. An explanation clarifies the focus while exercises give controlled practice.

Conversation practice A task lets students practise social and practical conversations based on their own experience or through role-play.

Speaking These sections give students the chance to exchange ideas. The final speaking task in each unit is a variety of longer tasks that draw the language and / or the themes of the unit together.

Listening These sections are introduced with a short description of the context. There is usually a pre-listening speaking task to generate interest or predict content, followed by tasks to guide students to understand the text and focus on vocabulary.

Reading These sections are introduced with a short description of the context. There is usually a pre-reading speaking task to generate interest or predict content, followed by tasks to guide students to understand the text and focus on vocabulary.

WHAT'S IN *OUTCOMES* TEACHER'S BOOK?

The Teacher's book is organised into three sections: Teacher's notes, Writing lessons and Communication activities. TEACHER'S NOTES provide guidance on how to use the 16 units and four REVIEWS in the Student's book. Each unit opens with a brief UNIT OVERVIEW that allows you to understand the main elements of the lesson very quickly.

Under the same headings as in the Student's book, the notes give clear aims and simple steps to provide a very easy path through the material. Answer boxes and audioscripts embedded in the notes ensure you have everything you need at your fingertips. Suggestions throughout the notes help you with ways to set up activities, check and clarify meaning, monitor, conduct feedback, etc. An icon 👥 indicates where you might want to use a **Communication Activity** (see next page). In addition, there's help through four mini features.

The **TIP** feature offers ideas on things such as:
- other ways to check meaning;
- how to adapt material for different groups such as mono or multilingual classes;
- bringing extra material into lessons.

The **NOTE** feature gives bite-size information about:
- places and people in the text;
- how cultures can differ.

The **ALTERNATIVELY** feature provides:
- a different way to stage an activity than the one suggested in the Student's book;
- ideas on how to make an activity more or less challenging.

The **OPTIONAL ACTIVITY** suggests:
- ways to extend an activity if students need to do more work.

The **WRITING LESSONS** section opens with a two-page introduction on teaching writing. It explains the approach to writing and suggests ways you can provide feedback to students. The introduction is followed by **Teacher's notes** and the answer key for the eight writing lessons.

The Communication activities section contains simple instructions on how to use the 32 photocopiable activities. The activities are designed to revise key grammar and vocabulary from the Student's book in a fun and varied way. There are quizzes, word puzzles, questionnaires, games, information gaps and short role-plays. Each unit has two activities calculated to take 10–15 minutes of class time.

OTHER *OUTCOMES* COMPONENTS

Outcomes Workbook The *Outcomes* Workbook thoroughly revises all the language areas that are in the Student's book. Each unit also has:
- a listening and a reading with tasks based on topics loosely connected to the theme of the unit and providing interest and extra challenges to students.
- **Developing Writing** that focuses on types of text students might write in their academic, professional and personal lives and further work on relevant language.

The *Outcomes* **Workbook** also comes with:
- **Audio CD** of recordings of the listening and reading texts.
- **Answer key** and **Audioscript** to aid self-study.

Outcomes **ExamView®** Writing tests to check your students' progress takes a lot of time and work but the **ExamView®** CD allows you to create tests and exams in as little as five minutes. What's more:
- all the tests are closely based on the Student's book.
- the software also generates the answer key.
- it provides a variety of exercise types (True / False, Multiple Choice, Yes / No, Matching, Short answer, etc.)
- tests can be printed, computer-based, or on the Internet.
- you can easily edit the questions and add your own.
- you can save all tests for another time.
- it's easy to reorder questions to avoid cheating.

MyOutcomes **online resource** Every copy of the *Outcomes* Student's Book has a unique code at the front of the book which provides access to My*Outcomes* online resource where they will find additional work on all the elements of the Student's book. There are:
- over 230 activities practising the grammar, vocabulary, pronunciation and conversations in the 16 units.
- additional listening, reading and speaking practice.
- reviews every four units to test students' progress.

Teachers can also use the online resource if they apply for an access code. Go to **myelt.heinle.com** and request an MyELT instructor account. This will allow you to set specific work for all your students and then receive their results. You can then store these results through the **Grade book**, so both you and your students have a record of their marks and progress.

OUTCOMES UPPER-INTERMEDIATE

In this introduction we try to answer these questions:
What are the goals of language students?
What is key language for students at this level?
What is key for teachers to help them teach?

KEY GOALS

The Common European Framework of reference (CEF) states that language learning and teaching overall goals should be:
1.1 to deal with the business of everyday life in another country, and to help foreigners staying in their own country to do so;
1.2 to exchange information and ideas with young people and adults who speak a different language and to communicate their thoughts and feelings to them;
1.3 to achieve a wider and deeper understanding of the way of life and forms of thought of other peoples and of their cultural heritage.
(Council of Europe, 2001, p3)

These ideas underpin everything we do in the *Outcomes* series. At Upper-Intermediate, we look at can-do statements for B2 level as a guide to what students might want to achieve.

Business of everyday life You can see the communicative areas that are dealt with in the *how to* sections of the contents and title strip that heads each unit. *Outcomes* has a strong practical thread. For example, students at Upper-Intermediate learn the grammar and vocabulary to:
- show people around your town / city pp. 14–15
- be more polite in business contexts pp. 110–111

For many students passing exams is also the business of everyday life, which is why *Outcomes* has a GRAMMAR REFERENCE with exercises on all the grammar you'd expect. Similarly, WRITING deals with both practical types of writing (formal and informal emails pp. 134–135) and exam-type writing (arguing your case pp. 132–133).

Communicating thoughts and feelings Practicalities are important, but just as important, and perhaps more motivating, is the ability to communicate in a way which reflects your personality, feelings and opinions. That's why most of the DEVELOPING CONVERSATIONS and CONVERSATION PRACTICE work towards practising typical conversations we have to establish and maintain friendships:

- disagreeing politely pp. 8–9
- passing on messages pp. 82–83

This is also why we constantly give students the chance to exchange their ideas, through SPEAKING, practice activities in VOCABULARY and GRAMMAR, the lead-ins to READING and LISTENING and discussions about the texts.

Understanding other cultures Students will best understand other cultures by talking with other students, which the various speaking activities in *Outcomes* always encourage. However, many classrooms may not have people from a large mix of backgrounds, which is why we use texts with international contexts and reflecting other cultures throughout the world – including Britain. Students come to realise they share many of the same desires and concerns! Among others, you'll read and hear about:

- living in another country pp. 46–47
- Chinese folktales pp. 100–101

Native speaker notes also draw attention to ways fluent speakers express themselves, which may be different to the neutral international language that we generally present.

KEY LANGUAGE

There were five guides to the input at Upper-Intermediate level – the communicative outcomes (outlined in *Outcomes Goals*), the frequency of words, 'naturalness' of usage, student autonomy and teacher–student expectations or interest.

For example, to describe films, music and books (pp. 8–13) students need to know a number of core adjectives which are presented and practiced in VOCABULARY. The practice gets them to think of language which might go with these words and the OVB provides further help in terms of collocations. GRAMMAR looks at adjectives and adverbs we typically use when talking about feelings and provides a fuller context for the vocabulary. LANGUAGE PATTERNS draws attention to the language around the chunk *(not) the kind of thing*. LISTENING then gives a model conversation. DEVELOPING CONVERSATIONS teaches expressions to disagree politely. PRONUNCIATION is based on the phrases they've learnt.

This is typical of the way language input is focused on helping students achieve the stated communicative outcome, but not all language learning can be developed in this way. A lot of vocabulary may be very frequent but not specific to any one topic (e.g. issue, unlike, refer). The language highlighted through texts is largely of this nature. The exercises and OVB, then show a range of natural collocations. Similarly, some grammar may

not be fundamental to a conversation in the way we saw with 'describing films, music and books'. Here, we make the choice based on what students and teachers expect to be covered at this level or have tested in exams. This may be 'exam grammar', but we try to give natural sounding examples.

Input is also decided on the basis that students need to learn outside the classroom. The *word families* strand in VOCABULARY, the OVB language boxes and READING, shows students how words are formed. This helps them recognise and learn new words in their own studies. The same motives underlie LANGUAGE PATTERNS, but with a focus on grammar.

Finally, students and non-native speaker teachers often express an interest in colloquial language and idioms. The NATIVE SPEAKER NOTE provides explanations and examples of this in contrast to the normal input which can be freely used and understood in contexts where English is a lingua franca.

KEY TO LEARN

There are many ways to learn but it seems there are a few essentials:

- Students need to notice.
- Students need to understand.
- Students need to practise – spoken, written, receptive.
- Students need to make mistakes.
- Students need to repeat these steps a lot.

Noticing and understanding Obviously the exercises in GRAMMAR and VOCABULARY encourage students to notice and understand. Visuals and clear explanations of vocabulary and examples of collocations in the OVB, reinforce meaning. The LANGUAGE PATTERNS exercise trains students to notice and consider how English compares with their own language.

Practice Students always have chance to practise language. This goes from very controlled 'remember and test', and gap-fills to freer role-play and personalised speaking. COMMUNICATION ACTIVITIES in this Teacher's book provide more practice.

Making mistakes Not all teaching and input can or should be provided by the coursebook. We all know from experience and research that people learn new language when they are struggling to express something and the 'correct' or better word is given. This is also why we have lots of speaking activities. They are not just opportunities for students to practise what they know; they are chances for them to try to say something new, stretch themselves and make mistakes, which you can then correct.

Repetition Seeing a word once is not enough! Some say you need to see and understand vocabulary ten times before you have learnt to use it! Maybe grammar takes even longer. Recycling and Revision is therefore a key part of the design of *Outcomes*. For example, the OVB, WORKBOOK and EXAMVIEW® allow unit-by-unit revision, while REVIEW after every four units ensures further revision at a later date.

With grammar, students can revise after the class by using the Grammar reference and exercises, the Workbook or the My outcomes online resource. Grammar structures are often looked at in several contexts over the course and at various levels. Review units test grammar and you can also create tests with ExamView®.

Apart from this revision we try to repeatedly re-use language from Vocabulary in Listening and Reading; in Grammar and Grammar Reference; in Developing conversations; in workbook texts; in exercises and texts in other units of the Student's book and even in other levels of the series. And as we have seen, Speaking and Conversation practice allow students to re-use language they've learnt.

In terms of speaking, research suggests that students can improve performance with repetition. Within the first two pages of each unit there are often several opportunities to have conversations around the same topic as we saw with 'describing films, music and books' through Vocabulary or Grammar practice, Developing conversations and Conversation practice. The Review units also encourage students to look back and repeat speaking tasks. There are also more ideas about revision in the Teacher's notes.

Key TO TEACH

Most teachers need or want material that:
- is quick and easy to prepare
- caters for mixed level classes
- motivates students

Quick and easy to prepare A coursebook is easy to use when the relation between input and outcomes is clear and we hope you already see that is the case with *Outcomes*. However, other aspects of the design should help you just pick up the book and teach:
- limited number of sections appear in all units.
- a regular structure to the units.
- a variety of familiar tasks.
- double-pages can exist as unique lessons but six-page units allow you greater flexibility.
- Straightforward rubrics in the Student's book fully explain tasks.
- Grammar and Vocabulary have clear links to texts.
- OVB follows the spreads of the book so you and students can easily look up words in class.

Mixed level classes Students often start at different levels within a class and so the input in *Outcomes* Upper-Intermediate revises and extends language encountered at Intermediate. However, the exercises and design of *Outcomes* also works for multi-level classes.
- **OVB** The *Outcomes* Vocabulary Builder allows weaker students to easily look up new words, before, during and after class, because it follows the spreads of the book. Stronger students benefit from the **OVB** because it gives extra input through collocation lists, extra language boxes and practice exercises.

- **Grammar** The short explanations help weaker students with exercises in the units. The Grammar reference helps weaker students with more examples, but stronger students will like the extra information that is always given.
- **Easy to difficult** Whether it is grammar or vocabulary, reading or listening, we usually move from easier to more difficult tasks in each section. For example, reading texts often allow language to be pre-taught, the first tasks are then based on general understanding and further tasks are more detailed.
- **Translation** Several exercises including Language Patterns encourage students to translate. Translation is particularly important for weaker students who benefit from the support of their mother tongue and bilingual dictionaries. In monolingual classes, especially, it allows stronger students to help others in the class by providing the translations.
- **Test and remember** Tasks like this are comforting for weaker students, but they can also be made more challenging for stronger students by asking them to remember more.
- **Native speaker notes** and **Language patterns** These offer extra input for stronger students and classes. You might consider dropping them for weaker classes.
- **Teacher's notes** There are loads more ideas for dealing with multi level classes in this book – particularly through the Tip and Alternatively features.

Motivating students As a teacher motivating students will be a major part of your job however, we know a coursebook can often work against student motivation by having irrelevant or boring content, unclear, unrealistic or unfulfilled outcomes or simply by a dull design. *Outcomes* helps you motivate students by having:
- outcomes matching students wants and needs
- a clear menu of input and outcomes at the start of each unit
- input and tasks that carefully match those outcomes
- a manageable number of keywords to learn in the OVB
- texts based on authentic sources that we think you'll find by turns informative, funny, even moving
- a range of speaking tasks that allow for play, humour and gossip, as well as serious discussion
- a fresh design with bright, interesting illustration

The CEF and Level There is not a direct correlation between publishers' levels and the CEF: completing Intermediate will not mean a student has reached B2 and completing Upper-Intermediate is not equivalent to reaching C1. That's because the CEF descriptions of level or the ALTE can-do statements do *not* exactly describe content, but describe someone's *performance* in a language. We have used can-do statements from the B2 level at Upper-Intermediate as a guide to what tasks and outcomes students want to achieve. However, students' performance in *doing* any of the speaking, reading, listening or writing tasks may be assessed using CEF scales as being B2 (+). If students are regularly outside the range of B1(+), B2 (+) they are probably at the wrong level for this material!

01 ENTERTAINMENT

UNIT OVERVIEW
The main aim of this unit is to enable students to talk about pictures and **to describe films, music and books.** They have practice in **disagreeing politely** and**talking about their impressions of paintings.** The main grammatical focus is **talking about habits** and ways of using **adjectives and adverbs** to express their opinions.

 Next class Make photocopies of **1A** p. 129.

SPEAKING

Aim
To lead in to the lesson and allow students to introduce themselves to each other.

Step 1 Tell students to think about their interests and what they do in their spare time. Then, put them into pairs to discuss. Ask them to find out what they have in common. Monitor closely and help out with any language problems.

GRAMMAR Habits

Aim
To present and practise useful expressions related to the frequency of habits.

Step 1 Tell students they are going to listen to eight answers people gave to different questions using the structure *Do you . . . . much?* Ask them to identify what each speaker is talking about the first time they listen. Play the recording and ask them to compare their answers in pairs; if necessary, play the recording again before checking in open class.

Answers
1 go shopping, go to the cinema, go clubbing sometimes
2 listen to music on his mp3 player
3 going to the theatre
4 go swimming
5 watch TV
6 play sports
7 go to the cinema
8 play computer games.

🔊 1.1
1: Yeah, at the weekends, of course. I go shopping, go to the cinema, go clubbing sometimes. I don't tend to during the week, though, because I've got to get up early for school and I've got homework, and basically my parents prefer me to stay at home.
2: Yeah, all the time. I take my mp3 player with me everywhere – it's, like, glued to my ears! All kinds of stuff as well – rock, pop, even some classical.
3: Not as much as I'd like to, because I really love it – especially musicals. I mean, I do go now and again, but the seats are so expensive I can't afford to go more than a couple of times a year.
4: I guess I might in the summer – if it's very hot. I find it a bit boring, just going up and down the pool. It's not really my kind of thing – and I'm not very good at it either.
5: Probably less than I think I do, if you know what I mean. It's always on in the background, you know, but I don't pay much attention to it most of the time. I will watch a big game if there's one on and the occasional film, but apart from that, most of it's rubbish.
6: Yeah, I guess so. I usually play football on a Wednesday and I go running now and again. I generally cycle to college as well – unless it's raining.
7: No, not as a rule. I tend to wait for films to come out on cable as I've got a nice, big, flat-screen TV at home. Oh, and I download quite a lot of stuff too.
8: Not as much as I used to. I was addicted to *The Sims* for a while until my parents banned me. I would sometimes play for five hours a day! I play other games now, but my parents control it a bit more.

Step 2 Tell students to listen again and write the question they think each person was asked. In pairs, they should compare answers before checking in open class.

Step 3 Tell students to listen again and complete the gaps individually with the correct expression. Before playing, check if they can remember any of the expressions. Check in pairs before checking in open class.

🔊 1.2 and Answers
1 I don't **tend to** during the week though.
2 **Yeah all the time!** I take my mp3 player with me everywhere.
3 Not as much **as I'd like to,** because I really love it.
4 **Very rarely,** to be honest, I guess I might in the summer.
5 I don't pay much attention to it most of the time. **I will watch** a big game, if there's one on...
6 Yeah, I guess so. I usually play football on a Wednesday and I go running **now and again.**
7 No, **not as a rule.** I tend to wait for films to come out on cable.
8 Not as much as **I used to.** I was addicted to *The Sims* for a while until my parents banned me. I would sometimes play for five hours a day!

Direct students to the grammar reference on page 136 if they still seem unsure.

Step 4 Get students to complete the sentences individually so that they are true for them. Monitor their use of language for a correction slot at the end. In pairs ask them to compare their statements. Do a correction slot on the board, write up examples of the correct and incorrect language and get students in pairs to identify and correct the incorrect language. Check in open class.

Step 5 Remind students of the structure *Do you . . . much?* and get them to write five questions. Give them some time to write their questions. Then, put students in pairs to ask and answer their questions and remind them to use the expressions from exercise B. Monitor and help out with any language problems. In open class do brief feedback on their language performance.

NATIVE SPEAKER ENGLISH

In English, people often use a general word when the topic is already known, *stuff* is a common expression like *thing*. Ask students what the sentences in the box could refer to, e.g. films, books.

VOCABULARY
Describing films, music and books

Aim
To introduce and practise using pairs of adjectives to describe opinions about films, music and books.

Step 1 Get students to read out the explanation box. Check understanding by asking, *Which word is repeated in each sentence?* (1 = *really*, 2 = *incredibly*), and *Why are they repeated?* (to add emphasis).

Step 2 Get students to look at the words in the box and check understanding and word stress of *dull* = not very interesting, *gripping* = keeps you interested, *disturbing* = make you feel extremely worried or upset, *catchy* = easy to remember, *over-the-top* = someone or something that is too extreme and seems silly, *weird* = very strange, *hilarious* = extremely funny, *uplifting* = makes you feel happier. Individually students complete the sentences and then compare in pairs. Check in open class.

Step 3 Elicit examples of films, books or music that fit the descriptions in exercise A. In pairs get students to discuss their opinions. Monitor and help out with pronunciation of the target language. Do brief feedback in open class.

DEVELOPING CONVERSATIONS
Disagreeing politely

Aim
To introduce students to different ways of disagreeing politely and give controlled practice of these.

Step 1 Get students to read the explanation box and check understanding: Is it the kind of thing the person likes? (No.) How do we know? (*It's not really . . .*) If we say *It's not my kind of thing*, do we sound polite? (No.) Tell them that when we want to soften our responses and be more polite, we use *not really, not that* and *a bit*.

Step 2 Get students to read the statements and responses and check any unknown vocabulary. Individually students match the responses and then compare in pairs and underline the expressions using *really, not that* and *a bit*. Check in open class.

> **Answers**
> 1 f = a bit more modern
> 2 a = I'm not that keen on
> 3 c = I'm not that keen on
> 4 e = It didn't really do anything for me
> 5 d = I'm not that keen on
> 6 b = I'm not really interested
> 7 h = a bit too poppy
> 8 g = a bit dull, a bit boring

Step 3 Put students in pairs or threes and ask them to tell each other about films, books and music they like and why. If their partner disagrees, tell them to use any of the underlined expressions in exercise B. Feedback in open class.

> **1A** see Teacher's notes p. 120.

LISTENING

Aim
To provide practice on listening and taking notes.

Step 1 Tell students they will hear two people taking about films and to take notes on how their tastes are the same or different. Briefly check *heavy* = something that is depressing (in this context). Play the recording, get students to compare in pairs and check in open class.

Tip With weaker students, you could divide them into As and Bs. Ask the As to take notes on what the first speaker says. Bs take notes on what the second speaker says.

> **Answers**
> **Similar** = they both like films, both like action films, although different ones,
> **different** = second speaker goes to the cinema most weeks, the first speaker waits for the DVD, first speaker didn't like *Old Boy* and the second speaker really liked it.

> **1.3**
> A: Do go to the cinema much?
> B: Yeah, a fair bit, I suppose. I tend to go most weeks.
> A: Really? That's a lot.
> B: Yeah, I guess so. I'd go more if I could though! What about you?
> A: Not that often, no – not unless I really want to see something that I know isn't going to come out on DVD for a while.
> B: Mmm. So what kind of things are you into?
> A: I don't know. All sorts, really, but I guess mainly action films.
> B: Such as?

> A: I don't know. I really·liked the first *Blade* film, *X-Men*, stuff like that.
> B: OK. Did you see *Old Boy* last night? It was on TV.
> A: Yeah, I started watching it, but I turned over.
> B: You didn't like it?
> A: It was so over-the-top, just so disgusting and then the plot! I don't know. It was all a bit too weird for my liking.
> B: Really? I love that film – the look of it, the music everything. It's just amazing. I think it's the fifth time I've seen it.
> A: Really? As I say, it was OK, but it's not really my kind of thing. Too much like horror really.
> B: I suppose so.
> A: So apart from *Old Boy,* what kind of stuff do you like?
> B: Oh, all kinds of things. As I say, I go most weeks, so you know . . . action films, comedies, foreign films - anything, really.
> A: Have you seen *Gold Diggers*?
> B: Yeah. Have you?
> A: No, but I've heard it's good. I was thinking of going to see it.
> B: I don't know. It is good, but it's pretty heavy, I found it quite disturbing, really. It's not the kind of thing you can watch and just switch off.
> A: Oh right. Maybe I'll give it a miss then.

Step 2 Get students to read the questions in B and in pairs check what they can remember. Then play the recording again. Check in open class.

> **Answers**
> 1 Speaker A: not that often, Speaker B: most weeks.
> 2 Speaker A: all sorts, action films, Speaker B: action films, comedies, foreign films, anything.
> 3 Speaker A: *Old Boy,* Speaker B: *Gold Diggers*.
> 4 Speaker A: over-the-top, disgusting, didn't like the plot, Speaker B: good but heavy, quite disturbing.

Tip Get students to read the audioscript on page 164 and underline any new or useful expressions. Compare in pairs. In open class go through any problems and share useful phrases.

LANGUAGE PATTERNS

Aim
To raise awareness of patterns with *the kind of*.

Step 1 Individually get students to read the explanation box and notice the pattern, *It's (not) the kind of . . .* thing / music / film. Tell them we use this to give a personal opinion about things we have seen, heard or read. Check understanding by getting them to explain what it refers to, e.g. sentence 1 = a good documentary, 2 = pop music.

Step 2 Ask students to translate the sentences into their own language. In monolingual classes, ask students to compare their translation. In multilingual classes, ask students to work in pairs and tell each other if the sentences were easy to translate into their language.

Step 3 Ask students to cover their English translations and use their translation to translate the sentences back into English. Then ask them to compare their translations in pairs against the book and discuss: who had the least mistakes, and what mistakes did they make? Why? Alternatively, if you prefer not to use translation ask students to notice the pattern, you could ask students for example sentences. Write the examples on the board and if they're wrong ask students to correct them or correct them yourself.

CONVERSATION PRACTICE

Aim
To practise the language learnt so far.

Step 1 Get students into new pairs to ask each other some questions starting *Do you read / listen to music / watch TV / go to the cinema much?* . Encourage them to use as much language as possible from their Student's books. Monitor and help out with any language.

Step 2 Do brief feedback in open class and then highlight any useful language or problems from monitoring.

 pp. 10–11

SPEAKING

Aim
To provide practise talking about art.

Step 1 Get students to look at the vocabulary box and check understanding: *product design* = the way a product is presented and packaged, *animation* = cartoons, *pop videos* = *music videos* to promote a song. Ask students to give examples of each type of art, e.g. *graffiti* is usually found on walls around the city or on public transport.

Step 2 In pairs or threes students discuss if they would classify them as art and why – and if not, why not. Then put students into small groups to discuss the questions. Monitor without interrupting and take notes on the language they use, vocabulary they needed and any errors.

Step 3 Do feedback in open class on the questions. Then write up the language you noted while monitoring, praising them on any good language, helping them develop their vocabulary and getting them to correct their mistakes.

Tip Get students to have a page in their notebooks where they write the feedback. Tell them to use the back of their notebook and make three boxes: vocabulary, grammar and pronunciation. Each time they make a mistake, they should

record it here. The next time they have a speaking activity, they should review their own typical mistakes and pay attention to them while speaking.

VOCABULARY Talking about pictures

Aim
To develop vocabulary related to talking about pictures.

Step 1 In pairs get students to look at the definitions. Tell them to decide which ones relate to the pictures.

Suggested answers
Statements 1, 6, 8, 9

Step 2 Get students to look at the sentences in exercise B and check understanding. Sentence 2 = Is she literally pulling her hair out? (No, it just seems that way.) Get them to notice the pattern after look and write on the board, e.g. *look + like + noun phrase, look + as if + clause*. Tell them we use this to say something seems that way but we are not sure. In pairs discuss which of the sentences about the Edward Munch picture they agree with. Do brief feedback in open class.

Step 3 Give students three minutes to memorise the phrases in exercise B. Then individually get them to complete the sentences in exercise C without looking. Compare in pairs and then check in open class.

Answers		
1 well	3 impression, look	5 must, like
2 as if / like	4 both	6 seems

LISTENING

Aim
To develop listening for specific information. To expose students to the adjectives and adverbs used in *Listening*.

Step 1 Tell students they are going to hear a guide in an art gallery telling a group of visitors about one of the paintings on the page, *Mr & Mrs Clark and Percy* by David Hockney and *Arnolfini* by Jan van Eyck. Get students to tell you what they can see in the two paintings. Then in pairs ask them to discuss the questions in A. Conduct brief feedback. With a weaker group write the painters' names on the board and complete with their suggestions. Also revise vocabulary from exercise A.

Step 2 Tell students to listen and answer the question in exercise B. After listening they compare in pairs, play the recording again and check answers in open class.

Answers
1 1971
2 Mr & Mrs Clark and Percy (the cat)

3 David Hockney's painting is loosely based on the one by Jan van Eyck although the positions are reversed
4 The lilies represent female purity and the cat symbolises infidelity and jealousy: Mr Clark had frequent affairs before and during their five-year marriage
5 Mr Clark fell into bankruptcy and addiction. His life ended tragically when he was murdered by an ex-lover in 1996. Mrs Clark continued to be one of Hockney's regular models for years
6 life-like, abstract, ambiguous, intimate

1.4

Now if you follow me through into the next room, we come to a far more modern piece of work, dating in fact from 1971. On the surface, this may strike you as a fairly conventional, life-like portrait. To the left, there's a young woman standing in front of an open door, and looking directly at the viewer, whilst to the right there's a young man sitting in a chair, with a white cat seated on his lap, pointedly looking away. Through the open door, we can see a balcony and beyond that the green garden of their town house. There are some flowers in a vase on the table, next to a book, and there's a phone and a lamp on the floor. Finally, to the very left of the picture, we see part of an abstract painting hanging on the wall.

However, beneath all of this, the work is actually a very ambiguous, multi-layered piece, heavy with symbolic meaning and with history. Called *Mr. and Mrs. Clark and Percy* and painted by David Hockney, the work was recently voted one of Britain's top-10 favourites and a knowledge of the behind-the-scenes story might help to explain some of the tension and drama in a piece which continues to fascinate us.

The couple in the painting are textile designer Celia Birtwell and fashion designer Ossie Clark, shortly after their wedding, at which the artist himself had been the best man.

The piece is loosely based on the 15th century work, the *Arnolfini* portrait, by Jan van Eyck, but the positions of the male and female characters have been reversed. The suggestion is perhaps that it was Mrs Clark who was the dominant partner in this particular relationship. The lilies on the table represent female purity, while the cat on Mr Clark's lap symbolises infidelity and jealousy. The roots of this symbol lie in the fact that Mr Clark had frequent affairs both before and during their five-year marriage. This played a part in the couple's eventual divorce three years later, and may explain part of the friction that seems apparent between the two sitters. We have the feeling that we have suddenly interrupted an intimate moment – a heated discussion, perhaps – and are not exactly welcome.

As a footnote, sadly Ossie Clark later fell into bankruptcy and addiction, and his life ended tragically when he was murdered by an ex-lover in 1996, a fact which lends a disturbing edge to the portrait. Celia Birtwell, meanwhile, continued to be one of Hockney's regular models for many years, and to this day remains a successful designer.

GRAMMAR Adjectives and Adverbs

Aim
To introduce the use of adjectives and adverbs and the language patterns that accompany them.

Step 1 Ask students to read out the explantation box, or read it out to them. Check understanding: *When do we use adjectives?* (Often before nouns.) *Which verbs are usually followed by adjectives?* (Be, look, seem, get, taste, etc.) *When do we use adverbs?* (To modify a verb, an adjective, another adverb or a whole clause or sentence.) *How do we form adverbs?* (Usually we add –ly, but there are some exceptions, e.g. *later*.)

Step 2 Individually ask students to choose the correct form in the sentences in exercise B. Then in pairs ask them to compare and explain their choice to their partner using the definition in the explanation box to help them. Check in open class. Direct students to the grammar reference on page 137 if they still seem unsure.

Answers	
1 fairly	5 loosely
2 pointedly	6 Unfortunately / frequent /
3 ambiguous	eventual / apparent
4 shortly	7 Sadly / tragically

PRONUNCIATION Adverbs describing sentences and clauses

Aim
To introduce stress patterns to emphasise adverbs.

Step 1 Get students to read the explanation box. Then put students in pairs or threes to mark the stress and pauses in the sentences. Then ask them to practise saying them. Monitor and help with the correct stress and pausing.

Step 2 Students listen and check the stress patterns. Pause after each one and get students to repeat them. If necessary, play the sentences clause by clause so students can hear the stress, pausing and intonation.

1.5
1 Interestingly, the painting used to have a different title.
2 Actually, no-one knows who the painter was.
3 Sadly, she died at the age of only 35.
4 The painting sold last year for 18 million, but amazingly, Van Gogh himself sold none in his lifetime.

> 5 Incredibly, Mozart was only six when he started performing in public.
> 6 The painting was damaged in a fire and, unfortunately, it couldn't be restored.

> monster and has help with a special weapon to defeat the monster. But, when the hero meets the monster they realise it's more of a challenge. They fight, have problems and are trapped, however the hero makes an amazing escape. Finally, the hero manages to kill the monster
> 3 Students' own answers.

SPEAKING

Aim
To practise language used to describe paintings.

Step 1 Put students into groups of three or four and tell them to choose a painting they like, or to find one on the Internet to talk about.

Tip You could set this for homework and complete the rest of the steps at the begining on the next lesson.

Step 2 Give them five minutes to make notes using the points given. Monitor and help out with language.

Step 3 Students now present their painting to each other, tell the other students to say whether they agree or not with the interpretation. You might like to model the activity first. Monitor and help with any language problems.

Step 4 In open class ask students if they agreed or not and why. Then highlight some correct use of language and correct any errors you noted while monitoring.

 pp. 12–13

 Next class Make photocopies of **1B** p. 130.

READING Part 1

Aim
To develop reading for specific information.

Step 1 Ask students to discuss if they have ever read a book or seen a film and thought the plot was very similar to another film or book, and to tell each other how they were similar and if it bothered them. Do brief feedback.

Step 2 Get students to read the questions in exercise B and check understanding: *fatal flaws* = something that makes it completely useless or wrong, *face a challenge* = to confront a situation. Then they read the first part and answer the questions in pairs before checking.

Note Hero is used here to mean either a male or a female.

Answers
1 They are all based around just seven basic plots, each featuring the same character types and events over and over again
2 There's a community threatened by a monster and a hero to save them. The hero prepares to meet the

READING Part 2

Aim
To develop reading for detail and be able to summarise the content of a text.

Step 1 Divide students into three groups and get them to read the texts: Group A File 1 page 156, Group B File 16 page 161 and Group C File 12 page 159. Tell them to read and identify the different plots. Monitor and help out as necessary.

Step 2 Put students into different groups so that each group has a student A, B and C. They then tell each other what they can remember about the different plots.

Step 3 In the same groups get them to look at the statements in C and identify if they refer to their texts. Do brief feedback in open class.

Step 4 In the same groups students complete the sentences in D using the words from exercise C. Check answers in open class.

Answers
1 transported	3 revenge	5 bullied
2 spiral	4 separated	6 temptation

SPEAKING

Aim
To provide fluency practice of talking about a book, film or story and discussing the plots.

Step 1 Put students into pairs to discuss the questions in exercise A. Monitor and help out with any language, making notes for a correction slot at the end.

Step 2 Do brief feedback on the questions. Then highlight any useful language and errors noted while monitoring.

Step 3 Get students to read the instructions in exercise B. Give them a couple of minutes to think and take notes. Then put students into pairs to tell each other the story, their partner guesses what they are talking about.

Step 4 Get a selection of students to tell the class if they guessed correctly and what helped them to do this.

 1B see Teacher's notes p. 120.

02 SIGHTSEEING

UNIT OVERVIEW
The main aim of this unit is to enable students to talk about **showing people around your town / city** and to **describe places, festivals and carnivals in more detail**. They have practice in **agreeing using synonyms** and to **hear and recognise short forms more easily**. The main grammatical focus is using **non-defining relative clauses** and **ways of using future forms**.

 Next class Make photocopies of **2A** p. 130.

SPEAKING

Aim
To lead in to the topic of making recommendations.

Step 1 Tell students they are going to imagine that four different groups of people are coming to their town to visit: a school trip of twenty 13-year-olds, four 18-year-olds, a young couple with two kids, a retired couple. In open class brainstorm ideas about what things interest the first group. Then put students into groups to brainstorm ideas for the other three groups. Do brief feedback in open class.

LANGUAGE PATTERNS

Aim
To help students notice useful expressions for making recommendations.

Step 1 Ask students to look at the sentences in the language patterns box. Get them to notice the basic pattern = someone / something recommends (which is optional), another person does / tries / uses something. Point out that the first two questions are more formal than the second two.

Step 2 Ask students to translate the sentences into their own language. In a monolingual class ask students to compare their translation. In multilingual classes ask students to work in pairs and tell each other if the sentences were easy to translate into their language and / or if *recommend* can be replaced with one word direct translation in all the sentences. Why / why not?

Step 3 Ask students to cover their English translations and translate the sentences back into English. Then ask them to compare their translations in pairs against

the book and discuss who had the least mistakes. Alternatively, if you prefer not to use translation ask students to notice the patterns. You could ask students for example sentences. Write the examples on the board, if the sentences are wrong ask students to correct them or correct them yourself.

VOCABULARY
Buildings and areas

Aim
To practise vocabulary related to buildings and areas.

Step 1 Tell students to look at the words in the vocabulary box and check understanding: *up-and-coming* = an area that is likely to develop, become successful or popular soon, *stunning* = extremely impressive, *trendy* = very fashionable, *grand* = very impressive, *rough* = an unpleasant place usually because of crime and violence, *residential* = area where people live, *affluent* = very rich, *high-rise* = very tall with many floors, *hideous* = very ugly, *run-down* = not well looked after, *deprived* = a place that doesn't have the essential things for a comfortable life. In pairs or threes students decide if they describe buildings, areas or both, and if they are positive or negative descriptions. Check answers as a class.

Answers			
Meaning	**Buildings**	**Areas**	**Both**
Positive	stunning, grand	up-and-coming, affluent	trendy, residential, historic
Negative	high-rise	rough, deprived	hideous, run-down

Step 2 Ask students to individually complete the sentences in B using the correct grammatical form of the verb. In open class do the first one as an example. In pairs they can compare their answers before checking in open class.

Optional Activity For extra vocabulary practise, ask students to think of three building / areas they know in their town or other well-known places. Then, in pairs, ask them to describe the place without naming it and their partner must guess which building / area it is.

LISTENING

Aim
To practise listening and taking notes, and to develop listening skills for specific information.

Step 1 Tell students they will hear a Scottish woman, May, and a Serbian woman, Ivana, taking about Belgrade (Serbia).

Step 2 Ask students to look at the chart and check understanding: where can you see big concerts or sports events? (The Arena.) In pairs ask students to predict the type of information they will hear before listening. Conduct brief feedback in open class.

Step 3 Play the recording. Then students compare in pairs. If necessary, play the recording again, pausing after each place and check students' understanding.

 2.1
M = May, I = Ivana
M: What a lovely day!
I: Yeah, it's nice, isn't it? It's been a really warm autumn.
M: So where are we?
I: Well, the bit we've just been through, with all the high-rise blocks, is what we call New Belgrade. It's the big up-and-coming area as all the new businesses are relocating here. And I don't know if you can see it or not, but just behind us, over to the right, is the Arena, where all the big concerts and sports events are held. It's one of the biggest entertainment venues in Europe.
M: Yeah, I think I did catch a glimpse of it.
I: That's where they held the Eurovision back in 2008.
M: Oh, OK. So I've seen it on TV, then.
I: And now we're crossing over the River Sava into Old Belgrade.
M: Wow! The river looks wonderful.
I: Yeah, it's great. In the summer, we often go out on little boats or have dinner down by the waterside.
M: Oh, that sounds lovely.
I: And just down there, there's a little street called Gavrila Principa Street, where Manakova Kuca – Manak's House – is located. It's an ethnological museum and it houses an amazing collection of old national costumes and embroidery and stuff.
M: OK. I'll check that out if I have time. What's that building over there?
I: Oh, that's St. Mark's Church.
M: Wow! It's a stunning building. How old is it?
I: Not that old, actually. It was built in the late 1930s or something, but it's on the site of a much older church. It contains the tomb of Stefan Dusan, who was perhaps the greatest Serbian emperor ever.
M: Oh, OK.
I: And if you want to walk around here later, you're quite close to the Kalemegdan Fortress, one of the most historic buildings in Belgrade. There's the Victor monument up there as well, which was erected after the First World War. It's one of the city's most famous landmarks.
M: Right. Well, I'll have to remember to take my camera with me up there, then.
I: And now we're coming up to Dedinje, which is one of the more affluent parts of the city. It's where all the celebrities and the old aristocratic families live – and a lot of the embassies are based here as well.
M: The houses certainly do look very grand.
I: Yeah, they're amazing, aren't they?

Optional activity In pairs or threes students talk about which of the places they would most / least like to visit in Belgrade and why. Alternatively, for homework ask students to write a short paragraph recommending places to visit.

GRAMMAR Non-defining relative clauses

Aim
To revise and practise adding extra information to sentences using non-defining relative clauses.

Step 1 Individually ask students to read the grammar explanation box. Write this sentence on the board: *Over to the right, is the Arena, where all the big concerts and sports events are held.* Then erase the relative clause (*where all the big concerts and sports events are held*) and change the comma to a full stop. Highlight that the sentence still makes sense. Get students to tell you how to add the information back into the sentence and write on the board. This will clearly set up the next activity. Then write the relative pronouns on the board and check what information comes after them. *Which*: thing or place, e.g. *most of which*: a large number of things; *by which time*: a specific time; *where*: a place; *when*: a time phrase; *whose*: belonging to a person or animal; *who*: a person. Elicit from students why we use non-defining relative clauses (to add extra information). Is it essential to the meaning? (No.) Do we use them more in writing or speaking? (Writing.)

Step 2 Individually students rewrite each pair of sentences in exercise A as one sentence. Monitor and help as necessary. Students then compare in pairs before checking in open class. Direct students to the grammar reference on page 139 if they still seem unsure.

> **Answers**
> 1 It contains the tomb of Stefan Dusan, who was perhaps the greatest Serbian emperor.
> 2 We're coming up to Dedinje, which is one of the most affluent parts of the city.
> 3 Just behind us, over to the right, is the Arena, where all the big concerts and sports events are held. (Note: 'where' replaces 'there'.)
> 4 I went to school with a woman called Zora, whose son plays professional football in England now.
> 5 I started working in that office over there in 2003, by which time the area was already starting to boom. (Note: 'by which time' replaces 'even then'.)
> 6 We produce bathroom tiles, most of which we export to northern Europe.

 2A see Teacher's notes p. 120.

DEVELOPING CONVERSATIONS Agreeing using synonyms

Aim
To introduce strategies of agreeing using synonyms.

Step 1 Get students to look at the explanation box. Ask them to identify the synonyms in the dialogue: *lovely / nice.* Check understanding: when do we use them? (To give opinions.) Why do we use them? (To show we agree.)

Step 2 Ask students to read the opinions and check understanding. Then get them to take turns expressing and agreeing with the opinions.

> **Answers**
> 1 Yeah, it's really ugly / horrible, isn't it?
> 2 Yeah, they're great / wonderful / fantastic, aren't they?
> 3 Yeah, it's amazing / impressive / fantastic, isn't it?
> 4 Yeah, it looks amazing / beautiful, doesn't it?
> 5 Yeah, it's pretty neglected, isn't it?
> 6 Yeah, it seems like quite a rich / affluent area, doesn't it?

CONVERSATION PRACTICE

Aim
To practise agreeing using synonyms.

Step 1 Ask students to individually read the instructions and prepare their tour.

Step 2 In pairs students role-play the conversation. If time, swap roles and repeat. Monitor and take notes on their use of language for a correction slot at the end.

 pp. 16–17

VOCABULARY Festivals and carnivals

Aim
To practise vocabulary related to festivals and carnivals.

Step 1 In pairs or threes students look at the words in the vocabulary box. Then get them to identify which of the items they can see in the photographs. Check answers in open class.

> **Answers**
> 1 silly string   3 a fireworks display
> 2 a costume, a parade   4 confetti

Step 2 Individually students match the nouns from exercise A to the groups of words in exercise B. Then they compare in pairs or threes before checking in open class.

> **Answers:**
> 1 mask   6 bonfire
> 2 float   7 steel drum band
> 3 silly string   8 firework display
> 4 sound system   9 parade
> 5 costume   10 confetti

Step 3 Give students time to choose five of the nouns from exercise A to describe a time they saw / wore / used them. Tell them they can make these up if necessary. When they are ready in pairs or threes they should explain where they were and what happened. Monitor and help out with any problems with language.

READING

Aim
To develop reading for general and detailed information.

Step 1 Tell students they are going to read an email about the Venice carnival. In groups students discuss what they know about Venice, its history, location, sights, etc. In open class ask students to share their ideas.

Note Venice is in the north east of Italy and consists of a series of little islands; the houses seem to rise out of the water and there are a lot of canals; it is considered a romantic place. The Venice carnival is one of the most famous carnivals in Italy and people dress up in costumes and masks, sometimes traditional ones from the Middle Ages.

Step 2 Individually they read the email quickly to see if their ideas are in the text. Check in open class.

Step 3 Students read the relative clauses in exercise B. Check: *fast* = not to eat food or very little for a period of time, usually for religious reasons. Then they read the email again and add in the extra information.

Answers				
1 i	3 g	5 j	7 f	9 e
2 d	4 a	6 b	8 h	10 c

Step 4 Individually students read the statements and decide if they are true or false. Then they underline the sentence that supports their answers. Get students to compare in pairs before checking in open class.

Answers
1 F: Chiaki stayed with Nina from uni, there's not enough information to say they all studied together.
2 T: prices really shoot up
3 F: my favourite costume is called the plague doctor
4 F: it takes place in the week leading up to Lent
5 T: people eat less
6 T: we ended up buying some ourselves and joined in the fun
7 F: the fireworks can be shocking, if you're not expecting it
8 F: she was going to but has uploaded more onto her website.

NATIVE SPEAKER ENGLISH BOX

Ask students to look at the Native Speaker English box. Tell them in informal spoken English we often use *uni* to refer to *university*.

Step 5 Get students to read the sentences in D and individually to look back at the email and find words that mean the same as those in italics. In pairs or threes students compare answers. Then check in open class.

Answers	
1 put me up	5 scary and sinister
2 completely packed	6 fattening
3 no wonder	7 transformed
4 stick with	8 set off

Step 6 Put students in pairs to discuss the questions in exercise E. Conduct brief feedback.

Step 7 Get students to look at the list of things to think about in F then read the email and underline useful expressions. Monitor and help them notice the informal writing style: contractions, dashes to add extra information, opening and closing language. Ask them to write their email, then to compare in pairs.

Tip If you don't have time in class, you could get students to write their email for homework. In the next class get them to look at each other's emails and check for any errors. Then get them to give their email to another student, and to write a reply for homework.

 pp. 18–19

 Next class Make photocopies of **2B** p. 131.

SPEAKING

Aim
To practise comparing and responding.

Step 1 Get students to look at the language in the vocabulary box and check understanding: *a bit tame* = not exciting, *dizzy* = feeling of things spinning, *set your pulse racing* = make you feel excited.

Step 2 Individually students rank the activities from 1 (like most) to 8 (like least) trying to use the language from the vocabulary box. Then in pairs they explain their choices to each other using the target language. Conduct brief feedback.

Tip With a weaker class, students could write their opinions before speaking. With a stronger class, you could get them to decide on the two they like the most and the two the like the least, and why.

LISTENING

Aim
To develop listening for specific information.

Step 1 Tell students they are going to hear six short extracts with people talking about rides and theme parks. Get students to listen to the recording and decide which photographs on the page are most similar to the attractions the speakers mention. Check answers in open class.

Answers

1 tower type ride	4 water slides
2 boat ride	5 medieval jousting
3 roller coaster	6 pirate ship

Step 2 Play the recording again and ask students to decide which speaker talks about the points in exercise B.

Step 3 In pairs or threes students compare and explain their choices, and see if they agree. If necessary, play the recording again. Check answers in open class.

Answers

1 Speaker 4 (planning permission, we're launching a campaign to stop it)
2 Speaker 1 (a door opens and they plunge 20 metres)
3 Speaker 5 (I'm dreading some bits, I'm going to go to the medieval show, I might just walk around the grounds)
4 Speaker 6 (I'm gonna be sick, you shouldn't have eaten before, I'll get you a tissue)
5 Speaker 3 (you've got to come with us next time, describing what happens)
6 Speaker 2 (it's boring, yawn, can't we have a break, stop moaning)

🎧 **2.2**

1 This year we're introducing a new ride called Hell and Heaven. The riders are strapped into seats and sit for anything between ten seconds and two minutes until, without warning, a door opens beneath them and they plunge 20 metres down into total darkness. Then devil figures appear and they're subjected to bursts of heat before suddenly getting shot back up into the light and up a 50-metre tower where they hang before dropping again. It's due to officially open in June, but I've taken part in the trials and I can tell you it'll really set your pulse racing.
2 A: What shall we go on next?
   B: Let's go on this one.
   A: No way! It's boring! Look at them – just floating along.
   B: It's nice. It's got tunnels and falls too. Look – you get splashed there.
   A: Yawn! Come on. Let's go on Dragon Kahn again.
   B: Can't we have a break? And there are no height restrictions on the boats either, so we can all go – your brother included.
   A: It's so annoying – why can't he be taller!!
   B: Erm, it's called biology! Now stop moaning. You'll spoil things.
   A: It's so unfair.
3 You've got to come with us next time. It's so cool. Oh, oh there's this one ride, yeah, it's just amazing. You go in this car really high up and you get really nervous, you know, with anticipation 'cos it goes quite slowly and I was holding really tight and going 'This is gonna

be awful, I wanna get off' and we got to the top and it just falls – falls really steeply – like almost vertical – and I just screamed and screamed and then we came up again and suddenly I'm going 'Wow, this is fantastic!' and it has all these loops and twists and turns and you go upside down and everything. It's amazing!
4 The company is applying for planning permission for a park with ten slides and four pools, so we're launching a campaign to stop it. There's already been a drought and this'll worsen the situation in the future. We understand the need for tourist attractions, but we want local government to investigate other sustainable alternatives, such as horse trekking and climbing. We've nothing against a park with slides – just not ones that'll put a further strain on water resources.
5 I'm dreading some bits. I went on a rollercoaster once and just got really bruised because of all the twists and turns. Still, I'm going to go to the medieval show anyway. It includes jousting, where they wear armour and try to knock each other off their horses. That should be good. Then I might just walk around the grounds, which are supposed to be really pretty.
6 A: Oh man! I think I'm gonna be sick!
   B: You shouldn't have eaten before.
   A: Well, it looked quite tame, but all that spinning around made me dizzy. One sec...
   B: I'll get you a tissue.

Step 4 In pairs students to look at the extracts in exercise D and complete with collocations. Students can check with the audioscript on page 165. Conduct brief feedback.

Answers

1 strapped	6 twists
2 plunge	7 permission
3 restrictions	8 launching
4 tight	9 strain
5 steeply	10 wear

Step 5 Individually students look at the questions in exercise E and think about their own experience. Elicit examples of different strains that tourism could put on society or on the environment. For example, in conversation five, the water ride would use a lot of water and this could put an extra strain on the environment, especially in places where there isn't much water each year. Put them into small groups of four or five to discuss the questions. Monitor and take notes on their use of language for a correction slot at the end.

GRAMMAR The future

Aim
To revise and consolidate the different future forms.

Step 1 Get students to read the grammar explanation box and check understanding: When do we use the present simple? (Timetables and dates.) When do we use the present continuous? (Fixed arrangements or plans.) When do we use *be going to*? (Intentions and predictions based on present evidence.) When do we use *will*? (Predictions based on opinion, decisions made at the moment of speaking.) When do we use *due / bound to*? (Something happening soon, high probability.) Students can compare in pairs or threes what they know / remember about the different meanings and the future forms. Monitor and note what problems they are having.

Step 2 In pairs students look at the sentences in A and correct them, justifying why. If necessary, students can check their answers with the audioscript on page 165. Check answers in open class. Check understanding: *might* = used when something is probable, *shall* = used for suggestions in the first person singular (*I*) and plural (*We*), *have got to* = used to mean a future obligation. Direct students to the grammar reference on page 139 if they still seem unsure.

> **Answers**
> 1 we're introducing = fixed future plan or arrangement
> 2 due to = something happening soon (formal)
> 3 'll really set = prediction based on opinion
> 4 shall = suggestion
> 5 've got to = future obligation
> 6 'll worsen = prediction based on opinion
> 7 'm going to go = intention
> 8 am going to be = prediction based on evidence
> 9 'll get you = decision made at the moment of speaking

Step 3 Get students to read the explanation box and check they understand: when we make predictions in English, what forms can we use? (*will* or *be going to*). Can we use the present continuous? (No.) Tell them that we can use different future forms without changing the meaning, and usually there are two alternatives.

Step 4 In pairs or threes students look at the sentences in exercise C. Ask students to decide which one or two sentences are incorrect and why. Check in open class.

> **Answers**
> 1 b is incorrect. a & c express predictions based on present evidence or situation. In addition, a *(will)* sounds more formal.
> 2 c is incorrect. a & b express future plans or decisions.
> 3 a & c are incorrect. b expresses a prediction based on present evidence, but is different from example 1 because it can clearly be seen.
> 4 c is incorrect. a & b express a suggestion or offer.
> 5 a & b are incorrect. c expresses a future obligation.
> 6 b is incorrect. a & c express a condition based on a real situation.

Step 5 Remind students that we prefer the present continuous when a decision has been made and that a plan is in place. Then students complete the text with the correct verb in the present continuous individually.

Step 6 In pairs or threes students compare answers. Then conduct feedback in open class.

> **Answers**
> 1 I'm really looking forward   4 are also hoping
> 2 I'm thinking   5 I'm expecting
> 3 is already planning   6 I'm dreading

PRONUNCIATION Elision and linking

Aim
To raise awareness of elision and linking sounds.

Step 1 Tell students to look at the sentences and guess what words might go in the gaps first. Tell students to listen and write what they hear. Check answers in open class. (Underlined in audio below.)

> 🔊 **2.3**
> … you get really nervous, you know, with anticipation '<u>cos</u> it goes quite slowly and I was holding really tight and going 'This is <u>gonna</u> be awful, I <u>wanna</u> get off' …

Step 2 Students read the explanation box. Tell students they are going to get more practice. Play each sentence and pause to get them to repeat.

Step 3 Students listen again and write the full form of the sentences. Get them to compare in pairs before checking in open class (answers in audioscript 2.4).

> 🔊 **2.4**
> 1 Have you ever been there?
> 2 I'm thinking of going there in the summer.
> 3 You should have seen him when he got off the ride.
> 4 I thought he was going to be sick!
> 5 I will take you because I'm going that way anyway.
> 6 I am going to leave now because I've got to finish some work.
> 7 Do you want to do that first or shall we leave it until later?

SPEAKING

Aim
To practise the language used in the unit.

Step 1 Allow students time to look through the different situations and plan what they want to say. (Tell them to choose three only if you are short on time.) Then ask students tell each other about their plans. Their partner should ask questions. Conduct brief feedback.

>   **2B** see Teacher's notes p. 120.

03 THINGS YOU NEED

UNIT OVERVIEW
The main aim of this unit is to enable students to **talk about wide range of objects** and to **describe what things are for**. They have practice in **explaining what went wrong**. The main grammatical focus is *so, if and to for describing purpose* and **indirect questions**. They have practice in **expressing useful things, problems with things and word families**.

 Next class Make photocopies of **3A** p. 132.

VOCABULARY Useful things

Aim
To lead in to the topic.

Step 1 Get students to look at the pictures in File 15 on page 160 and discuss the questions in pairs. Conduct brief feedback in open class.

Step 2 Ask students to close their books and put them in small groups. Ask them what things they remember from the photographs for each category without looking back at the pictures. You might like to give them a time limit, then stop them and get them to compare how many they got in each category with another group before checking in open class.

> **Answers**
> The office / study = Packing tape, blu-tac, drawing pin, a padlock, gaffer tape, safety pin
> The kitchen = packing tape, safety pin, elasticated rope, a padlock, safety pin
> Clothes = safety pin
> DIY = packing tape, a padlock, gaffer tape, safety pin, caribiner
> First Aid = safety pin

NATIVE SPEAKER ENGLISH *DIY*

Tell students to read the box and ask them if *DIY* is popular in their country. In English-speaking countries there are a lot of stores where people can buy things cheaply to make improvements to their houses.

Step 3 Put students in pairs, Student A looks at File 15 on page 160 and Student B closes their book, A then asks B the questions. Then they swap roles. Monitor and help out with vocabulary. Then check answers in open class.

> **Answers**
> **Student A:** *to tie things together* = a rope, a wire, a rubber band, string, *to put up a poster or notice* = sticky tape, *to wash and hang up your clothes to dry* = rope, wire (clothes) pegs; *if there's a crack in your roof and it's leaking* = a stepladder a (plastic) bowl a mop and bucket; *so you can mend a rip in your clothing* = needle and thread, pins (small basic kind for sewing).
> **Student B:** *to keep papers together* = staples, a stapler, clips (paperclips and bulldog clips), *to put up a picture* = a hammer, a drill, a stepladder, a nail, a screw, wire; *to prevent something rubbing or to protect your body* = arm / elbow pads, cotton pad, a plaster / band-aid, a bandage; *if you knock over a cup and it smashes on the floor* = a cloth, a dustpan and brush, a mop and bucket; *so you can see better in the dark* = a torch.

GRAMMAR *so, if* and *to* for describing purpose

Aim
To introduce *so, if* and *to* for describing purpose.

Step 1 Put the following sentences on the board. Ask students what pattern comes after *to, so* and *if*. To = verb, *so* = a clause (sentence), *if* = a clause (sentence) that depends on the first part.
1 I need a safety pin <u>*to mend a rip in my skirt*</u>.
2 Can I have a paper clip <u>*so I can keep these papers together*</u>.
3 It's a thing you can put on the floor <u>*if there's a lot of cables*</u>.

Step 2 In pairs ask students to look back at the *Vocabulary* exercise and complete the sentences in A. Check answers.

> **Answers**
> 1 to   2 so   3 if

Step 3 In pairs or three students look at the other items in B and think of a common and one less common purpose for each. Put them in larger groups to compare ideas. Compare as a class and ask students to decide on the best uses.

Suggested answers

a thread:	You use it to sew a rip in your clothes. If you can't remember something you could tie it round your finger.
a nail:	You use it to put up a picture. If the sole of your shoe is falling off, you could use it to repair it.
a bandage:	You use it to cover a cut or burn on your arm or leg. You could use it to tie a parcel.
a lighter:	you use it to light a cigarette, candle or gas oven. You could use it to burn a loose thread on your shirt.
a bucket:	You put water in it to clean the floor. You could use it as a seat for a young child.

 3A see Teacher's notes p. 121.

DEVELOPING CONVERSATIONS
Explaining and checking

Aim
To develop speaking strategies for explaining what you say and checking what other people say.

Step 1 Tell students to listen to the two short conversations and decide which of the things in the photographs they are talking about. Check answers.

Answers
Conversation 1 = blu-tac   Conversation 2 = caribiner

🔊 3.1
Conversation 1
A: What's the name of that stuff you use to put posters up?
B: Can you be a bit more specific?
A: Yeah, sorry, I mean that stuff – it's a bit like chewing gum or something, but it doesn't actually feel that sticky.
B: What? You mean blu-tac?
A: Yeah! Is that what they call it?

Conversation 2
C: It's, um … what do you call those things climbers use. They're made of metal. They're like a hook.
D: What? You mean the thing you use to connect yourself to the rope?

C: Yeah, they have a sort of springy gate thing. You see people using the small ones as key rings sometimes.
D: Yeah, yeah. I know exactly what you mean – I don't know! Do they have a special name – aren't they just clips?

Step 2 Get students to read the explanation box and help them notice the language pattern = to explain things we can use. *That stuff – it's a bit like...* + noun phrase, or *They have a sort of...*+ noun phrase. To check you understand you can use: *What? You mean...* + noun phrase, *What? you mean the thing you use to...* + verb phrase.

Step 4 Ask students to look at exercise B and tell them to think of some things from the home or office that they don't know the name of. Tell them to use the target vocabulary to explain these items to their partner. Their partner then checks they understand by drawing the item. They then swap roles.

LISTENING

Aim
To develop listening for specific information.

Step 1 Tell students to listen to the conversation and answer the questions in A. Check in pairs then as a class.

Answers
1 a corkscrew
2 to open a bottle of Californian grape juice
3 a wooden spoon
4 a cloth, to wipe up the juice

🔊 3.2
A: I brought you a present.
B: Wine?
A: No! I know you don't drink. No, it's Californian grape juice! I had some at a friend's the other day and it was really delicious.
B: Really?
A: Apparently, they have all sorts of varieties.
B: Yeah? Well, thanks! Shall we have some now?
A: Sure! Have you got a corkscrew?
B: Ah, that's a point, actually. I'm not sure I have actually. Let me have a look. There's so much stuff in these drawers. Most of it's rubbish. I really should clear it out. Mmm. I don't think there's one here. Can't you use a knife?
A: I don't think so.
B: You need a stick or something to push it down. Would a pencil do?
A: It wouldn't be strong enough.

B: What about a wooden spoon? You could use the handle.
A: Yeah, that should do. Let's see... Oh no!!
B: Oh, it's gone everywhere!
A: Sorry! Have you got a cloth?
B: Yeah. I think we need a mop and bucket as well.
A: Sorry.
B: Don't worry about it. These things happen. You might want to rub some salt into that shirt or it'll leave a stain.
A: Really?
B: Well, it works for other things.

Step 3 In pairs get students to complete the sentences from the conversation. Tell them it might be more than one word in each gap. Then play the recording again to check answers.

Answers

1 Can't you	5 You could use
2 or something	6 should
3 do	7 things happen
4 strong enough	8 it'll leave a stain.

SPEAKING

Aim
To provide fluency practice on language used so far.

Step 1 Put students in small groups to discuss the questions. Monitor and take notes on their use of language for a correction slot at the end.

CONVERSATION PRACTICE

Aim
To practise asking for things and solving problems.

Step 1 Divide students into AB pairs. A looks at File 17 on page 161 and B at File 21 on page 162. Tell students that they are going to ask for different things and they have to solve different problems. Tell them to choose one problem in the pictures and then ask another student for a solution using the model provided. Tell them to continue their conversations until they find a good solution.

 pp. 22–23

SPEAKING

Aim
To practice fluency.

Step 1 Tell students to look at the photographs and decide what things they can see that people might collect. [*Wine bottles*, *vintage hubcaps* = (cover for wheels on a car), *badges*, *toyshop*, *car reflectors*, *Russian dolls*.]

Step 2 Get students to think about the kind of people who collect these things and write down six questions they could ask them.

Suggested answers
When did you start collecting (wine bottles)?
How and why did you start collecting them?
How many do you have?
Where do you keep them?
What do your friends think about your collection?
Do you have things from different countries or places?

Step 3 In pairs or threes tell them to ask and answer each other the questions they wrote. If they don't collect things, ask them to think of someone they know who does or imagine they collect one of the things in the photographs. Monitor and take notes on their use of target language for a correction slot at the end.

READING

Aim
To develop reading for specific information.

Step 1 Ask students to read the blog and answer the questions individually. Check answers in pairs then as a class.

Answers
1 All kinds of things: vacuum cleaners, old doors, windows, records, newspapers, children's toys.
2 There's a bit of Mr. Trebus in all of us. The writer also collects things that are no longer useful.
3 Mr. Trebus: that they were useful, The writer: instructions and guarantees in case things break down, coins because they might be useful.
4 Student's own opinion.

Step 3 In pairs or threes students correct the sentences about Mr. Trebus. Monitor and help out if necessary.

Answers
1 His house became a *health* hazard.
2 he was a veteran of the *Second World War*.
3 he was a *tank* commander.
4 The trauma of *what he lost when he left Poland* caused his obsession.
5 He settled in *Britain* after the war.
6 He sorted the junk into piles of *similar things*.
7 He acquired *every record Elvis Presley had ever made*.
8 The neighbours complained about infestations of *rats*.
9 He resisted *eviction*.

Step 4 In a monolingual class, get students in pairs or small groups to translate the words in bold into their language. In a multilingual class, tell them to translate into their language, then with their books closed back into English.

Alternatively If you prefer not to use translation, ask students to write a different sentence using the words in bold.

VOCABULARY Word families

Aim
To introduce and practise word formation using suffixes.

Step 1 Write the following words on the board: *development, developmental, tidy, tidiness* and ask them which word is the noun and which one is the adjective. *Develop* + suffix *ment* forms the noun, *develop* + *-ment* + *-al* forms the adjective; *tidy* is the adjective and verb, *tidi* + *-ness* forms the noun (note: changing the *y* to an *i* forms the noun).

Step 2 In groups ask students to think of other words they know ending with the suffixes in the box. Ask them to answer the questions in A. Check answers in class.

Answers
Suffixes that do not form nouns = adjectives: -al, -less, -ious, -y; verbs: -ise.

Step 3 In pairs students complete the expressions with the nouns from the blog. Check answers as a class.

Answers
1 obsession	3 caution	5 intentions	7 meanness
2 eviction	4 fear	6 optimism	8 pessimism

Step 4 In small groups students discuss if the words in the box refer to Mr. Trebus and / or the writer. Check understanding of *well-intentioned* = someone who tries to help but often makes things worse. Check answers as a class.

Answers
Obsessive = both, They keep and collect a lot of old and what most people think are not very useful things. Well-intentioned = the writer has a number of batteries in his drawer he has been meaning to take to the recycling centre. Pessimistic = the writer has a number of instructions and guarantees for things in case they break down. Optimistic = Mr. Trebus has resisted eviction. Cautious = both, they keep things because one day they might be useful. Mean = Mr Trebus is mean because the rats are annoying his neighbours and his wife.

Step 5 Tell students to read the question in exercise D and give them a couple of minutes to make notes. Then ask them to discuss in pairs / threes. Monitor and take notes on their use of target language for a correction slot at the end. Remind them to record this feedback in their notebooks.

SPEAKING

Aim
To develop fluency in responding to information.

Step 1 Tell students that when people respond to blogs they sometimes don't use their real identity but invent an alias, e.g. in the last blog the person's identity is *Greengoddess*. Individually students read the responses to the blog and decide which they like or agree with the most. Monitor and help out with any language. Then they compare in pairs.

Step 2 Tell students they are going to write their own comment to add to the blog. Give them time before writing to think about what they will say.

Step 3 In small groups tell them to read each other's comments and to say what they think of them.

Tip You could get students to put their comments on the wall and ask students to read them and make notes about their reactions.

 pp. 24–25

 Next class Make photocopies of **3B** p. 133.

SPEAKING

Aim
To provide fluency practice and introduce the language they will be looking at in more detail in the unit.

Alternatively Omit this stage and go straight to *Listening*. Then use this speaking activity to consolidate the listening.

Step 1 Ask students to read the statements and then put them into small groups to discuss the questions. Conduct brief feedback.

LISTENING

Aim
To develop listening for general and specific information.

Step 1 Get students to read the questions in exercise A and then play the recording. Ask them to compare their answers in pairs. Check answers in open class.

Answers
1 a tie, it's not him (not his style)
2 not very successful because he doesn't have a receipt

Step 2 In pairs students read the statements and decide if they are true or false. Play the recording again to check.

Answers
1 F it was a birthday present
2 F it was bought a couple of weeks ago
3 T it's not very me

4 F
5 F he doesn't have a clue (doesn't know)
6 T try not to get upset, sir
7 F it cost £90

🔊 3.3

S = sales assistant, C = Customer

S: Who's next, please?

C: Oh hello. I wonder if you can help me. I was given this tie for my birthday a couple of weeks ago and I believe it came from your store. I was wondering if I could possibly get a refund on it as it's ... well, it's just not very ME, if you know what I mean.

S: OK. It was purchased two weeks ago, you say?

C: Yes, that's right. Give or take a day or two.

S: Right.

C: But this is the first chance I've had to come in to the store. I was too busy working before.

S: And do you still have the receipt for it?

C: Um ... no, I don't, no. As I said, it was a present.

S: So – without meaning to be rude – how can you be sure it actually came from us?

C: Well, it was from my girlfriend and I did see her coming home the day before my birthday with a bag from your shop, and I did also see exactly the same ties for sale in your menswear department a minute ago, so I'm assuming it must have come from here.

S: Well, to be honest, we can't really take it back without proof of purchase. Would you happen to know how your girlfriend paid for it? Do you know if it was by cheque or by credit card or ...?

C: Look. I honestly haven't a clue. I obviously wasn't with her when she bought it, was I!

S: OK. Please try not to get quite so upset, sir. I'm just trying to do my job here.

C: No, I know. I'm sorry. It's just that ninety pounds is an awful lot of money for a tie – and it does seem a terrible shame if I'm never going to wear it.

S: Indeed, but I'm afraid that under the circumstances, I'm not going to be able to offer any kind of refund or exchange. I suggest you go home and try to find a receipt of some sort. Perhaps your girlfriend kept it?

Step 3 In pairs ask students to discuss what they would do next if they were the customer. Play the recording to see if their ideas are talked about.

Step 4 Get students to read the questions in exercise D and think about them as they listen. Then they compare their answers in pairs before checking in open class.

Answers
1 & 3 student's own opinion
2 Ending 1: resigned   Ending 2: frustrated.

🔊 3.4

S = sales assistant, C = Customer (as above)

C: But I know I won't be able to get hold of the receipt or any other proof she bought it here without letting

her know and she'd be so disappointed, she really would. She's had so many other problems recently – I really don't want to upset her. Please, is there really nothing you can do?

S: I am sorry, sir. It's just that we're not actually legally obliged to accept returns of this kind at all, so there's really nothing else I can do to help.

C: Oh well. I suppose I'll just have to force myself to wear the tie once in a while. Thanks for your help, anyway.

Ending 2

C: Yes, but that would mean having to tell her I've been trying to get a refund on the stupid thing!

S: That's not strictly our problem. I'm afraid, sir.

C: No, of course not. It never is, this kind of thing, is it!

S: I'm sorry you feel that way, sir, but I've done all I can for you.

C: Well, it's just not good enough, is it! Do you think you could call the manager, please? I've had just about enough of this.

S: I'm afraid the manager is out at the moment. Would you like me to give you her number?

C: When do you expect her back?

S: It could be any time today.

C: Oh, that's just marvellous, that is!

S: I should tell you, though, that she'd probably tell you exactly what I've just told you. No proof of purchase, no refund.

C: Great! Well, thanks a lot for your help! That's the last time I ever come here! I'll take my business elsewhere in future.

LANGUAGE PATTERNS

Aim

To draw students' attention to patterns using *without*.

Step 1 Ask students to read the examples in the box. Draw their attention to *without* + *verb* + *-ing* as a way of being polite and *went without* = live without something you need.

Step 2 Ask students to translate the sentences into their own language. In monolingual classes ask students to compare their translation. In multilingual classes ask students to work in pairs and tell each other if the sentences were easy to translate and / or if *without* in all the sentences can be replaced with one word direct translation.

Step 3 Ask students to cover their English translations and translate the sentences back into English. Then ask them to compare their translations in pairs against the book and discuss who had the least mistakes. What mistakes did they make? Why? Alternatively, if you prefer not to use translation ask students to notice the patterns. You could ask students for example sentences and write these on the board. If the sentences are wrong, ask students to correct them or correct them yourself.

GRAMMAR Indirect questions

Aim
To revise ways of asking indirect questions.

Step 1 Ask students to read the grammar explanation box. Remind them that in direct questions we need an auxiliary verb or *to be* and the word order = question word + auxiliary + subject + verb. And that in indirect questions the word order is the same as normal sentences = subject + verb + object.

> **Answers**
> How did your girlfriend pay for it?
> Was it by cheque or credit card?

Step 2 Individually ask students to rewrite the direct questions in exercise B as indirect questions. Monitor and help out as necessary. Check in pairs, then in open class.

> **Answers**
> 1 Do you happen to know how long the guarantee lasts?
> 2 Do you know where the toilets are?
> 3 Excuse me. Do you know if you sell wire?
> 4 Hello. I was wondering if I could speak to the manager?
> 5 Would you happen to know when the sofa will be delivered?
> 6 Sorry to bother you, but do you think you could bring me the next size up?

Step 3 In pairs students match the responses to the questions in exercise C. Monitor and help out with any problems. Then play the recording to check the answers.

> **Answers**
> a 3   b 1   c 2   d 6   e 5   f 4

> 🔊 **3.5**
> 1 A: Do you happen to know how long the guarantee lasts?
>   B: I'm not sure, actually, but it's usually at least a year.
> 2 A: Sorry. Do you know where the toilets are?
>   B: If you go up the stairs, the Ladies' is on your left.
> 3 A: Excuse me. Do you know if you sell wire?
>   B: Yes. There should be some in the hardware department on the second floor.
> 4 A: Hello. I was wondering if I could speak to the manager?
>   B: Certainly. I'll put you through now.
> 5 A: Would you happen to know when the sofa will be delivered?
>   B: It says on the computer it should go out tomorrow.
> 6 A: Sorry to bother you, but do you think you could bring me the next size up?
>   B: Of course. I'll just grab you one from the racks.

Step 4 Tell students that we use indirect questions to sound more polite and that it is important to use the correct pronunciation. Play the recording and get students to repeat the questions. Then in pairs ask them to practise asking and answering the questions. Direct students to the grammar reference on page 141 if they still seem unsure.

>   **3B** see Teacher's notes p. 121.

VOCABULARY Problems with things

Aim
To introduce and practise vocabulary related to having problems with things.

Step 1 Individually ask students to complete sentences 1–5 using the words in the vocabulary box. Then they compare in pairs before checking in open class.

> **Answers**
> 1 screen   2 part   3 flash   4 outfit   5 strap

Step 2 Get students to read the words in the second vocabulary box and check *it jumps* = when a CD or DVD is scratched and the reader moves quickly over the track.

Step 3 Individually students complete the sentences using the words in the vocabulary box. Then they compare in pairs before checking in open class.

> **Answers**
> 6 funny   7 allergic   8 ripped   9 scratched   10 cracked

Step 4 Put students in pairs / threes to look at the pictures and match them to the problems listed and discuss if they have ever had these problems.

> **Answers**
> 1 picture 4   5 picture 3   9 picture 1
> 2 picture 9   6 picture 10   10 picture 7
> 3 picture 5   7 picture 8
> 4 picture 6   8 picture 2

SPEAKING

Aim
To provide fluency practice of returning things.

Step 1 Tell students they are going to role-play some conversations between the shop assistant and the different customers in the picture. Ask them to look at the audioscript on page 166 to underline any expression they want to use. Then, in pairs students take turns to have the conversations. Monitor and take notes on the uses of the target language for a correction slot at the end.

04 SOCIETY

UNIT OVERVIEW
The main aim of this unit is to enable students to **talk about the government and their policies and how the economy is doing** and to **discuss social issues**. They have practice in **responding to complaints**. The main grammatical focus is *so* and *such* and *the . . . , the . . .* + comparatives and ways of **using expressions to describe economics, society and the government**.

 Next class Make photocopies of **4A** p. 134.

VOCABULARY

The government, economics and society

Aim
To give practice in guessing meaning from context.

Step 1 Tell students to read the explanation box and check understanding: who does *they* refer to in the sentence? (The government.) Whose policies does *their* refer to? (The government's.) Tell them that *they* is used when talking in general about the government or to other groups of officials like the council, the police, etc. Ask if it's the same in their language.

Step 2 The aim of this exercise is to train students to look at the information before and after a word to help them understand the meaning. Write the first sentence on the board, using a different colour for the word in bold. Tell them to look at the second part, *They've done a lot to help the poor.* Ask students: Does this have a good effect on society? (Yes.) Has it changed society for the better? (Yes.) So what does *make a difference* mean? = have a good effect on something.

Step 3 In pairs or small groups students look at the other sentences and guess the meaning. Then get them to check in the *Vocabulary builder*. Check the answers in open class.

Answers
1 *non-existent* = if something is non-existent, it doesn't exist at all
2 *recession* = if there is a recession, there is less business activity in a country, so people make less money and some people lose their jobs
3 *soft* = to describe someone not strict enough
4 *gone bankrupt* = if a company is bankrupt, it can't pay all its debts and so cannot continue to exist
5 *booming* = the economy is booming, it is growing quickly and is very successful

6 *shortages* = not enough of something
7 *shot up* = increases very quickly
8 *boost* = to boost something means to improve it or increase it, *standing* = your reputation, based on what other people think of you
9 *undermining* = to weaken or make it less effective
10 *to make ends meet* = you just manage to buy everything that you need to live, even though you have very little money

Step 4 In groups ask students to decide whether the statements in exercise A are true or false for their country and say why. Do brief feedback in open class.

LANGUAGE PATTERNS

Aim
To draw students' attention to some common patterns for talking about government policies.

Step 1 Ask students to read the examples in the box. Draw their attention to the quantifier words: *a lot, a huge amount, enough, little, not...anything* to emphasise how much the government is doing or not doing.

Step 2 Ask students to translate the sentences into their own language. In monolingual class, ask students to compare their translation. In multilingual classes, ask students to work in pairs and tell each other if the sentences were easy to translate into their language.

Step 3 Ask students to cover their English translations and using their translation translate the sentences back into English. Then ask them to compare their translations in pairs against the book and discuss who had the least mistakes and what what mistakes they did make. Alternatively, if you prefer not to use translation ask students to notice the pattern. You could ask students for example sentences and write these on the board, if the sentences are wrong ask students to correct them or correct them yourself.

LISTENING

Aim
To develop listening for specific information.

Note With a weaker class, you could revise the vocabulary from issues raised in *Vocabulary* on the previous page. Ask students what issues they remember and put them on the board, e.g. helping the poor, crime, recession, drug control, unemployment, water shortages, inflation, government policies, national unity, cost of living. Then play the recording and ask students to listen for the topics the speakers mention. Check in open class by putting a tick (√) against those they spoke about on the board. (tuition fees, unemployment, voting, job prospects, cost of living). Then go on to Step 1.

Step 1 Tell students they will hear two university students from different countries and that they should take notes on what they say about the questions in A. Listen and then compare in pairs. Check in open class.

> **Suggested answers**
> The first speaker's country sounds better as they have done some controversial things, but the economy and job prospects are booming, easy for foreigners to get work.

🔊 4.1
A: So what do you think of your president?
B: Oh, I can't stand him. He's so arrogant.
A: Really? Whenever I see him on TV he comes across as being OK.
B: Ah, it's all marketing. You hear some people say he's boosted our standing in the world, whatever that's supposed to mean, but he's done nothing for people like me – just put up tuition fees for students.
A: I know. I saw. It's three thousand euros or something a year now, isn't it?
B: More than that!
A: Really! I don't know how you manage. The cost of living there's so high.
B: Tell me about it! I'm going to be so far in debt by the time I graduate, I'll be paying it back for years.
A: Is it easy to find a job there?
B: Well, this is it. Unemployment's shot up recently. It's really worrying. If you ask me, they've been so concerned with supposedly 'green' laws like banning plastic bags, they've totally ignored the economy and now it's a complete mess.
A: So when's the next election? Can't you vote against them?

B: It's next year, but I'm not going to vote.
A: No?
B: No. They're all as bad as each other. The opposition are so busy fighting among themselves that they're not going to make any difference.
A: I know what you mean, but there must be someone worth voting for. I mean, like our government has done a few controversial things – stuff I didn't agree with – but, you know, they've done good things as well. I mean, the economy's really booming.
B: Yeah? Maybe I should think about emigrating there after uni.
A: You should. Honestly, there's such a skills shortage that companies are paying really good money now. They're desperate for people.
B: You don't think the language would be a barrier?
A: Not necessarily. Quite a few multinationals have set up there recently and they use English and there are other jobs, and you'd pick our language up. They've actually done a lot to cut back on bureaucracy too so it's much easier for foreigners to get work than it used to be.
A: Yeah? I'll have to think about it. It'd be nice to escape my debts, anyway!

Step 2 In pairs or threes get students to complete the sentences in exercise B with the missing preposition. Monitor to help out with any problems of understanding, but avoid helping with the prepositions. Play the recording to check their answers.

> **Answers**
> | 1 on | 3 about, in | 5 against | 7 for | 9 on |
> |---|---|---|---|---|
> | 2 for | 4 with | 6 among | 8 with | |

Step 3 In pairs students discuss the questions in exercise C. Conduct brief feedback in open class.

GRAMMAR *so* and *such*

Aim
To practise language patterns with *so* and *such*.

Step 1 Get students to read the two example sentences and check understanding: *What is cause of the problem*? (Sentence 1 = the opposition are so busy fighting among themselves, sentence 2 = There's such a skills shortage.) *What is the result*? (Sentence 1 = they're not going to make any difference, sentence 2 = companies are paying really good money now.) Tell them that we use *so* and *such* to link the cause and result of a situation.

Step 2 Get them to read the explanation box and choose the correct alternative to complete the grammar rules. Check understanding = *What word follows so in the first sentence?* (Busy.) *What part of speech is it?* (Adjective.) *What words follow such in the second sentence?* (A skills shortage.) What part of speech are they? (Indefinite article + adjective + noun.) Get them to notice the patterns after so (+ adjective) and such [+ article (+ adjective) + noun].

Answers
1 so   2 such   3 don't have to

Direct students to the grammar reference on page 141 if they still seem unsure.

Step 3 Individually ask students to complete the sentences in exercise B with *so or such*. Then they compare in pairs before checking in open class.

Answers
1 so   2 so   3 such   4 such   5 so   6 such

Step 4 In pairs, ask students to write possible endings to the sentences. Then in groups compare their sentences. In open class share ideas.

Suggested answers
1 they have employed a consultant to promote their image.
2 it's getting more difficult to find affordable food.
3 they are too tired to enjoy themselves.
4 they couldn't prosecute.
5 people had to wear masks when they went outside.
6 he was forced to resign.

Step 5 Tell students to think about any news stories they've heard involving the situations in exercise B and what happened in the end. Give them some time to think of what they want to say. Then put them into small groups to share their opinions. Monitor and help out with any language problems. Do brief feedback in open class.

 4A see Teacher's notes p. 121.

DEVELOPING CONVERSATIONS
Responding to complaints

Aim
To introduce useful phrases to respond to complaints.

Step 1 Get students to read the responses in the explanation box and check understanding. Tell students that in English people often respond to an opinion in a polite way by using phrases that signal partial agreement or disagreement.

Step 2 Individually ask students to match the complaints in 1–6 to the responses in a–f. Then they compare in pairs or threes before checking in open class.

Answers
1 b   2 d   3 a   4 e   5 f   6 c

Step 3 In pairs ask students to write one extra possible way of responding to the complaints in 1–6.

Suggested answers
1 I know what you mean, I can hardly make it to the end of the month these days.
2 I know, and it's harder to find work when you are older.
3 Well, maybe, but I like the energy it gives me.
4 Tell me about it, I don't go out at all after dark.
5 Well, maybe, but the new shopping centre should bring more tourists.
6 I know what you mean, but if you know how to work the system it's OK.

Step 5 In pairs ask students to talk about possible ways of responding to the sentences in C. Conduct brief feedback.

Suggested answers
1 I know, what can we do about it though?
2 Well, maybe, but there are a lot of low cost airlines opening routes soon.
3 I know what you mean, but not everyone is the same.
4 I know, they are even trying to negotiate with them.
5 Well, maybe, but it takes a long time to make a difference.
6 I know what you mean, but there is an election soon.

CONVERSATION PRACTICE

Aim
To practise responding to complaints.

Step 1 Put students in AB pairs and get them to look at File B on page 157. Tell them to decide on their roles and follow the instructions to role-play the conversation. Monitor and take notes on their use of language for a correction slot later. Conduct brief feedback.

 pp. 84–85

 Next class Make photocopies of **4B** p. 135.

SPEAKING

Aim
To provide practice talking about social issues.

Step 1 Get students to read the social issues and check understanding and word stress of *gender discrimination* = where people are treated differently because they are female or male; *bullying* = behaviour that frightens or hurts someone weaker or smaller; _family breakdown_ = situation where the main family unit separates; _homelessness_ = people who live in the streets and have no home; _school dropout rates_ = the number of young people who leave school before they have completed their compulsory education; _drug and alcohol abuse_ = some people get addicted to alcohol and drugs and it affects their health.

Step 2 Ask students to individually rank the items from 1 (the most important) to 10 (the least important) in their society. Put them in pairs or threes to explain their choices. Remind them of the expressions of agreeing and disagreeing, e.g. _I know what you mean, but . . . , I know!, Tell me about it!, Well, maybe, but..._ Monitor and take notes on their language.

Step 4 In open class encourage pairs of students to tell each other their opinions and why.

 4B see Teacher's notes p. 212.

LISTENING 1

Aim
To develop listening for specific information.

Step 1 Tell students they are going to hear five short news extracts and decide which of the issues from the _Vocabulary_ box is discussed in each one. Play the recording. Students compare in pairs and check in open class. If necessary play the recording again.

Answers	
1 homelessness	4 the destruction of the
2 gender discrimination	environment
3 racism	5 family size

4.2

1 The government will today launch a new initiative aimed at getting vulnerable young people off the streets and into hostels. The move is a response to growing concern about the number of teenagers sleeping rough on the streets of the capital, many of whom, it is feared, are in danger of becoming involved in drugs and other criminal activity.
2 A senior executive at one of the country's leading law firms is today almost half a million euros richer after winning her case against her employers, McLintock and Rice. Judith Fenton had claimed she was denied promotion as a direct result of telling colleagues she was pregnant. The court ruled in her favour and she was awarded compensation of four hundred and eight-seven thousand euros.
3 Police are today conducting investigations after a young Asian student was attacked near the city centre by a group of white youths late last night.

The attack was captured on CCTV and a senior policeman has announced he believes it may well have been racially motivated. The 19-year-old vicim being treated in hospital and is believed to have suffered several broken bones.
4 A tiny pressure group has claimed victory over one of the country's richest men. Multi-millionaire Ronald Stamp had been planning to build a hotel and entertainment complex on a privately owned beach on the north-east coast. However, following protests by local residents, the group Save Our Seaside took legal action to prevent what they claimed would amount to 'vandalism on a huge scale' – a claim that was yesterday upheld in court.
5 A woman from East Sussex last week became the country's youngest grandmother. At the age of 29, Tracy Bell is now the proud granny of a baby boy, Kevin. Bell's daughter, Caroline, aged 14, said she had initially been too scared to break the news to her mother, and had waited until a doctor had confirmed she was indeed pregnant. Mrs. Bell, however, seems resigned to the situation, stating that as she is already bringing up five children, one more will make little difference.

Step 2 In pairs or threes ask students to read the statements in exercise B and decide which of the news extracts mentions each idea. Play the recording again to check the answers.

Answers		
speaker 1 c	speaker 3 a	speaker 5 b
speaker 2 d	speaker 4 e	

Step 4 In pairs or small groups, ask students try to add the verbs in the box to the nouns 1–8 to make a common phrase. Ask students to read the audioscript on page 167 to check their answers – tell them they appear in the same order as in the exercise.

Answers
1 launch a new initiative (speaker 1)
2 win her case (speaker 2)
3 be denied promotion (speaker 2)
4 conduct investigations, (speaker 3)
5 suffer several broken bones (speaker 3)
6 claim victory (speaker 4)
7 uphold a claim (speaker 4)
8 become a grandmother (speaker 5)

Step 5 Get students to read the questions in exercise E and give them a couple of minutes to think about their opinions. Then put students into pairs to discuss.

Tip If time, get students to share opinions in open class by referring to one group and saying '_I heard you talk about x, tell us about it_'.

LISTENING 2

Aim
To develop listening for general and specific information.

Step 1 Tell students they will hear two friends discussing one of the stories from the news extracts. Ask them to read the questions and then play the recording. In pairs they compare answers. Check answers in open class.

> **Answers**
> 1 gender discrimination at work (speaker 2 from the news extracts)
> 2 typical double standards
> 3 having children and a career

> 🔊 **4.3**
> A: Did you see that thing on the news about that woman who's been suing the firm she works for?
> B: I was just reading about that, actually. She won, didn't she?
> A: Absolutely. It was shocking what happened to her. It was such typical double standards!
> B: Well, maybe – but it was a lot of money. I'm not so sure about it all, to be honest. If you ask me, if you're in that kind of that situation, you have to decide what you want. Either you try and get promoted or you focus on having kids. You can't have everything in life, can you?
> A: That's such rubbish! You can't really believe that. This is the twenty-first century! Surely a woman's allowed to have children and a career!

Step 2 In pairs ask students to read the statements in exercise B and decide which ones they heard in the conversation. Play the recording again to check their answers.

> **Answers**
> 1, 5, and 9 were used

Step 3 In the same groups ask students to decide which of the sentences could be used to talk about the other news stories.

> **Answers**
> extract 1 sentences 4, 6, 7 and 8
> extract 2 sentences 1, 2, 3, 4, 7
> extract 3 = sentences 10, 11 and 12
> extract 4 = sentences 2 and 3
> extract 5 = sentences 1 and 7

NATIVE SPEAKER ENGLISH *Mind you*

Step 1 Get students to read the box and check understanding: *In the examples does the speaker agree completely with what was said before?* (No, they are sympathetic but add their own opinion, sentence 1 = it

was a lot of money, sentence 2 = the last initiative didn't work out well, sentence 3 = he was provoked.)

PRONUNCIATION Stressing *and* and *or*

Aim
To draw attention to stressing *and* and *or* for emphasis.

Step 1 Get students to read the explanation box and ask them if the same is true in their language.

Step 2 Play the recording and get students to repeat the sentences with the same stress pattern.

> 🔊 **4.4**
> They told her, 'You either have kids or you can get promoted.' (x 2)
> I mean, they can have a career and a family. (x 2)

Step 3 In pairs ask student to practise saying the sentences with and without the stress on *and* / *or*, the other student has to say if it was stressed or not.

Step 4 In small groups ask students to discuss if they think the sentences in B are true. Conduct brief feedback.

SPEAKING

Aim
To provide fluency practice in talking about news stories.

Step 1 Tell students to write a short conversation in pairs about one of the other four news stories they heard in *Listening* 1. Tell them to start by asking: *Did you see that thing on the news / in the paper about...?* They should answer by giving a comment about how they feel about it. Then they should continue the conversation by agreeing / disagreeing and add a comment. They should use at least one sentence from exercise B in *Listening* 2. Tell them to look back at their notes and the pages of the units to find at least two other pieces of useful language.

Step 2 Put students into groups of four and tell them to act out their dialogue to another pair. Monitor and correct any language problems. Conduct brief feedback on the most interesting news story they heard about.

 pp. 30–31

READING

Aim
To develop reading for general and specific information.

Step 1 Tell students they are going to read an article about economist Jeffery Sachs and global problems. Individually students look at the words in the box and if they don't know any words they can look them up in the *Vocabulary builder*. Then, get students to put the words in the four categories. Monitor and help out as necessary.

Step 2 Put students into pairs and ask them to explain their choices to each other.

> **Answers**
> Population: family planning, child mortality rate, birth rate
> Farming: crop yields, seeds, soil
> Underdeveloped countries: scarce resources, poverty, deprived
> Aid: donors, measures, project

Step 3 Tell students they are going to read an article about global issues, and get them to read the questions. Get students to read the headline and in pairs to predict what they think the article will say before reading.

Step 4 Individually ask students to read the article and to answer the questions. Ask them to check in pairs before checking in open class.

> **Answers**
> He is concerned about: poverty and hunger, global warming, AIDS and malaria pandemics.
> His solutions are: provide every child in poverty with an anti-mosquito net, free school meals, supplying fertilizers, access to family planning, basic health care and clean water supplies.

Step 5 Put them in pairs and ask them to explain the article to each other using the words from Exercise A.

GRAMMAR *the...*, *the...* + comparatives

Aim
To introduce and practise a comparative pattern to show how an increase or decrease causes a change.

Step 1 Write the following sentence on the board: *The longer we wait to save the planet, the worse the problem will become.* Check understanding: *What is the problem?* (How to save the planet.) *What is the consequence?* (The problem will get worse.) Then ask them *How do we emphasise an increase or decrease in something causing a problem? (The..., the ... + comparative.)* Tell them to read the explanation box.

Step 2 Ask students to individually find the sentences in the text and complete them. Then they compare in pairs before checking in open class.

> **Answers**
> 1 higher the ..., greater
> 2 more secure ..., fewer
> 3 longer ..., greater ..., larger

Step 3 Ask students to individually complete the sentences in exercise B with one word. Do the first one as an example. Ask them to compare in pairs before checking in open class.

> **Answers**
> 1 the / the
> 2 are / more
> 3 the / less
> 4 more / and / there
> 5 are / better
> 6 fewer (few is used before plural nouns) / have

Direct students to the grammar reference on page 141, if they are still unsure.

Step 4 Individually ask students to write sentences using *the...*, *the...* comparatives and the words in the box in C.

Step 5 In pairs or small groups students discuss the issues and use their statements to help make their point. Monitor and correct them on their pronunciation and take notes on their language.

Step 6 Divide students into As and Bs. Get As to read File 2 on page 156 and Bs to read File 11 on page 158. Give them time to prepare what they want to say.

Step 7 Put students in AB pairs and get them to role-play the conversation. Do brief feedback and a correction slot at the end.

SPEAKING

Aim
To provide fluency practice in expressing and responding to opinions.

Step 1 Ask students to read the article about *Millennium Promise*, then in pairs / threes ask them to discuss the questions in A. Monitor and help out with any problems.

Step 2 Ask students to work in groups of four or five and tell them they should all agree on one activity to help *Millennium Promise*. When they have chosen the activity, discuss when and where to do it, how to advertise it and who should do what. Conduct brief feedback.

Optional activity If time, ask each group to present their ideas or poster to the class. Decide together who has the best idea and who is the most organised.

Overall Aims

It is rarely enough to meet and use 'new' language and skills once. In reality, people learn these things by being exposed to them and activating them again and again. Therefore each of the four review units are designed to revise material covered in the previous four units. They also introduce a *Learner training* section (helping students to become more aware of their learning style / strategies and enabling them to learn more effectively). The first two pages are designed to revise the material in a fun, interactive way. The second two pages are more traditional listening, grammar and vocabulary exercises, which could be given as a progress test. In addition, these test pages expose students to exam-type questions they are likely to meet in common English exams.

LEARNER TRAINING

Overview

Research has shown that effective language learners develop strategies for dealing with a range of situations, from making sense of unknown language to recording and reviewing language. The *Learner training* feature encourages students to review their own strategies, whether implicit or explicit, as well as developing new strategies so they become more effective language learners and users.

Aim

To raise students' awareness about the factors involved in learning and remembering vocabulary.

Step 1 Tell students to read the statements about learning vocabulary individually and then in small groups to discuss the questions. Monitor and help out with any problems with language or ideas.

Step 2 Conduct feedback in open class by asking them what strategies or things they could do to help them remember vocabulary and put these ideas on the board, e.g. use vocabulary cards = on one side write the new word or expression and on the other write one of the following: the meaning, a sentence with the expression, a drawing or a translation. Then while you are waiting somewhere, you can test yourself by looking at the word or expression and see if you can remember.

GAME

Overview

Games are valuable for language learners because as they become involved in the activity they become less self-conscious about speaking in a foreign language and less worried about making mistakes. In addition, games help develop classroom dynamics and they are fun – it's important to enjoy learning!

Aim

To recycle some of the language covered in the units, in a fun, student-centred way.

Step 1 Put students into A / B pairs. Ask student A to look at the questions in the green squares and student B to look at the questions in the yellow squares. They should find the answers in the units and try to memorise them. They may need longer than five minutes for this.

Step 2 Tell students to play the game in pairs. They should take turns to throw a coin and move one of their squares for heads and two of their squares for tails. Their partner should check the answer in the relevant part of the book. If they get the answer right, they move forward one square (but not answer that question until their next turn). If they get the answer wrong, their partner tells them the answer and they miss a turn – and use the coin again for their next turn. The first student to reach the last square is the winner. If you want to extend the activity, students could swap colours and play again.

CONVERSATION PRACTICE

Overview
In this activity students decide for themselves which conversation they want to repeat. Two students perform the task in front of a third, who acts as 'judge'. Having an audience normally means students perform better. The judge also has to listen carefully because they have the responsibility for marking their classmates. This whole process has the added advantage of promoting learner autonomy.

Aim
To provide fluency practice in the different topics practised so far and to raise students' awareness of their speaking ability by asking them to observe and assess each other.

Step 1 Put students into groups of three and tell them they can refer to the *Vocabulary builder* if they need to. They should take turns to be pairs of speakers and an observer. Each pair should choose one of the topics, look back at the relevant part of the book and take a few minutes to prepare. They then have the conversation while the third student (the observer) listens and takes notes on how well they communicated, their strengths and weaknesses with use of language and any common errors. At the end, the observer gives a mark out of 10 to each person and explains the mark using their notes as a guide (1= poor, 10= excellent). Then they swap, change roles and repeat the activity with a different topic. Monitor and help out where necessary. Finish with a brief correction slot.

ACT OR DRAW

Overview
This is an enormously popular game amongst people the world over because it is so much fun. The gap between the actor's / artist's performance and the 'guesser's' ideas leads to a lot of laughter and a lot of language use as well.

Aim
To revise and practise vocabulary in a fun way.

Step 1 Put students into groups of three or four and ask them to take turns to act or draw the words / phrases in the box chosen at random. They should not speak while they are acting or drawing. Their partner should guess the word / phrase. Then they swap.

QUIZ

Overview
This game is best played in teams of two or three in order to promote speaking. It's a good idea to give students a realistic time limit. The pressure also increases energy levels and makes the game more exciting.

Aim
To revise and practise more vocabulary from the units.

Step 1 Put students into pairs or threes and ask them to answer as many questions as possible. You could do this as a race so that the first pair / three to finish with the correct answers are the winners.

Alternatively
You could do this activity as a 'pub quiz', with you reading out each question and groups of three or four students secretly writing down the answers. Then in open class each group swaps their answers with another group. You read the answers and they mark each other's answers. The winner is the group with the most correct answers.

> **Answers**
> 1 You might sing along with a **catchy** song or have it in your head all day.
> 2 An **ordeal** is a bad thing to go through.
> 3 You might **seek** help, assistance, information, etc.
> 4 You might need a **disguise** if you want to hide your identity.
> 5 If you **fulfil** an ambition or dream, you achieve it.
> 6 You might **steer clear of** an area, if it's dangerous or rough, or a person if you don't want to talk to them.
> 7 The opposite of a **stunning** building is a hideous building.
> 8 You could **launch** a new product, a rocket, an advertising campaign, etc.
> 9 You **acquire** things by buying them, being given them or by collecting them.
> 10 If you **settle** in a town or a city, you get a job, a house and maybe start a family.
> 11 Things that use or contain **wire** could be = a coat hanger, an electric cable, a mobile phone aerial.
> 12 A film, book or performance can **leave you cold**.
> 13 (Answer depends on where you are.)
> 14 You can use, glue, a nail or a screw to **join together** bits of wood.
> 15 A politician might use an advertising campaign, a new law or an appearance at a local festival to **boost** their **standing**.

COLLOCATIONS

Overview
Collocations are words that usually go together such as *do me a favour* and *a pressing problem*. Until relatively recently the concept of collocation was not an area that was covered in vocabulary teaching. However, computational linguistics has shown how important a force collocation is in language. This activity helps to develop students' awareness of the importance of collocation in natural language generation.

Aim
To revise and practise some common collocations from the first four units and to give students learner training in using the *Vocabulary builder*.

Step 1 Put students in A / B pairs and tell them to test each other on collocations from units 1–4. Student A looks at unit 1 of the *Vocabulary builder* and reads out a collocation, with a gap where there is '~'. They should say 'blah' for the gap and student B should say the missing word. They could do 6–8 collocations and then swap.

PRONUNCIATION

Overview
These activities encourage students to be reflective about sounds and to develop their 'inner ear'. The main aim is not to make students native-speaker-like but to develop their ability to understand spoken English as well as to improve their own intelligibility when speaking to other non-native and native English speakers.

Aim
To revise and practise voiced and unvoiced consonants.

Step 1 Tell students to read the explanation box. Then tell them to practise saying the consonants in exercise A by repeating them to themselves. Tell them to put their fingers on their throat, so that they can hear the vibration on the voiced consonants in the second column, e.g. v/ /b/, /d/, etc.

Step 2 Tell students to individually repeat the phrases in exercise B. Monitor and help out with pronunciation. Then in groups they practise saying the phrases to each other. Tell them to decide who they think has the best accent – they should try to copy that person.

DICTATION

Overview
Dictation is a great way to practise language (vocabulary and grammar) and skills (listening and writing) in one activity. Students like it because it's challenging and really tests their ability to listen and understand the main information when someone is speaking.

Aim
To give students practice in note taking.

Step 1 Tell students they are going to hear a short extract from one of the texts they read in units 1–4 and that they will hear it only once. Tell them they won't have to time to write everything, but they should listen and take notes. Play the recording only once.

> **🔊 R1.1**
> Venice was absolutely amazing. You would've loved it. I stayed with Nina, who I'm sure you remember from uni. It was really kind of her to put me up – and it meant I didn't have to struggle with trying to find a hotel, which would've been almost impossible! The city was completely packed with tourists for the whole ten days, and prices really shoot up.

Step 2 Put students into groups of three or four and tell them to work together to write the whole text from their notes. Then they can compare what they have written with the audioscript on page 167.

Note
Listening and the rest of the review unit could be used as a progress test. The suggested scores are given below each exercise. Alternatively, these exercises could be done individually or in pairs and then checked in pairs, or you could put students in teams and they do them as a quiz / competition. If students need help you can direct them to the relevant pages of the grammar reference or the *Vocabulary builder*.

 pp. 34–35

LISTENING

Aim
To develop listening for general information.
The audio is 🔊 R1.2.

Exercise A answers				
1 d	2 c	3 f	4 e	5 b
Exercise B answers				
1 b	2 f	3 c	4 a	5 d

GRAMMAR

Exercise A answers

1 which	4 by which
2 usually	5 both correct
3 both correct	6 none

Exercise B answers

1 They're bound to win.
2 It's so messy I can't find anything in here.
3 I'm dreading making the speech
4 It might possibly rain this afternoon.
5 She only helps out once in a while.
6 I don't tend to / tend not to go out on Friday nights.

Exercise C

1 We're thinking of buying
2 I always carry a pen to write
3 They're such welcoming people
4 There were lots of rides, most of them
5 correct
6 There was so little traffic
7 correct
8 in the carnival look weird.

LANGUAGE PATTERNS

Answers

1 would	3 go	5 Not / Without	7 campaign
2 to	4 some/any	6 went	8 for

PREPOSITIONS

Answers

1 on	3 on	5 to	7 in
2 at	4 in	6 in	8 at

WORD FAMILIES

Answers

1 optimism	5 compensation
2 anxiety	6 bureaucratic
3 caution	7 racially
4 obsession	8 permission

COLLOCATIONS

Answers

1 setback	5 interpretation
2 temptation	6 target
3 challenge	7 controversy
4 hazard	8 spiral

PHRASAL VERBS

Answers

1 have	3 stick	5 put	7 joined	9 cut
2 dressed	4 shot	6 setting	8 came	10 go

VOCABULARY

Answers

1 loosely	3 subjected	5 combat	7 uplifting
2 poverty	4 upheld	6 dull	8 overcome

05 SPORTS AND INTERESTS

UNIT OVERVIEW
The main aim of this unit is to enable students to **talk about what they do in their free time** and **how fit they are** and to **talk about lucky escapes**. They have practice in **checking they heard things correctly**. The main grammatical focus is *should(n't) have, could(n't) have* and *would(n't)* **have** and the **present perfect simple and continuous** and ways of **expressing health and fitness, football and life,** and **lucky escapes.**

SPEAKING

Aim
To lead in to the topic.

Step 1 Individually ask students to read the statements and decide which statements are true for them, and which are true for other people they know. Tell them that it's not necessary to find someone for each statement.

Step 2 Put students into groups of four to compare their ideas.

Step 3 Conduct brief feedback by asking a student from each group to tell the rest of the class what interests or hobbies they had in common. Then do a correction slot. Remind them to record their common errors in their notebooks.

LISTENING

Aim
To develop listening for specific information.

Step 1 Tell students they are going to hear three conversations about free-time activities and to answer the questions in A. Then play the recording and get students to compare in pairs or threes. If necessary, play the recording again and pause after each speaker to check the answers.

Answers
1 Conversation 1: belly dancing; Conversation 2: a fencing workshop; Conversation 3: knitting group.
2 Conversation 1: this will be her first class, Conversation 2 she started at school, Conversation 3 for about six months.
3 Conversation 1: she saw an advertisement; Conversation 2: she tried it at her PE (physical education) class at school; Conversation 3: When he was giving up smoking.
4 Conversation 1: maybe, he'd feel a bit self-conscious; Conversation 2: no, just the thought of doing that kind of exercise makes him sweat, Conversation 3: Yes, at first he thinks it's a bit boring, but then changes his mind when he finds out a lot of women go there.

5.1
Conversation 1
A: What are you up to later?
B: Oh, I'm going to a belly dancing class.
A: You're doing what?
B: Belly dancing. You know, like...
A: Yeah, I know what it is. I just had no idea that you did that.
B: Well, I don't really. It's actually the first class.
A: Oh OK. So why belly dancing?
B: I've been thinking about doing something to get a bit fitter and I've never liked sport particularly. I find jogging and swimming and stuff like that a bit boring, you know – and then I saw this class advertised and I thought it'd be fun.
A: Yeah, I guess so. I should really do something as well. I've put on five kilos since January.
B: Really? It doesn't look it. You've got a lovely figure.
A: Well, I don't feel like I have! And I'm really unfit. I had to run for the bus this morning and it took me about ten minutes to get my breath back!
B: Well, why don't you come with me?
A: I don't know. I think I'd feel a bit self-conscious.
B: Come on! You can't be worse than me. I'm totally uncoordinated! It'll be a laugh.
A: Well, maybe.
Conversation 2
C: Are you around this weekend at all?
D: No, I'm going to a fencing workshop all day Saturday.
C: You're going where?
D: This fencing workshop. It's like a master class with this top Russian fencer.
C: Wow! I didn't even know you did fencing? How did you get into that?
D: Oh, we actually used to do it at school. In PE, we had the option to try out all kinds of sports and I just really got into it and then I joined a club and then I started competing a bit more seriously, you know.
C: I had no idea. Well, what about Sunday? I'm going to have a wander round the flea market in the morning.
D: To be honest, I think I'm just going to have a lie-in and chill out at home. I'll be exhausted after Saturday.
C: Fair enough. Just the thought of doing that kind of exercise makes me sweat!

Conversation 3
E: What're you doing this evening? Do you fancy meeting later?
F: No, I can't. I've got my ... um ...my um knitting group tonight.
E: You've got what?
F: My knitting group.
E: Since when?
F: I've been doing it for about six months now. I took it up because I was giving up smoking and a friend suggested doing it. She said it'd give me something to fiddle with instead of cigarettes, so I joined this group and it's been really good. I feel so much healthier now and I actually really like the knitting. I just find it very, very relaxing.
E: OK, but isn't it just full of old women, this group?
F: No, not at all. Well, I mean, I am the only man, but most of the women are quite young.
E: Ah.
F: What? What's 'Ah' supposed to mean?
E: Nothing.

Step 2 Tell students to read the statements in exercise B. Tell them to listen and choose the correct word in each statement. In pairs they compare answers. If necessary, play the recording again. Then check answers in open class.

Answers
1 up to	5 flea	8 it up
2 figure	6 lie-in	9 fiddle
3 breath (noun)	7 Fair enough	10 isn't it.
4 master		

Step 3 Get students in pairs or threes to discuss the questions in exercise C. Conduct brief feedback.

NATIVE SPEAKER ENGLISH

What are you up to?

Step 1 Ask students to read the exampl es in the box and check they understand by asking: what can you use instead of *what're you up to later? (What are you doing?)* Is this formal or informal? (Informal.)

VOCABULARY Health and fitness

Aim
To introduce vocabulary related to health and fitness.

Step 1 Ask students to look at the words in the vocabulary box. Check and drill the word stress: *stamina, healthy lifestyle, flexibility, hand-eye co-ordination, speed, strength*.

Step 2 Ask students to match the words in the box with the sentences 1–6, then compare in pairs. Check as a class.

Answers
1 stamina
2 speed
3 flexibility
4 strength
5 hand-eye coordination
6 healthy lifestyle

Step 3 Check understanding and elicit word stress: *keep up with* = make progress at the same speed as others, *flab* = loose, fat flesh, *clumsy* = someone who is not careful and is always breaking, dropping or knocking over things. Then ask students to individually complete the sentences in B and then compare in pairs. Check answers in open class.

Step 4 Put students into pairs or threes to discuss the questions in exercise C. Conduct feedback in open class.

DEVELOPING CONVERSATIONS
Checking what you heard

Aim
To raise students' awareness of common strategies to check what you've heard.

Step 1 Get students to read the two example sentences in the explanation box and check understanding: how does the person check they heard correctly? (*You've got what? You're going where?*) Tell them we often add a question word at the end of a clause to check we heard something correctly and that this turns the statement into a question. Tell them we also stress the question word. (See stress in audioscript below.)

Step 2 Ask students to listen to the examples. Ask them: What happens to B's voice in each case? (It rises at the end on the question word.)

5.2
A: I've got my knitting group tonight.
B: You've got what?
A: I'm going to a fencing workshop all day.
B: You're going where?

Step 3 Ask students to individually complete the sentences in exercise B with similar questions to those in the example. Tell them to pay attention to the verb tense, some are in the past and some are negative. Monitor.

Step 4 Put students in pairs to compare their answers, then check in open class.

Answers

1 You run how far?
2 You do what?
3 You went where?
4 She's into what?
5 You didn't get up till when?

Step 5 Put students in pairs to practise reading the dialogues, taking turns to be A and B. Monitor, making sure their voices rise at the end of the checking questions.

CONVERSATION PRACTICE

Aim
To provide fluency practice of talking about free time.

Step 1 Divide students into As and Bs and tell them they are going to talk about a hobby or interest they have. Tell them to prepare both roles because they practise twice, first as A and then as B.

Step 2 Then put students into pairs to talk about their unusual hobby or interest. Monitor and take notes on their language for a correction slot at the end.

 pp. 38–39

 Next class Make photocopies of **5A** p. 136.

SPEAKING

Aim
To provide fluency practice talking about sport.

Step 1 Ask students to read the questions in exercise A and to ask you the questions in open class to provide a clear model. Then put them in pairs to discuss the questions. Monitor and conduct brief feedback.

VOCABULARY Football and life

Aim
To practise expressions related to football and life.

Step 1 In pairs or threes students read the statements in exercise A and help each other with the words in bold. If they like they can check in the *Vocabulary builder*. Monitor, but try not to help too much with vocabulary, as the aim is for students to check meaning for themselves.

Step 2 In groups students discuss what other sports the words could be used in and how sentences 7–13 could be used for non-sporting things. Check ideas in open class.

Suggested answers

1 *sent off* = any sport involving a ball
2 *goalkeeper* = hockey, ice hockey, water polo
3 *fouled* = most sports involving a ball, Note: not tennis
4 *post and bar* = most sports involving a ball and two teams
5 *dived* = all sports involving a ball
6 *thrashed* = all sports
7 *close* = all sports
8 *tackled* = most sports involving a ball and two teams
9 *greedy* = most sports involving a ball and two teams
10 *substituted* = most sports involving a ball and two teams
11 *got promoted* = most sports involving a ball and two teams
12 *sacked the manager* = all sports
13 *fixed* = all

Answers

Used about non-sporting things:

7 *close* = short distance or time away, shave, friends
8 *tackled* = deal with a difficult problem,
9 *greedy* = eat or drink more than you need, want more money, things or power than you need
10 *substituted* = use something new or different instead of what it's normally used for,
11 *promoted* = given more responsibility at work
12 *sacked the manager* = at work
13 *fixed* = any result in a competition

Step 3 Ask students to individually choose five of the words in bold to talk about that have happened to them or people they know in sport or in other areas of life. Give them time to think about what they want to say.

Step 4 Get students in pairs to discuss their experiences. Monitor and take notes on their use of the target language from *Vocabulary* for a correction slot at the end.

READING

Aim
To develop reading for general and specific information.

Step 1 Ask students to discuss the questions in exercise A in pairs. Conduct feedback and write their ideas on the board.

Step 2 Tell students to read the text quickly and see if their ideas were mentioned in the text. Note any other ideas not on the board. In open class check their ideas.

Step 3 Ask students to read the statements and decide which of them the writer would agree with. They should explain why by referring to the information in the text. They compare answers in pairs before checking as a class.

Answers

1 yes – in the first paragraph: people suffering from mild depression

---

2 no – in the second paragraph: Competitive sports teaches us...

3 no – in the second paragraph : Sure, we're not all naturally sporty

4 no – in the third paragraph: Obviously, these are not necessarily bad – especially reading

5 no – in the third paragraph: Playing sports helps to build relationships...

6 yes – in the fourth paragraph: So making sport...

7 no – in the fourth paragraph: I'm reminded of a scene in a film...

8 no – in the last paragraph: No-one looks aback at their life and says...

9 yes – in the last paragraph: No, what we remember...

Step 4 Individually students read the text again and mark the text to show where they agree or disagree with the writer's opinion. Then in pairs or threes they discuss their opinions. Conduct brief feedback in open class.

 5A see Teacher's notes p. 122.

GRAMMAR *Should(n't) have, could(n't)have, would(n't) have*

Aim
To introduce and practise modal verbs to express regret.

Step 1 Individually students read the explanation box. Check understanding: Sentence 1 – *Did I stick to the rules?* (Yes.) *Was it a mistake?* (Yes.) So if we do something and we think it was a mistake we say *I should've* and the result is certain; in the past we say *I would've*. Sentence 2: *Did I work more?* (No.) *Was I successful?* (No.) *How sure am I?* (Not very.) *Did I buy a new car?* (No.) So if we didn't do something and the result is not certain we say *I should've*; in the past we say *I could've*. Then get them to complete the rules. Check answers in open class.

Answers
1 should've	3 Would've
2 shouldn't have	4 could've

Step 2 Ask students to complete the sentences in exercise B individually. Tell them to pay attention to the tense, e.g. present or past, then compare in pairs. Check answers in open class.

Answers
1 should've saved
2 shouldn't have been disallowed
3 should've stuck to
4 should've been sent off
5 shouldn't be, should've passed
6 should've thrashed, shouldn't have bought

Step 3 Tell students to listen to the recording and write down the six sentences they hear. If necessary, play each sentence

twice. In pairs students compare with the audioscript on page 168. Check in open class by getting students to dictate them to you and you write them on the board.

 5.3
1 I <u>should've joined</u> a <u>gym years</u> ago.
2 I <u>shouldn't</u> have <u>eaten</u> so <u>much</u>.
3 You <u>should've gone</u> to <u>bed earlier</u>.
4 I <u>shouldn't</u> have been <u>substituted</u>.
5 He <u>should never</u> have been <u>sent off</u>!
6 We <u>should've gone</u> somewhere <u>else</u>.

Step 4 Play each sentence and get students to tell you which are stressed (sounds stronger), tell them in spoken English we stress the important information (in a way it reads like a telegram). Then use the sentences on the board to mark the stress.

Step 5 In pairs students practise saying the sentences to each other and help with the pronunciation.

Step 6 In new pairs ask them to imagine what happened in the situations. Check their ideas in open class.

Possible answers
1 The person has just been told they are overweight.
2 The person feels sick.
3 The person is tired and can't concentrate.
4 The person tackled an opponent fairly.
5 The person didn't hit an opponent, she was pushed by the opponent.
6 The people are not happy with the restaurant they went to because of the bad service.

SPEAKING

Aim
To provide fluency practice of expressions learnt so far.

Step 1 Tell students to read the topics and choose one to talk about. Tell them to look at their notes and try to use the language they have learnt so far including *should(n't) have / could(n't) have / would(n't) have*. Give them time to think about what they want to say.

Step 2 In pairs or threes students tell each other about their topic. Monitor and take notes on their language for a correction slot at the end.

 pp. 40–41

Next class Make photocopies of 5B p. 137.

LISTENING

Aim
To develop listening for general and specific information.

Step 1 Ask students to look at the vocabulary box and check understanding. Also get them to look at the sentence frames and notice the patterns that come after the sentence frames, e.g. *I think it'd be* + adjective, *I think I'd really enjoy it because I like* + noun or verb phrase, *I don't have* + noun phrase, *I'm not* + adjective + *enough*, *I'd be scared of* + verb-*ing*, *I'd worry about* + verb-*ing*.

Step 2 Put students in pairs or threes to discuss the questions in exercise A. Conduct brief feedback.

Step 3 Tell students they are going to listen to three people – Chloe, Molly and Kyle – talking about Molly's uncle and to decide which of the activities in exercise A he has done. Then play the recording and get students to compare answers in pairs. Check as a class.

Answers
Handstands, ice-skating, hang-gliding, roller-skating, windsurfing

5.4
C: I must go and send my cousin an email in a minute.
M: Oh, OK.
C: I've been meaning to go round and see him, because he's not been well, but Kyle's a bit reluctant to drive me round there because it'd mean spending time with my uncle.
M: Really? What's wrong with him?
K: He's just mad, that's all.
M: He's not, he's just...
K: Annoying?
M: No!
K: Crazy? Exhausting?
M: Chloe – just ignore him. Kyle – you can be so horrible sometimes.
K: Listen, Chloe, the last time we went to see him he had a thing about handstands. We were sitting outside a café, just having a coffee and chatting and he suddenly just got up and did a handstand – right next to all the tables! He kept it up for about half an hour!
C: That does sound a bit odd. How old is he?
M: About 50.
C: 50!
K: I told you! He's crazy.
M: He is not! He's just one of these people who can't sit still. I mean, he's always loved sport and when he does something new, he really gets into it. Like he took us ice-skating once. Do you remember?
K: How could I forget?

M: I mean, we were exhausted after about an hour, but he just kept on skating – and we watched him going round and round for another hour.
K: It was like he'd just completely forgotten we were there! And what about the hang-gliding?
C: Hang-gliding?
M: Yeah, he used to go hang-gliding. Obsessed with it, he was. He went practically every weekend for about three years.
K: Until he had an accident. He fell something like 1,000m without a parachute.
C: You're joking!
M: No, it's true.
C: So what happened?
M: Well, he'd borrowed someone else's glider for some reason and they didn't have a parachute, but he went up anyway. And he was caught in really bad weather and the hang-glider broke and he fell.
C: And he wasn't badly injured?
M: Well, he went through some trees, which broke his fall. He had hairline fractures in his shoulder and his neck and some minor cuts and bruises, but basically he was OK. He was incredibly lucky he didn't die.
C: Absolutely!
K: Anyway, then we saw him about three weeks later roller-skating in the park, even though he still had his neck in a brace!
C: My God! But he did give up the hang-gliding after that?
M: Not exactly, no. He tried it once more – to overcome any fear. I mean, he just wanted to prove to himself he could do it, but since then ... no. The last few years he's been really into windsurfing. He's actually always liked it – he did it when he was younger – but the last few years, that's been his main obsession. He lives on the coast, so he goes nearly every day.
C: Right. I'm starting to think Kyle might be right!
K: And you haven't heard all of it. For the last few months he's been rubbing lemon juice into his skin and his hair every day! He says it gets rid of dandruff and he was going on and on about how amazingly healthy it is.
M: OK, OK! It's true. He is a little bit mad, but he's a nice guy and he's fun to be with.
K: In small doses!

Step 4 In pairs ask students to read the sentences in exercise C and decide if they are true or false and why. Play the recording and check their answers.

Answers
1 F: he did one if front of them while they were having coffee
2 F: Molly and Kyle were exhausted after an hour
3 F: he went practically every weekend
4 T: not exactly, he tried it once more after that but since then, no
5 T: he's been doing it for the last few years

6 T: he lives on the coast
7 F: he rubs it into his skin and hair, it gets rid of dandruff
8 T: in small doses (for short periods of time)

Step 5 Put students in pairs or threes to discuss the questions in exercise E. Conduct brief feedback.

LANGUAGE PATTERNS

Aim
To draw students' attention to ways of emphasising information by repeating a word.

Step 1 Tell students to read the language pattern box.

Step 2 Ask students to translate the sentences into their own language. In a monolingual class, ask students to compare their translations. In a multilingual class, ask students to work in pairs and tell each other if the sentences were easy to translate into their language.

Step 3 Ask students to cover their English translations and use their translations to translate the sentences back into English. Then to compare their translations in pairs against the book. Alternatively, if you prefer not to use translation ask students give you some example sentences.

GRAMMAR Present perfect continuous / simple

Aim
To consolidate the use of the present perfect continuous and simple.

Step 1 In pairs ask students to read sentences one to four and decide if the meaning of the sentence is a or b. Do the first one as an example by asking *In sentence* 1 *When did he start thinking about visiting?* (In the past), *Does he still think about it now?* (Yes). Tell them that when we emphasise an intention, activity or feeling that started in the past and continues up to the present, we use the present perfect continuous. Check answers in open class.

Answers			
1 b	2 b	3 b	4 a

Step 2 Get students to read the explanation box to answer the question in exercise B, e.g. it's an action that started in the past and is still true now.

Step 3 Ask students to read the sentences in exercise C individually, match the sentence halves and compare in pairs before checking in open class.

Answers							
1 c	2 b	3 h	4 f	5 a	6 g	7 d	8 e

Step 4 In pairs students discuss the question in exercise D. Direct students to the grammar reference on page 144 if they still seem unsure.

Answers
1 activity repeated over time (all morning)
2 & 3 intention that is still going on now
4 feeling that is still going on now
5, 6 & 8 express actions completed before now which have a present result
8 *hear* is a verb which is hardly ever used in the *-ing* form.

Step 5 Ask students to individually complete the sentences so that they are true for them. Then to discuss in pairs. Monitor and take notes for a correction slot at the end.

 5B see Teacher's notes p. 122.

VOCABULARY Lucky escapes

Aim
To introduce and practise ways of expressing what happened to them in an accident.

Step 1 Get students to read the problems, then check understanding and elicit word stress: *hairline fracture* = very thin break or crack in a bone, *tore* (past of tear) a *ligament* = damage a muscle so that it pulls apart, *sprain* = stretch or turn too much, *knock out* = hit so hard you (nearly) lose consciousness, *pass out* = faint.

Step 2 In pairs or threes ask students to discuss which of the problems in exercise A is worse. Check ideas as a class.

Step 3 Write the conversation on the board without *hairline fracture* and *broken his leg*, e.g. *He had a ...*, *He... completely*. Ask students what words are missing. Then in pairs they write two more conversations like this, but leave blanks for the vocabulary from exercise A.

Step 4 In groups of four, one pair takes a turn to read the dialogue and the other pair has to say what's missing.

SPEAKING

Aim
To provide fluency practice.

Step 1 Ask students to individually choose one of the speaking activities in exercise A. Remind them that they can tell an imaginary story, or tell a true story about an accident they (or someone they know) has had.

Step 2 In pairs or small groups they tell each other what happened; encourage them to respond as in exercise B. Conduct brief feedback.

06 ACCOMMODATION

UNIT OVERVIEW

The main aim of this unit is to enable students to **talk about places they have stayed in** and **settling in somewhere.** They have practice in **discussing and dealing with problems.** The main grammatical focus is **modifiers and** *have / get something done* and ways of **expressing where you stayed** and **understanding idioms.**

 Next class Make photocopies of **6A** p. 138.

SPEAKING

Aim
To lead in to the topic.

Step 1 Get students to look at the places in the vocabulary box and check understanding: *self-catering apartment* = a flat you rent for a holiday and can do your own cooking, *a camping van* = bigger than a car and you can sleep in it. Put students into small groups to discuss the questions. Conduct brief feedback.

VOCABULARY Where you stayed

Aim
To introduce and practise expressions to describe places.

Step 1 Ask students to read the statements in exercise A and decide if they are describing good places or bad places or either. Ask students to compare in pairs then check answers as a class.

Answers				
1 bad	3 good	5 bad	7 bad	9 either
2 good	4 bad	6 good	8 good	10 either

Step 2 In pairs ask students to look at the pictures on the page and describe them using the vocabulary from exercise A. Conduct brief feedback in open class.

Answers
1 It's in the middle of nowhere, could have stunning views, the weather is terrible and the sea is rough.
2 People are camping in tents, the campsite is flooded and everything has got filthy.
3 The place is a bit of a dump.
4 A posh hotel that looks welcoming.

LISTENING

Aim
To develop listening for specific information.

Step 1 Tell students to listen to the two short conversations and to answer the questions in A. Ask students to compare their answers in paris then listen again to check.

Answers
Conversation 1 = 1: They camped on the festival site and then in a flat of some people they met at the festival, 2: some local people put them up for a couple of nights , 3: absolutely poured down, whole place was flooded and they got completely soaked – tent, sleeping bags everything, everything covered in mud.

Conversation 2 = 1: They stayed in a hotel, 2: stayed in an amazing place on the south coast – right on top of the cliffs, overlooking the ocean, stunning sunset, hardly anyone there, nice just chilling out, drinking tea and chatting to other people, 3: the hotel was a bit cut-off, the minibus only went in the morning and in the evening.

♺ 6.1
Conversation 1
A: Have you ever been to Hungary?
B: Yeah, I went to the Sziget festival a couple of years ago.
A: You went where?
B: The Sziget. I don't know if I'm pronouncing it right, but it's an enormous music festival in Budapest. It's held on this island in the middle of the Danube.
A: Oh right. So where did you stay?
B: We camped on the festival site. It was a bit of a nightmare, actually, because it absolutely poured down while we were there. The whole place was flooded and we got completely soaked - tent, sleeping bags, everything. Everything ended up covered in mud. It was crazy.
A: Couldn't you stay somewhere else?

B: Well, we actually did in the end. We met these really nice Hungarians who lived in the city and they put us up for a couple of nights.

A: Wow, that was generous! So would you go again?

A: Absolutely. We had a whale of a time in spite of the weather. I hardly slept the whole time we were there. There was so much going on.

Conversation 2

A: Did you go away in the holiday at all?

B: Yeah, I went to Turkey.

A: In August? Wasn't it a bit hot?

B: It was boiling, but then I love the heat – and you get quite dry heat there.

A: I guess. So did you enjoy it?

B: Yeah, it was brilliant. We stayed in this absolutely amazing place on the south coast – right on top of the cliffs, overlooking the ocean.

A: Sounds nice.

B: It was. Wait, I've got a picture of it somewhere on my mobile.

A: Let's have a look. Wow! Look at that sunset. That's stunning!

B: I know. It was like that nearly every night.

A: That's great. Were there any other places nearby? It looks as if it's in the middle of nowhere.

B: It was a bit cut-off, yeah. It was a few kilometres along this winding track to the nearest village – well, town – but they had a minibus to take people there in the morning and to bring them back in the evening.

A: Wasn't that a pain, having to rely on the bus? Didn't they run more often than that?

B: No. It was a bit of pain, if I'm honest, but considering how cheap the place was, it was fair enough. I mean, you could walk back if you really couldn't bear to hang around and there was a little bay you scramble down to from the hotel. It was a great place as there was hardly anyone there. It was also actually really nice just chilling out, drinking tea and chatting to the other people in the hotel. It was cool.

A: Mmm. I think I'd get a bit restless after a couple of days. I don't really like being stuck in one place.

LANGUAGE PATTERNS

Aim
To draw students' attention to some common patterns using *considering* to express contrast.

Step 1 Ask students to read the examples in the box. Check understanding of *considering* = show that your opinion about something is affected by a particular fact.

Step 2 Ask students to translate the sentences into their own language. In a monolingual class, ask students to compare their translation. In a multilingual class, ask students to work in pairs and tell each other if the sentences were easy to translate into their language.

Step 3 Ask students to use their translation to translate the sentences back into English. Then ask them to compare their translations in pairs against the book and discuss who had the least mistakes. Alternatively, if you prefer not to use translation ask students to notice the patterns.

GRAMMAR

Modifiers

Aim
To introduce expressions to describe places.

Step 1 Ask students to read the grammar explanation box. Point out that *completely* and *absolutely* are strong modifiers and go with strong adjectives, e.g. *completely deserted, absolutely incredible. Really* is unusual because it can go with strong and neutral adjectives, e.g. *really empty, really deserted*.

Step 2 Students look at exercise A individually and correct the mistakes. In pairs they compare before checking in open class.

Answers
1 It was a bit of a nightmare.
2 We got really / completely soaked.
3 It was quite nice.
4 correct
5 correct
6 There were hardly any people there.

Direct students to the grammar reference on page 144 if they still seem unsure.

Step 3 Individually students look at exercise B and decide which modifiers go with each group. Then in pairs they compare before checking answers in open class.

Answers
1 a bit of a (+noun phrase)
2 hardly (+ verb phrase)
3 absolutely (+ strong adjective)
4 a bit (+ adjective or noun)
5 very (+ adjective)

Step 4 Tell students to use some of the words and modifiers to talk about places they've been to or visited on holiday. Put students into small groups to share their experiences.

 6A see Teacher's notes p. 122.

PRONUNCIATION
Modifiers, stress and meaning

Aim
To show how changing stress can affect meaning.

Step 1 Read the explanation box to students and emphasise the stress, e.g. It was quite <u>easy</u>. Ask, *Do I think it was easy?* (Yes), *How do you know?* (The stress was on the adjective = *easy*) then change the stress, e.g. *It's <u>quite</u> easy.* Ask, *Do I think it was easy?* (a little), *How do you know?* (The stress was on the modifier = *quite*.)

Step 2 Tell students they will listen to the beginning of six sentences and to decide which of the two options is the best ending for each, depending on the stress. Play the first one as an example and pause to check the option. Repeat the process for each sentence, or play the rest without pausing.

> 🔊 **6.2**
> 1 It was quite near the beach.
> 2 The beach was quite crowded.
> 3 It was a bit overwhelming.
> 4 The surrounding area's quite nice.
> 5 The food was pretty good.

> **Answers**
> 1 b   2 a   3 b   4 a   5 b

Step 3 Tell students to practise saying sentences 1–6 in pairs in two different ways: first they stress the modifier, then the adjective. Monitor and help with pronunciation.

DEVELOPING CONVERSATIONS
Negative questions

Aim
To practise negative questions to show surprise or opinions.

Step 1 Get students to read the explanation box. Model the examples by emphasising the words in italics, e.g. *Couldn't you stay somewhere else?* Ask them if they do the same in their own language.

Step 2 Tell students to complete the questions with the correct negative form, tell them to read both lines and decide what tense to use. In pairs students compare answers before checking in open class.

> **Answers**
> 1 wasn't   2 don't   3 have   4 weren't   5 isn't

Step 3 Tell students to look at exercise B and individually write negative questions about the sentences. In pairs they compare answers before checking answers in open class.

> **Answers**
> 1 Wasn't it expensive?   3 Isn't it scary?
> 2 Won't it be crowded?   4 Didn't it feel awkward?

Step 4 Tell students to continue the conversations and try to use more negative questions. You could develop one on the board, eliciting ideas from students.

CONVERSATION PRACTICE

Aim
To use the language practised in the unit so far.

Step 1 Tell students they are going to have conversations about places they've stayed in recently. If they haven't stayed anywhere recently, they can use their imagination. Give them time to prepare what they want to say.

Step 2 Put students in new pairs to have their conversations. Monitor and take notes on their use of language for a correction slot at the end.

 pp. 44–45

 Next class Make photocopies of **6A** p. 139.

LISTENING

Aim
To develop listening for general and specific information.

Step 1 Put students in groups to discuss the questions in A. Conduct brief feedback.

Step 2 Tell students to listen to the recording and match each conversation to one of the pictures. In pairs they compare answers and then check answers in open class.

> **Answers**
> conversation 1 = picture 4
> conversation 2 = picture 1
> conversation 3 = picture 3
> conversation 4 = picture 2

> 🔊 **6.3**
> **Conversation 1**
> A: I have a booking under the name of Bergen.
> B: Hmm. I'm sorry sir. We have no record of any reservation.

A: That can't be right. I spoke to someone just over a week ago.
B: Well, did you receive a confirmation by email or text?
A: Should I have?
B: That's our normal procedure, yes.
A: No. I haven't had anything.
B: Well, I'm afraid there's nothing I can do.
A: Haven't you got any rooms available?
B: I'm afraid not.
A: Oh, that's great, that is.

Conversation 2

C: Hello. I was wondering if you could help. My room's not very warm. Is there any way I can turn down the air-conditioning?
D: I'm afraid it's all controlled centrally.
C: Can't you do anything about it? I mean, you seem to have it on full blast. It's absolutely freezing!
D: I'm sorry, but we haven't had any other complaints about it.

Conversation 3

E: What do you mean you're not going to give us our deposit back?
F: Look at the state of the place. It's filthy!
E: Well, it wasn't particularly clean when we moved in.
F: And what about the washing machine? That'll need to be replaced.
E: That's hardly our fault. It's ancient. It was already falling apart – and I hardly think it's worth a whole month's rent.
F: Well, it's the combination of things. When you take everything into account – the stuff which is broken and missing, the mess – it all adds up.
E: What? To over a thousand points? You're taking the mickey! I can't believe you think we're going to pay that! It's ridiculous!

Conversation 4

G: I warned the landlord that boiler was a health hazard again and again.
H: I know. I remember you telling me ages ago.
G: They promised to fix it, but they just kept putting it off. Honestly, I'm furious about it!
H: I'm not surprised. Still, you were right to have it checked and to get it repaired. I mean, you could've suffocated while were you sleeping.
G: Well, you hear about carbon monoxide poisoning all the time, don't you?
H: It doesn't bear thinking about.
G: The thing is, though, I'm completely out of pocket now.

Step 3 Tell students to listen again and match two of the eight statements to each conversation. Play the recording and then get students to compare in pairs. Check answers.

Answers
conversation 1 = statements a & d
conversation 2 = statements c & g
conversation 3 = statements b & f
conversation 4 = statements e & h

Step 4 Get students to discuss the questions in D in pairs. Conduct brief feedback.

NATIVE SPEAKER ENGLISH Sarcasm

Ask students to read the box and check they understand. Tell students that we often say the opposite of what we mean when we want to show anger or be funny and we say it with a falling voice and stress the information word.

SPEAKING

Aim
To practise fluency when complaining about accommodation.

Step 1 Put students into pairs to choose three situations that they would like to role-play. Give them some time to write and practise their dialogues.

Step 2 When students are ready, put two sets of pairs together and they take turns to read their dialogues to the other pair, who has to decide which situation they are talking about. Monitor and take notes on their use of language for a correction slot at the end.

GRAMMAR *have / get* something done

Aim
To introduce and practise the passive construction *have / get something done*.

Step 1 Get students to look at the sentence from *Listening*. Ask them if they remember what they were talking about and to compare their ideas with a partner (the boiler in conversation 4). Check in open class.

Step 2 Get students to read the explanation box. Make reference to the sentence in step 1 and concept check *have / get something done = Do we know who checked and repaired it?* (No.) *Is it important to know?* (No.)

Step 3 In open class look at the first example in exercise B and elicit different ways to complete the sentence. Then put students into pairs to complete the rest.

Suggested Answers
1 your foot, your arm, or any other part of the body
2 the picture, the photograph, the painting
3 my coat, or any other item of clothing, my carpet
4 her tattoo / old car / mole, birthmark
5 bag, money, passport, wallet or purse, bicycle, car
6 my car, my roof, my central heating, my television
7 rewired, redecorated
8 cut, done, dyed, styled, permed, straightened

Tip You could make it into a competition by getting students to make as many combinations as possible and the winner is the pair with the most correct combinations.

Step 4 In groups get students to talk about the things in exercise C. Monitor for a correction slot at the end.

 6B see Teacher's notes p. 122.

VOCABULARY Understanding idioms

Aim
To revise and practise some common idioms.

Step 1 Ask students to read the explanation box. Check *taking the mickey* = say something to make someone look silly. Individually tell students to replace the definitions in sentences 1–8 with the idioms in the box. In pairs or threes they compare their answers. Check answers in open class.

Answers
1 out of pocket
2 through rose-coloured glasses
3 having a whale of a time
4 in small doses
5 make ends meet
6 cost an arm and a leg
7 taking the mickey out of
8 finding my feet.

Step 2 Individually students think of three situations in which they could have used any of these idioms. You could give model first and get students to guess the idiom, e.g. *On my last holiday, I went to a great museum, I really enjoyed myself = you had a whale of a time.* Then they tell each other and guess the situations in pairs.

 pp. 46–47

READING

Aim
To develop reading for general and specific information.

Step 1 Tell students that they are going to read a series of emails about Ben, who has moved to Hong Kong from Britain. Ask them to look at the pictures and describe what they can see, e.g. *Hong Kong = a busy street market, Britain = also a street market, the houses are not high rises.*

Step 2 Tell students to discuss the question in pairs about his change in living. Monitor and help with language.

Step 3 Ask students read the first email individually to find out how many of the things they thought of are mentioned. Then they compare in pairs and tell them to discuss if they are surprised by his reaction. Why / Why not?

Step 4 Put the following categories on the board, *weather, Ben's first impression, work, accommodation,* and ask what Ben said about these things in the first email. Then in pairs they discuss what changes they might expect to have happened. Then tell students to read the second email and find out if they were correct. Check answers in open class.

Answers
Ben is finding the work very busy and at a fast pace. He finds the people and the TVs very noisy. Generally, he has a lot of frustrations and is thinking of leaving.

Step 5 Put students in groups and tell them to discuss the questions in exercise D.

Step 6 Tell them that individually they are going to read two more emails from Ben and to answer the questions in exercise E. Check answers in open class.

Answers
1 He decides to travel around China and is getting more used to the life and culture. He finds people more in touch with their culture than in Britain, where they watch reality TV and have no interest in their culture.
2 His home-life is easier and he has a maid. The food is amazing. He's got married and has a son.
3 He probably became so busy at work and in his personal life that he had no time to keep in touch.
4 He seems open to the new experience and his attitudes have changed. He seems happy with his life.
5 Student's own opinion.

Step 7 Tell students to match the verbs from the four emails with the words they were used with. Then they compare in pairs before checking in open class.

Answers
1 gaze out of the window   5 honk their horns
2 get over my jet lag   6 sort out my flat
3 get down to work   7 take pride in what they do
4 go very smoothly   8 email me

LISTENING

Aim
To develop listening for general and specific information.

Step 1 Put *culture shock* on the board and check understanding = feeling nervous or uncomfortable in a different culture or situation. Then elicit categories of things it could include, e.g. food, weather, people's habits and customs, living conditions, etc. Then put them into pairs or threes to discuss the questions in A.

Step 2 Tell students they are going to hear a short extract from a radio programme about culture shock and they should listen and see how similar their ideas are. Play the recording and check as a class.

🔊 **6.4**

One often hears that something was a culture shock – most often when people arrive in a new country, but also when they enter other kinds of new environments. However, it is usually described as being similar to jet lag – something which you experience for a couple of days and then get over – all you need is a good night's sleep! The reality is, however, that undergoing any big change – whether it's moving house, changing jobs or going to university – will bring about a 'culture shock'. Far from being a single event which is quickly forgotten, it is a process which may take several months – even years – to fully recover from. Psychologists more commonly call this process acculturation and highlight four distinct phases that nearly everyone goes through. These are elation – the joy and wonder you first have, where everything is so new and different; resistance – when things settle into a routine and you start to see everything which is bad in your new situation. You look back through rose–coloured glasses on your life before the change. This resistance is then followed by the transformation phase, where you swing more to the other extreme and start looking down on your previous existence and its culture. You may refuse to mix with people you used to know or who speak the same language. You might put them down when you do. Finally, people reach a state of integration where cultural differences are acknowledged and accepted and people appreciate both their own heritage and their new life.

That's the ideal situation, according to psychologist Perry Graves. 'Everyone goes through the initial stages, but not everyone finishes the complete cycle. This can cause problems because they often don't recognise the phases of acculturation. For example, some people drop out of university in their first year, saying they don't relate to the middle-class values or that it has nothing to do with reality and so on. In reality, these opinions are actually a symptom of the resistance stage. In other cases, people get stuck in a transformation phase, which may stop them moving on to new experiences or lead to them cutting themselves off from their roots, from people they've known for years and years. That can lead to a deep sense of unhappiness and to feelings of frustration.'

Step 4 Tell students to listen again and answer the questions in B. They compare in pairs then as a class.

Answers
1 It happens not only in a new country but also other kinds of new environments = moving house, changing jobs or going to university.
2 It is a process which may take several months and even years to get over.

3 Elation, resistance, transformation, integration.
4 *elation* = the joy and wonder, where everything is so new and different, *resistance* = when things settle into a routine and you start to see everything which is bad in your new situation, *transformation* = where you swing more to the other extreme and start looking down on your previous existence and its culture. *integration* = where cultural differences are acknowledged and accepted.
5 It can lead to unhappiness and feelings of frustration.

Step 5 Tell students to look back at the four emails and find examples of the things listed in C. In pairs they compare answers before checking in open class.

Answers
1 first email, first paragraph = It's been with my mouth hanging open...
2 first email, first paragraph = am slowly finding my feet
3 second email, last paragraph and third email first paragraph = he talks about leaving and then decides to stay
4 first email, last paragraph = 15th floor, stunning view
5 second email, second paragraph = have a moan about things
6 not mentioned
7 third email, first paragraph = back home people just aren't interested anymore,

Step 6 Put students into small groups to discuss the question in D. Conduct brief feedback.

SPEAKING

Aim
To provide fluency practice.

Step 1 Tell students to think about a time when they experienced culture shock. Give them five minutes to make notes.

Step 2 In groups students take turns to have the conversations. Monitor for a correction slot at the end.

 5B see Teacher's notes p. 122.

07 NATURE

OVERVIEW

The main aim of this unit is to enable students to **talk about weather and natural disasters** and **plants and animals** as well as **issues connected to animals**. They have practice in **exaggerating**. The main grammatical focus is **narrative tenses and participle clauses** and ways of **expressing weather, natural disasters, plants and trees**.

 Next class Make photocopies of **7A** p. 140.

VOCABULARY
Weather and natural disasters

Aim
To introduce and practise vocabulary related to weather and disasters and to lead in to the topic.

Step 1 Ask students to look at the pictures and identify what they can see from the words in the vocabulary box and check understanding of *a famine* = serious lack of food.

Step 2 Put students into pairs and tell them to discuss the questions in exercise B. Conduct brief feedback.

Step 3 Tell students to work individually and to match the weather expressions in the box to the descriptions / comments 1–10 in exercise C. Remind them that two of the words will be used twice. Then in pairs they compare answers before checking in open class.

> **Answers**
> | | | | | |
> |---|---|---|---|---|
> | 1 a storm | 3 heat | 5 rain | 7 mist | 9 wind |
> | 2 fog | 4 cold | 6 snow | 8 rain | 10 wind |

Step 4 Tell students to underline any new expressions or collocations in exercise C and to compare with a partner. Check briefly in open class.

> **Suggested answers**
> Sentence 2 *it's lifted* = the fog has gone away
> sentence 5 *soaked* = get very wet
> sentence 6 *melted* = snow or ice turns to water
> sentence 8 *eased off* = not as severe, *spitting* = very light rain, *pouring* = very heavy rain
> sentence 9 *knock off* = cause you to fall off
> sentence 10 *slight breeze* = very light wind

Step 5 Put students into groups and tell them to discuss the questions in exercise E. Tell them to ask follow-up questions. Monitor and correct any language problems.

LISTENING

Aim
To develop listening for specific information.

Step 1 Tell students they are going to hear two people sharing experiences of extreme weather conditions. Then get them to read the questions in exercise A and play the recording. In pairs students compare answers before checking in open class.

> **Answers**
> 1 Italy (Rome) and Israel (Acre)
> 2 The first speaker experienced a storm with enormous *hailstones* then they saw *lightning*. The second speaker also experienced a storm. However, it started with lightning, then *thunder*, then it started spitting before it poured down.
> 3 The first speaker thought it was amazing but was also scared, the second speaker thought it was spectacular, the first speaker *pulled over* and waited, the second speaker ran to the nearest café.

> **♪ 7.1**
> A: We got caught in this incredible storm on our way to visit friends in Rome.
> B: Yeah?
> A: Yeah, it was amazing! One moment we were in sunshine, the next we saw like a line on the road ahead and we drove through it and it was hail! Incredible – these enormous hailstones just started bouncing off the car! They were like as big as golf balls.
> B: Really?
> A: Well, maybe I'm exaggerating a bit, but they were pretty big and it was pretty scary.
> B: I bet.
> A: And then the lightning started. It was lighting up the whole sky. In the end, we pulled over to the side of the road till it all blew over.
> B: Right.

A: And then it cleared up again – almost as quickly as it'd started.

B: It's amazing, isn't it? It actually reminds me of a time I was in Israel. We were visiting this town called Acre. Actually, I guess we should've realised because it'd been boiling all day – very humid and sticky – and then in the evening we were just taking a walk along the old walls – you get this great view across the bay to Haifa.

A: Uh huh.

B: And anyway suddenly we saw this incredible forked lightning across the bay followed by a faint rumble of thunder, and it just continued. It was so spectacular, we were just, like, transfixed watching it because, you know, it was still dry where we were. It was amazing – I could've watched it for hours, but then suddenly it started spitting and then just two seconds later the heavens opened and it started pouring down.

B: Oh no.

A: And of course we hadn't brought an umbrella or anything, so we just ran to the nearest café we could find and honestly it can't have been more than a minute but we got absolutely soaked. I must've poured like a litre of water out of my shoes.

B: No, seriously?

A: I swear – sitting there in the café I think it was the wettest I've ever been!

GRAMMAR Narrative tenses

Aim
To revise and consolidate narrative tenses (past simple, past continuous and past perfect).

Step 1 Remind students of *Listening* and ask, *When did the stories happen?* = in the past, *How many different tenses can you use to tell a story in the past?* = three: past simple, past continuous and past perfect. Tell them to look at the box and in pairs decide what the form of each tense is and when these tenses are used. Direct students to the grammar reference on page 145 if they still seem unsure.

Tip To give extra support, ask students to read the audioscript on page 170 and find examples of the tenses to help them see when we use them.

Suggested answers
Form = past simple = regular verbs add 'ed' irregular verbs vary, past continuous = *was / were* + subject + verb-*ing*, past perfect = *had* + past particple regular + *ed* or irregular.
Used = past simple = completed action in the past, past continuous = action in progress in the past, past perfect = a time frame leading to another in the past.

Step 2 Tell students to work individually and to complete the summary of the second story from exercise A by putting the verbs in brackets into the correct tense. Then they compare in pairs before checking in open class.

Answers
1 were visiting / visited
2 had been
3 were taking
4 saw
5 started
6 hadn't brought
7 ran
8 could

Step 3 Ask students what they remember from the first story in *Listening* and put their ideas in note form on the board. In pairs they re-tell the story using the prompts on the board. Monitor and help with problems with the tenses.

Step 4 Get a strong pair to re-tell the story to the class. Then play the recording to check their ideas.

 7A see Teacher's notes p.123.

NATIVE SPEAKER ENGLISH
like / something like

Ask students to read the box and check they understand, tell them that the word *like* has many meanings and here it shows we are not being exact, e.g. *Did the person literally empty a litre of water from their shoe?* (No.) *How do we know?* (They said emptied *like a litre*), *Why?* (They didn't know exactly the amount of water.)

DEVELOPING CONVERSATIONS
Exaggerating

Aim
To present and practice expressions used to exaggerate opinions when telling stories.

Step 1 Ask students to read the explanation box.

Step 2 In pairs students use the ideas in exercise A to have similar exchanges to the example in the box. You could do the first one as an example with a strong student in open class. Monitor and help out with any language problems.

Answers
1 we got really / pretty / fairly / a bit / quite wet
2 it hasn't rained for a long time
3 she's a bit bigger than me
4 it was pretty / fairly / quite deep
5 she speaks quite a few languages
6 it was miserable the whole time we were there
7 we were pretty / fairly / a bit / quite chilly
8 it was fairly / pretty / quite / really / a bit foggy
9 it's really / very good

Step 3 Individually students look at exercise B and choose two or three of the things and write sentences like the ones in the previous exercise. Then in pairs they read their sentences to each other and have similar conversations to the ones in exercise A. Monitor and help with any problems.

CONVERSATION PRACTICE

Aim
To practise the language learnt so far.

Step 1 Tell students to think of some extreme weather they have experienced recently and to take notes on what happened. If they haven't experienced any, they could imagine some. Tell them to exaggerate if possible.

Step 2 Then get students to talk to three or four different people in the class and have conversations about their experiences. Tell them they should try to respond with a similar experience saying *Actually, that reminds me of …* Monitor and take notes on their correct use of language for a correction slot at the end.

 pp. 50–51

SPEAKING

Aim
To provide fluency practice talking about animal rights issues.

Step 1 Individually tell students to read the statements in the speech bubbles and check understanding and word stress of *vivisection* = performing operations on living animals for scientific experiments, *indefensible* = impossible to defend. Tell them to decide how far they agree with each of the ideas about animals, e.g. very strongly agree, strongly agree, not sure, disagree, strongly disagree, very strongly disagree. Give them time to prepare.

Step 2 In pairs students share their opinions and see if they agree. Monitor and help with any language problems.

Step 3 Ask a selection of students to share their opinions.

READING

Aim
To develop reading skills for specific information.

Step 1 Tell students they are going to read four articles about animal-related issues. Get them to look at the words in the vocabulary box and check understanding and word stress of *intimidation* = make someone feel frightened, *soaring* = increasing very quickly, *a will* = legal document that tells what to do with your money and property after you die, a *dare* = you do something even if it may be dangerous or shocking to do it, *subsidies* = money paid by the government or other organisation to help pay the cost, *insights* = an opportunity to learn or understand more about something. Then in pairs they discuss the question in A.

Suggested answers
Intimidation of laboratory staff + provide invaluable insights = could be a story about how staff have been threatened to cover up the way animals have been treated
Wages are soaring + subsidies = the government or other organisation are helping companies cope with the cost of paying salaries
A will is being contested + her rightful inheritance = a story about a woman who is due to get a lot of money but someone in the family doesn't want her to get it
Try them for a dare + maggots = a story about how people's eating habits are changing and persuading people not to each too much meat.

Step 2 Divide the class into two groups, A and B. Tell group A to read the two articles on the right of the student's book page and group B to read the two articles in File 9 on page 158. Monitor and help out with any language.

Step 3 Put students in same letter pairs to discuss what they have understood in each article.

Step 4 Then tell them to change partners and work with a partner from the other group. They should try to summarise the articles without looking at their notes and share opinions about the issues raised. Tell them to start with A: *Did you see that article in the paper about …* B: *No, what was that?* Monitor and help with any problems.

Step 5 When they have finished tell them to read the other two articles and see if there is anything their partner forgot to mention. They can compare and help each other.

Step 6 In the same pairs tell them to look at the statements in exercise E and decide which article they refer to. Then check answers in open class.

Answers
1 article three	4 article three	7 article two
2 article four	5 article one	8 article one
3 article two	6 article four	

Step 7 In pairs tell students to discuss the questions in exercise F. Conduct brief feedback.

GRAMMAR Participle clauses

Aim
To present and practise participle clauses.

Step 1 In open class ask students to read the two examples: a and b in exercise A and ask them if the verb in each clause is active or passive. a = active (*feature*) b = passive (*are aimed at*). Then concept check by asking, *What have they added to the menu?* (A range of dishes.) *How is the menu defined?* (Which feature the insects.) Tell them we can add information to define the previous noun in two ways: by using a relative clause (as in the example) or a participle clause (the *-ing* or *-ed* form of the verb). The form of the verb after the noun depends on whether the verb is active or passive. Then ask them to work in pairs and how could they shorten the start of each clause in bold to make a participle clause. Then get them to look back at the articles to check their answers. Check understanding by asking, *What ending do we use with an active verb? = -ing, and with a passive verb? = -ed.*

Answers
a Since adding a range of dishes featuring insects to the menu … .
b The £18 million centre was intended to allow experiments aimed at … .

Direct students to the grammar reference on page 145 if they still seem unsure.

Step 2 Tell students individually to choose the correct form in exercise B. Do the first one with them on the board. Then get students to compare in pairs before checking in open class.

Answers
1 abandoned(passive)
2 living (active)
3 moving (active)
4 suffering (active)
5 studying (active)
6 sold (passive)
7 donated (passive)
8 thrown (passive)

Step 3 In open class ask students if the number of animals abandoned by their owners has increased or gone down over recent years in their country and get them to explain their ideas.

Step 4 Put students into pairs and get them to discuss if the other numbers / amounts in exercise B have increased or gone down recently and to explain their ideas. Monitor if they using participles correctly.

 pp. 52–53

Next class Make photocopies of **7B** p. 141.

VOCABULARY Plants and trees

Aim
To introduce words related to plants and trees.

Step 1 Tell students to look at the vocabulary box and check understanding: *stem* = long, central part of a flower, *leaves* = flat, green part that grows on a branch or stem, *weeds* = a wild plant that grows in places you don't want. Then ask students to work individually to complete sentences 1–10. In pairs students compare answers then check in open class.

Answers
1 weeds
2 seeds
3 herbs
4 palm tree
5 leaves
6 oak
7 stems
8 roots
9 flower (verb)
10 bushes

Step 2 Get students to work in teams of four or five and to write down the names of as many flowers, herbs and trees as they can. Tell them they could nominate one secretary who writes the words and that the others tell them what they know, or they can use a dictionary if they want to. Set a time limit of three minutes.

Step 3 After three minutes tell them to stop. Ask each team how many flowers they have and then ask the team with the most to write them on the board, ask the rest of the class if they have any others to add. Then do the same with herbs and finally trees.

Suggested answers
Flowers = rose, tulip, daffodil, crocus, carnation, gardenia, iris, orchid, sunflower, snowdrop
Herbs = basil, rosemary, thyme, chives, coriander, parsley, dill, mint, sage, vanilla
Trees = oak, palm, willow, elm, fir, maple, pine, poplar, cypress, cedar

Step 4 Ask students to read the questions in exercise C and to discuss them in pairs. Monitor and help out with any problems with the target language.

LANGUAGE PATTERNS

Aim
To draw students' attention to some common patterns using prepositions in relative clauses to add information to a noun.

Step 1 Ask students to read the examples in the box. Draw students' attention to the position of prepositions in relative clauses (which add information about a noun).

Step 2 Ask students to translate the sentences into their own language. In a monolingual class, ask students to compare their translation. In a multilingual class, ask students to work in pairs and tell each other if the sentences were easy to translate into their language.

Step 3 Ask students to cover their English translations and using their translation translate the sentences back into English. Then ask them to compare their translations in pairs against the book and discuss who had the least mistakes? And what mistakes did they make? Why? Alternatively, if you prefer not to use translation just draw students' attention to the patterns.

LISTENING

Aim
To develop listening for general and specific information.

Step 1 Tell students they are going to listen to five conversations connected with plants and that they need to match one of the statements in a–f with each conversation. Also tell them there is one statement they will not use.

Step 2 Play the recording and get students to compare in pairs. If necessary, play the recording again and check answers after each conversation.

> **Answers**
> conversation 1 = sentence c, conversation 2 = sentence b, conversation 3 = sentence f, conversation 4 = sentence e, conversation 5 = sentence a. sentence d is not used.

🎧 7.2
Conversation 1
A: Oh dear! Those don't look very healthy.
B: I know. I bought them to cheer up the flat a bit. You know, a bit of colour and greenery, but they just look depressing now! It's strange. I've been watering them every day.
A: Maybe that's it. The soil's probably too wet. I think it rots the roots.
B: You're joking! You mean I'm drowning them?
A: I guess so!
Conversation 2
C: What are these flowers? They're lovely.
D: They're a menace!
C: What do you mean?
D: They just so invasive! They take over the whole place. None of the other plants can survive – and they're really difficult to get rid of as well.
C: But they look so nice.
D: Yeah, but they're not native to this country and they're destroying the local varieties.
C: That's too bad. I still like them, though.

Conversation 3
E: I wanted to take them something to say thank you for having me to stay and so I bought some flowers.
F: Fair enough.
E: Anyway, I handed them over and you know that feeling when you know you've put your foot in it, yeah? She kind of gave me this tight smile and nodded, but, you know, they were quite a big bouquet.
F: You kind of expect something different, yeah?
E: Exactly. Anyway, she said something to her husband and he took them away and there was a bit of an awkward silence and then we just carried on with the evening.
F: How weird!
E: Yeah. I thought so, but then I was telling someone about it and they told me people there only give those flowers when someone's passed away!
F: Oh no!
E: It was like I was cursing her or something – hoping it was she'd have a funeral!
Conversation 4
G: You're going to do what?
H: Gather mushrooms. Isn't gather right?
G: Yeah, yeah – gather, pick, whatever. It's just, I don't know, I've never met anyone who does it.
H: No? Everyone does it here in Poland. Why don't people do it in Britain?
G: Well, it's dangerous, isn't it? Don't you worry about picking the wrong one and poisoning yourself? Some of them are lethal, aren't they?
H: We're brought up doing this. We know from when we're children what's OK and what's not. And it's good – you feel more connected with nature. Last time we went we saw a deer – really close.
G: Yeah? Wow! It sounds great.
Conversation 5
I: Here, take this. It should help.
J: What's in it?
I: It's just a herbal tea my gran makes. It's basically fennel seeds and leaves with a touch of lemon and honey. She swears by it.
J: I've never had fennel.
I: It's nice. It's got an aniseedy kind of taste. It's great. It'll really settle your stomach.

Step 3 Put students into pairs and get them to read the pairs of words in exercise B, check understanding of *rot* = go bad, *get rid of* = to remove or throw away something unwanted, *awkward* = feel uncomfortable and embarrassed, *settle* = make calm. Then ask them to discuss how the expressions were used in each conversation and tell them to look at the example.

Step 4 Play the recording again and tell students to listen and read the audioscript on page 171 to check. When the recording has finished get them to underline the expression in the audioscript. (Answers in audioscript.)

PRONUNCIATION Linking

Aim
To introduce and provide pronunciation practice of how words are linked together.

Step 1 Tell students to read the explanation box and draw their attention to the blue arrows underneath the consonant sound and vowel sound in the first two examples. Check that in *take* the *e* is not pronounced and that the final sound is *k*. Tell them this is a very common feature of spoken English and it will help them when listening to English.

Step 2 Tell students to listen and write down the ten sentences they hear. Play the recording.

Step 3 Tell students to compare their sentences. Play the recording again and get students to dictate the sentence back to you and you write it on the board.

> **🔊 7.3 Answers**
> 1 They're really difficult to get rid of.
> 2 It shot out of the bushes.
> 3 We waited till it all blew over.
> 4 It's beginning to ease off.
> 5 We 're brought up doing it.
> 6 My gran swears by it.
> 7 It almost knocked me off my bike.
> 8 Were you affected by it?
> 9 The company has pulled out of it.
> 10 Experiments are being carried out on them.

Step 4 Tell students to work individually and to decide which words link together. If they are not sure tell them to look at the explanation box again. Then get them to compare their answers in pairs. Check answers as a class (above).

Step 5 Play the recording again and pause after each sentence. Tell students to repeat with the same pronunciation.

Step 6 Tell students to read the example in exercise D and draw their attention to *they* as the pronoun. Then tell them that all the sentences that they wrote in exercise A are from this unit. Individually, can they remember what things the pronouns have replaced in each case? If they are not sure, they can look back through the unit or their notes. Then tell them to compare in pairs before checking in open class.

> **Answers**
> 1 They're really difficult to get rid of. = 'they' refers to some weeds that were invasive.
> 2 It shot out of the bushes. = 'it' refers to a fox (sentence 10 in exercise A *Vocabulary* plants and trees)
> 3 We waited till it all blew over. = 'it' refers to the storm (first speaker in the first listening in the unit)
> 4 It's beginning to ease off. = 'it' refers to the rain (sentence 8 in exercise C *Vocabulary* Weather and natural disasters)
> 5 We're brought up doing it. = 'It' refers to picking mushrooms (fourth speaker in previous listening)
> 6 My gran swears by it. = 'it' refers to fennel tea (fifth speaker in previous listening)
> 7 It almost knocked me off my bike. = 'it' refers to the wind (sentence 9 in exercise C *Vocabulary* Weather and natural disasters)
> 8 Were you affected by it? 'it' refers to natural disasters in *Vocabulary* Weather and natural disasters
> Note: this answers is hard to find, students might need extra support.
> 9 The company has pulled out of it. = 'it' refers to a project (reading in File 9)
> 10 Experiments are being carried out on them. = 'them' refers to animals (reading in File 9)

SPEAKING

Aim
To provide fluency practice talking about plants and animals.

Step 1 Tell students to read the questions in exercise A and check understanding. Give them some time to prepare.

Step 2 In groups students take turns to have the conversations. Monitor and take notes on their use of language. Conduct brief feedback.

> **7B** see Teacher's notes p. 123.

08 LAW AND ORDER

UNIT OVERVIEW
The main aim of this unit is to enable students to **talk about crimes and what they involve** and **the powers the police have**. They have practice in **describing different kinds of punishment and giving opinions about prison life**. The main grammatical focus is **modals + present and past infinitives** and **nouns and prepositions** and ways of **expressing crimes, agreeing and disagreeing and adding comments and questions**.

 Next class Make photocopies of **8A** p. 142.

SPEAKING

Aim
To lead in to the topic of crime.

Step 1 Put students into small groups and tell them to discuss the questions in A. Conduct brief feedback.

VOCABULARY Crimes

Aim
To introduce and practise expressions related to crime.

Step 1 Ask students to look at the pictures and the words in the vocabulary box and say which crimes they can see.

Step 2 In pairs ask students to compare their ideas. Monitor and help out as necessary. Then conduct feedback.

Answers			
speeding	riot	burglary	kidnapping

Step 3 In pairs ask students to test each other. Student A describes what happens during some of the crimes in the vocabulary box and student B has to guess the crime.

Step 4 Conduct brief feedback by getting students to describe a crime and the others have to guess the crime.

Step 5 Ask students to read the vocabulary box in exercise C and check understanding. Then ask students to look at the example and point out that the words are not in the same order as in the box. Then get students to complete sentences 2–9. Then in pairs they compare answers before checking in open class.

Answers		
2 caught, doing		4 came back, vanished
3 found, stabbed		5 smashed, set

6 broken into, stolen	8 seized, held
7 came up to, grabbed	9 went off, killed

Step 6 In pairs students discuss what crimes from exercise A are described in sentences 1–9 in exercise C. Check answers in open class and check their pronunciation.

Answers
1 identity theft
2 speeding
3 a murder
4 a disappearance
5 a riot
6 a burglary
7 a street robbery
8 a kidnapping
9 a bombing

Step 7 Individually get students to choose four of the crimes in exercise C and think of real examples that they know or have heard of / read about. Give them time to make notes about it using the new language from this page. Then put students into small groups to discuss what happened. Conduct brief feedback.

LISTENING

Aim
To develop listening for specific information.

Step 1 Tell students they are going to listen to three conversations about crimes and to answer the questions in A.

Step 2 Play the recording and then put students in pairs to compare their answers and then listen again to check.

Answers
Conversation 1 crime: a street robbery, victim: the girl in the conversation, criminal: some lads
Conversation 2 crime: a murder, victim: a schoolgirl, criminal: they don't know
Conversation 3 crime: a kidnapping, victim: an ex-girlfriend, criminal: some guy

8.1

Conversation 1

A: How was your holiday? B: Fine – apart from getting robbed.

A: Oh, you're joking! What happened?

B: Well, it was stupid, really. I should've been more careful. I was sitting in a café and these lads came up to me with a map asking for directions. I said I didn't understand and they walked off. Then I suddenly realised my bag was gone.

A: Oh no!

B: I'd left under my chair and one of them must've grabbed it while they were talking to me.

A: That's terrible! Did it have much in it?

B: Fortunately not. My purse was in my pocket.

A: Still, it can't have been very nice.

B: Yeah, it was a bit upsetting, but I didn't let it spoil the holiday.

A: Well, that's good.

Conversation 2

C: What're you reading about?

D: Oh, it's about that girl who got stabbed outside her school.

C: Oh, I know. It's awful! They really should do something about kids carrying knives.

D: I know. Apparently, she might've been involved in some kind of gang.

C: Oh really. So do they know who did it?

D: I don't think so, but I mean, someone must've seen it – it was broad daylight.

C: I know! I guess people could be just too scared to come forward and talk to the police.

D: Hmm. It must be awful for the parents, losing a child.

C: Absolutely! Did you see them on TV last night?

D: No.

C: It was dreadful. Really upsetting.

Conversation 3

E: That's ridiculous!

F: What?

E: Did you see this thing about this guy being arrested for holding his ex-girlfriend captive?

F: No. Doesn't sound that funny.

E: Well, it is kind of because he did it to get her to do his ironing and the washing up!

F: The ironing? You are joking, aren't you?

E: Well that's what it says here. Says he seized her in a pub, dragged her into his car, drove her home and forced her to do his ironing.

F: And this was his *ex*-girlfriend.

E: Yeah. Not that that should make any difference.

F: Absolutely. But you wonder, what was he thinking?

E: He's just a dinosaur. You can see why she dumped him!

Step 3 Ask students to listen again and to make notes on the questions in B. Then in pairs they compare before checking in open class.

Answers

Conversation 1 = the woman was sitting in a café when these lads came up to her with a map asking for directions, she said she didn't understand and they left. Then she realised they must have grabbed her bag. Fortunately it didn't have much in it, her purse was in her pocket. She didn't let the experience spoil her holiday.

Conversation 2 = the second man is reading a newspaper article about a schoolgirl who was stabbed outside her school. Apparently she might've been involved in a gang, no-one appears to have seen anything.

Conversation 3 = a man was arrested for holding his ex-girlfriend captive. He seized her in a pub, drove her home and forced her to do his ironing.

Suggested answers

Conversation 1: It could be seen that the victim brought it upon herself, she was in a new city and should have paid more attention to her bag

Conversation 2: the victim didn't bring it upon herself, she was just doing what she does every day and was attacked for no apparent reason

Conversation 3: the victim didn't bring it upon herself, she was just the victim of a bad person.

Tip With a strong class you could get them to work in pairs and make notes on what they remember before listening. With a weaker class, you could exploit the audioscript on pp. 170–171 by getting students to read and listen and underline any information about what happened.

DEVELOPING CONVERSATIONS

Comments and questions

Aim

To practise making comments and questions.

Step 1 Get students to read the explanation box and check understanding. *Which expression is a comment to what someone previously said? = Oh you're joking. Is it really a joke?* (No). Tell them that we often use *You're joking* when we are surprised by what someone says. Sentence 2: *Which expression is a comment to what someone previously said = That's terrible. Is the speaker sympathetic?* (Yes.) *Which expressions ask for more information?* = sentence 1 = *What happened?* and sentence 2 = *Did it have much in it?*

Step 2 Individually tell students to read the words in exercise A and make comments and suggestion by re-ordering the words, tell them they need to add exclamation and question marks. In pairs students compare their answers before checking in open class.

> **Answers**
> 2 That must've been awful! Were you OK?
> 3 Oh no! Did they take anything very valuable?
> 4 That's dreadful! What were the parents thinking?
> 5 What a shame! Were you insured?
> 6 That's terrible? Did you report it to the police?
> 7 You're joking! Do they know who did it?
> 8 It's awful! What must his family be going through?

Step 3 Get students to read the prompts in exercise B and to think of a comment and a question in response to each.

Step 4 Put students in pairs to have their conversations using the prompts. Tell them to continue the conversations as long as they can. Monitor for a correction slot at the end.

GRAMMAR
Modals + present and past infinitives

Aim
To practise modals + present and past infinitives.

Step 1 Write the following examples from *Listening* on the board: *One of them must have grabbed it, It must be awful for the parents* and ask them which conversation they come from = sentence1 from conversation 1 (the street robbery) and sentence 2 from conversation 3 (the kidnapping). Then check understanding: Sentence 1 = *When did it happen?* (In the past.) *How do we know it's in the past?* (*must've* + past participle). *Was she careful?* (No.) *Was she nearly 100% sure that's what happened?* (Yes.) Tell them that when something happened in the past and we regret what happened we use *should've* + past participle. Sentence 2 = *When did it happen? (In the present.) How do we know it's in the present? (Must + base form of the verb.) Is the person expressing a strong sympathy with the parents?* (Yes.) Tell them that when something happens in the present and we want to express a strong sympathy, we use *must* + base form of the verb.

Step 2 Individually students look at exercise A and decide which sentences are in the present and which are in the past. Then they compare in pairs before checking in open class.

> **Answers**
>
> | | | |
> |---|---|---|
> | 1 past | 4 past | 6 present |
> | 2 present | 5 present | 7 present |
> | 3 past | | |

Step 3 Tell students to match the words in italics to the ideas in a–f. Tell them the ideas in a–f explain the meaning of the modal verb. Then in pairs they compare before checking answers in open class. Direct students

to the grammar reference on page 146 if they still seem unsure.

> **Answers**
> 1 g   2 e   3 f   4 c   5 a   6 b   7 d

Step 4 Tell students to read the situations in exercise B and to take notes on their opinions, what caused the situation and what the characters might be feeling. Remind them to use *should / might / must / can't* + past and present infinitives. In pairs tell them to share their opinions.

 5A see Teacher's notes p. 123.

CONVERSATION PRACTICE

Aim
To practise using the language learnt so far.

Step 1 Tell students they are going to have similar conversations to the ones in *Listening*. They can talk about crimes which have happened to people they know or that they have heard about in the news recently. Give them time to prepare what they want to say.

Step 2 In new pairs students have their conversations. Monitor for a correction slot at the end.

 pp. 56–57

SPEAKING

Aim
To practise fluency when talking about punishments.

Step 1 Put students in pairs and tell them to discuss the questions in A. Draw their attention to the structures they should use. Monitor and help out with any language problems. Conduct brief feedback.

LISTENING

Aim
To develop listening for general and specific information.

Step 1 Get students to look at the pictures and quickly in open class say what is happening in each one.

> **Suggested answers**
> 1 a prisoner doing hard physical labour
> 2 a prisoner in solitary confinement
> 3 a prisoner doing community service
> 4 prisoners dancing

Step 2 Tell students they are going to hear a phone-in programme about prisons and to listen to the introduction then answer the questions in B. Play the recording and then get students to compare in pairs before checking in open class. If necessary, play the recording again before checking.

Answers
1 Picture 4
2 dancing to Michael Jackson's *Thriller* as an experimental approach to physical fitness
3 It is claimed it has dramatically improved discipline in the prison

---

🎧 8.2
Now, many of you may have seen the remarkable video clip showing hundreds and hundreds of Filipino prisoners – all dressed in orange uniforms and dancing to Michael Jackson's *Thriller*. This ... um ... experimental approach to physical fitness has attracted worldwide attention and was apparently all the brainchild of Byron Garcia, a security consultant at the Cebu Provincial Detention and Rehabilitation Centre in the Philippines. The dancing is compulsory and has, it is claimed, dramatically improved discipline in the prison. So, the question is, is this something we can learn from over here. Would our prisons be better places if we introduced mass dancing hours? And if not, why not? And does anyone have any other ideas on how can we make prisons work better? We want to hear what you think, as ever.

Step 3 Tell students to read the questions in exercise C and to think about their opinions. Then put students in pairs to discuss the questions. Conduct brief feedback.

Suggested answers
Picture 1 advantages: helps team building, can make the prisoner feel sorry for what they did, disadvantages: prisoners can escape, not very humane.
Picture 2 advantages: punishes the prisoner for bad behaviour, gives them time to think about what they did, disadvantages: very small space and prisoner could be claustrophobic, not very humane.
Picture 3 advantages: it is more beneficial to society, can help prisoner think of their role in society, disadvantages: people think this is an easy option and doesn't punish the criminal, people may feel threatened.
Picture 4 advantages: helps team building, makes the prisoners feel they are doing something to help society, disadvantages: gives the prisoners an easy time when they should be punished, shows society that prison could be fun.

Step 4 Tell students to listen to the phone-in programme and decide if Gary (the presenter) and the callers Doreen and Nigel think prisoners have a hard time in prison. Play the recording and then get students to compare in pairs. If necessary, play the recording again before conducting feedback.

Answers
Doreen = she thinks prisoners have an easy time, says it's like a holiday camp, Nigel = he thinks they have a hard time, prison is hard, Gary = agrees more with Nigel.

🎧 8.3
G=Gary, D=Doreen, N=Nigel
G: OK, I think we have our first caller. Yes, hello. Doreen in Birmingham.
D: Oh hello, Gary. Yes, well, what I wanted to say was that I think we've got it all wrong, the way we're doing things.
G: Why's that, then, Doreen?
D: Well, they're like holiday camps, aren't they, prisons today. These people, these CRIMINALS, they're animals! They've done horrid, wicked things and yet they're living in there better than some of us are living out here on the outside. TVs, they've got, video games, mobiles, all manner of technology ... visits from their wives, all sorts. They lead a life of luxury, most of them.
G: Well, that's certainly one way of looking at things.
D: It's true, I'm telling you! So I think the idea of free dance classes - well it's ridiculous! The world's gone mad, Gary.
G: And what would you like to see instead, Doreen?
D: What I want is a return to the good old days. I want them punished. Make them work Gary.
G: That's not a bad idea, Doreen. What kind of thing did you have in mind? Making clothes, perhaps? Or cleaning the streets?
D: Breaking rocks would be better. Just hard, hard, nasty, dirty, physical work. Breaking rocks in the sun, that's what I'd have them all doing.
G: OK. Well, Doreen. I can't say I'm with you on that one, but thanks for taking the time to call. And our next caller is ... Nigel. Nigel in Manchester. Hello.
N: Oh hello, Gary. Good morning. Yes, well, firstly, I'd just like to say that - with all due respect – Doreen doesn't seem to know what she's talking about. Anyone who thinks that prisons are fun needs their head examined. And as for the suggestion that breaking rocks would help – well, God save us all! The way I see it, the main problem with prisons today is that we place too much emphasis on punishment and don't pay enough attention to rehabilitation - to helping these people lead useful, independent lives of their own once they are released.
G: Nigel, I couldn't agree more. I could not agree more.
N: And as a result re-offending rates are appalling! Young offenders go into prison for the first time and they make contacts, meet other, more professional, criminals and they come out and go on to commit ever more serious crimes.
G: I know what you mean, Nigel.
N: What I'd like to see, Gary, is inmates, prisoners, learning skills that'll help them avoid a life of crime once they've been released. Fine, make them do work that's useful for society while they're inside, or give them dance hours or whatever, but also teach them how to read and write, teach them computer skills, teach them how to learn. It's the only way we'll ever break this vicious circle of crime and prison and crime again.

Step 5 Get students to read the statements in exercise E and check understanding, *inmates* = polite term to refer to prisoners, *breed* = make a negative situation develop more.

Step 6 Tell students to listen to the phone-in again and mark a tick (√) when Gary, Dorren and Nigel agrees with a statement and a cross (X) when they disagree. If the information is not given, leave the box blank. Play the recording and then get students to compare in pairs.

> **Answers**
> 1 Gary (G), Doreen (D) and Nigel (N) all agree
> 2 D disagrees, G & N don't say anything
> 3 G doesn't say anything, D agrees, N disagrees
> 4 G & N don't say anything, D agrees
> 5 G & N agree, D disagrees
> 6 G & D agree, N disagrees
> 7 G & N agree, D doesn't say anything
> 8 G & N agree, D doesn't say anything
> 9 N agrees, G & D don't say anything

LANGUAGE PATTERNS

Aim
To draw students' attention to some common patterns to emphasise nouns by putting them at the end of the sentence.

Step 1 Ask students to read the examples in the box. Draw their attention to the pronouns at the beginning of the sentence. Check by asking concept questions: *What are 'they'?* = prisons. *Who is 'he'?* = my uncle. Tell students that when we want to emphasise nouns when speaking and keep the attention of the listener we can put them at the end. Ask, *Is it formal or informal English?* (Informal).

Step 2 Ask students to translate the sentences into their own language. In a monolingual class, ask students to compare their translations. In a multilingual class, ask students to work in pairs and tell each other if the sentences were easy to translate into their language.

Step 3 Ask students to cover their English translations and using their translation translate the sentences back into English. Then ask them to compare their translations in pairs against the book. Alternatively, if you prefer not to use translation ask students to notice the patterns.

VOCABULARY Agreeing and disagreeing

Aim
To practice expressions of agreeing and disagreeing.

Step 1 Tell students to look at the audioscript on page 172 and find expressions used to agree and disagree.

> **Answers**
> Agreeing: That's not a bad idea, I couldn't agree more, I know what you mean
> Disagreeing: I can't say I'm with you on that one, I'd just like to say that – with all due respect

Step 2 Get students to read the vocabulary box and complete sentences 1–8 in exercise B with one of the words in the box. Check answers in pairs then as a class.

> **Answers**
> 1 way   5 agree
> 2 point   6 complete
> 3 with   7 see
> 4 mean   8 idea

Step 3 Tell students to work in pairs and decide which four expressions in exercise C show you agree, which one shows you half-agree and which three show you disagree. Check answers in pairs then as a class.

> **Answers**
> Agree = I'm with you on that, I know what you mean, I couldn't agree more, that's not a bad idea.
> Half agree = I agree with you up to a point.
> Disagree = Well, that's one way of looking at things, that's complete rubbish, I don't really see it like that myself.

GRAMMAR
Nouns and prepositional phrases

Aim
To present and practise noun and prepositional phrases.

Step 1 Ask students to read the example in the explanation box and check understanding: *What is the main problem with prisons?* = we place too much emphasis on punishment and don't pay enough attention to rehabilitation. Tell them that to emphasise a point of view in English we can introduce the opinion with a noun or prepositional phrase = *The main problem with prisons is ...* . Direct students to the grammar reference on page 147 if they still seem unsure.

Step 2 Individually students read statements 1–8 and decide if they agree or disagree and why. Give them time to review the expressions of agreeing and disagreeing from *Vocabulary* before discussing in pairs. Conduct brief feedback.

Step 3 Tell students to choose four of the sentences in exercise A and make new sentences by changing the prepositional phrases. Monitor.

SPEAKING

Aim
To practise fluency using the language taught so far.

Step 1 Tell the class they are going to role-play a phone-in programme on the issues of prison and punishment. Divide the class into three groups: A, B and C. Tell group A they are the presenter of the programme and to look at File 4 on page 156. Tell group B they are the guests on the programme and to look at File 21 on p. 159 and prepare their role. Tell group C they are the callers and could look at audioscript 8.2 to get ideas. Give each group time to read and prepare their roles, tell them they can help each other with what they want to say in their groups.

Step 2 Put students into ABC groups. Tell them to role-play the phone-in. Conduct brief feedback.

 pp. 58–59

 Next class Make photocopies of **8B** p. 143.

READING

Aim
To develop reading for general and detailed information.

Step 1 Tell students they are going to read an article about a mother's problems with her teenage son and that the words in bold in exercise A all appear in the article. Tell students to match the summaries in 1–8 with the extracts from the newspaper articles a–h and that they can look up any words they do not know in the *Vocabulary Builder*. In pairs they compare their answers before checking in open class.

Answers			
1 c	3 a	5 d	7 e
2 f	4 h	6 g	8 b

Step 2 In pairs tell them to discuss what the connection might be between the words in bold in exercise A and the home life of a teenager. Do brief feedback in open class.

Step 3 Tell students to read the article and check if their ideas are mentioned. In pairs they compare.

Step 4 Tell students to read the questions in exercise D and to read the article to discuss the questions in pairs. Check answers in open class.

Answers
1 a simple question about what time he might be home from a party
2 to show her son that her behaviour is actually reasonable, this has no effect on her son

3 being an evil dictator, she might as well begin acting like one
4 stealing the small change from her bedside table, put up with his emotional blackmail, being told he wishes he'd never been born
5 she promised (vowed) never to subject him to the strict discipline her parents subjected her to
6 to drag any of his girlfriends into the living room and show them pictures of him as a child
7 student's own opinion

Step 5 Tell students to complete the sentences in E with the correct form of the verbs from the article. Check understanding: *storm* = used as a verb meaning to leave quickly and making a noise, *get away with* = to do something wrong and not get discovered, *put up with* = tolerate someone's actions or behaviour. Then in pairs they compare before checking in open class.

Answers	
1 gets away with	4 storming
2 put up with	5 turn
3 change	

Step 6 Tell students to read the questions in exercise F and discuss in pairs. Conduct brief feedback.

NATIVE SPEAKER ENGLISH

might as well

Ask students to read the box and check they understand by asking, *Does the mother want to act like a dictator?* (No.) *Does she feel she has no reason not to?* (Yes.) Tell them that we use the expression *might as well* to mean *have no reason not to*.

SPEAKING

Aim
To provide fun fluency practice.

Step 1 Tell students to make a list of six 'household crimes' = behaviour that you find unacceptable, e.g. not washing up after dinner.

Step 2 Tell students in pairs to discuss and suggest suitable punishments. Conduct brief feedback.

 8B see Teacher's notes p. 123.

LEARNER TRAINING

Aim
To raise students' awareness about their views on reading.

Step 1 Tell students to individually read the students' views on reading in exercise A and to think about the positive and negative aspects of each approach. Give them a couple of minutes to think about their opinions. Monitor and help out with any ideas.

Step 2 Put students into groups to discuss their opinions. Ask them if they would consider changing their reading habits after this discussion. Conduct brief feedback at the end in open class.

GAME, CONVERSATION PRACTICE & ACT OR DRAW

For aims and suggested procedure, see Review 01, pp. 32–35.

QUIZ

Answers
1 A footballer might **get sent off** because he hit an opponent, he insulted the referee, etc.
2 If you **take the mickey** out of someone, you make fun of them in a friendly way.
3 You might **put off** doing something because you don't really want to do it, like doing your homework, going to the dentist, etc.
4 Friendly staff, a comfortable atmosphere, etc. make a place **welcoming**.
5 You suffer from **jetlag** when you travel by plane from one time zone to another, you can **get over it** by adjusting your sleep pattern to the new time zone a couple of days before you leave, or by staying awake in the new time zone until it's time to go to sleep there.
6 Herbal tea, warm milk, etc. can help **settle your stomach**. The problem might be that you feel nervous or anxious about something.
7 Someone might **storm out of** a room or meeting because they are angry or upset.
8 **Bribery** is when you offer money or something valuable in order to get someone to do something for you; **blackmail** is when you threaten to do

something unpleasant or reveal a secret unless they give you money.
9 If a child **vanishes**, they disappear; money, a car, a stain, etc. can all vanish.
10 People often have to **put up with** transport being late, a colleague at work, noisy neighbours.
11 **Fog** is a thick cloud that makes it difficult to see all around; **mist** usually happens in the morning and is close to the ground.
12 Finding it more difficult to walk, greying hair, eyesight gets worse, etc. are things you associate with **ageing**.
13 People often **moan about** the weather, the price of things, public transport, etc.
14 You can **chill out** by reading a book, sitting on the beach and listening to the waves, chatting with friends, listening to music, etc.
15 You might stay in a **self-catering** apartment because you want some privacy, it's easier to do what you want to do or it's cheaper than a hotel.

COLLOCATIONS

For aims and suggested procedure, see Review 01, pp. 32–35.

PRONUNCIATION

Stress in compound nouns

Aim
To revise and practise stress in compound nouns.

Step 1 Tell students to read the explanation box. Then in pairs they decide where they think the main stress is in each of the compound nouns in exercise A.

Step 2 Play the recording and tell students to check their answers. Then play the recording again and tell them to repeat the words with the correct stress.

🔊 R2.1 and Answers
volun<u>teer</u> work
a <u>mas</u>ter class
<u>crosswords</u>
<u>rack</u>et sports
a <u>com</u>ic fair
a <u>fit</u>ness fanatic
a <u>goal</u>keeper
<u>in</u>jury time
<u>rock</u> climbing

a <u>cam</u>per van
a <u>health</u> hazard
a <u>for</u>est fire
<u>hail</u>stones
<u>identity</u> theft
a <u>street</u> robbery
the <u>death</u> penalty
com<u>mun</u>ity service
a rehabili<u>ta</u>tion centre

Step 3 Put students into pairs and tell them to take turns explaining each compound noun, without saying the actual words. Their partner should guess the correct noun.

DICTATION

For aims and suggested procedure, see Review 01, pp. 32–35.

 pp. 62–63

LISTENING

For aims and suggested procedure for the rest of the review, see Review 01, pp. 32–35. The audio is 🔊 R2.2.

Exercise A answers				
1 e	2 d	3 c	4 b	5 f

Exercise B answers				
1 c	2 e	3 f	4 d	5 b

GRAMMAR

Exercise A answers			
1 a	3 c	5 c	7 a
2 a	4 c	6 b	8 c

Exercise B answers
1 I had my passport stolen while I was on holiday.
2 She mustn't have heard you – she wouldn't ignore you.
3 They might be waiting outside.
4 Advertising aimed at children should be banned.

Exercise C answers	
1 was sitting	6 saw
2 opened	7 were doing
3 looked	8 ran off
4 was	9 chased
5 had caught	10 had to

PREPOSITIONS

Answers			
1 for	3 with	5 to	7 off
2 in	4 on	6 to	8 to

LANGUAGE PATTERNS

Answers
1 Considering how little exercise
2 correct
3 He went on and on
4 correct
5 you were talking to?
6 I'm interested in at all.
7 nowadays, to do voluntary work.
8 overwhelming, to visit / visiting India

FORMING WORDS

Answers		
1 volunteers	4 uncoordinated	7 exaggeration
2 flexibility	5 resistance	8 dramatically
3 exclusion	6 harassment	

PHRASAL VERBS

Answers		
1 settled	3 passed	5 put
2 put	4 hang	6 puts

COLLOCATIONS

Answers			
1 tent	3 insight	5 phase	7 bomb
2 ankle	4 match	6 weed	8 seed

Note If students are finding this difficult direct them to Units 5–8 in the *Vocabulary builder* for more information on collocations.

VOCABULARY

Answers		
1 fires	5 seized	9 disappearance
2 flooding	6 captive	10 detention
3 thunder	7 release	
4 ease off	8 suspicion	

09 CAREERS AND STUDYING

UNIT OVERVIEW
The main aim of this unit is to enable students to **talk about good and bad aspects of working life** and **explain feelings about the future**. They have practice in **giving better presentations**. The main grammatical focus is **conditionals with present and past tenses** and **ways of expressing working life and starting presentations**.

VOCABULARY Working life

Aim
To introduce expressions related to working life.

Step 1 In pairs ask students to discuss whether the statements in A are good or not and why, in addition what are the causes and / or results of each thing. Do the first one as an example. Check answers in open class.

Suggested answers
1 got promoted = good thing because it makes you feel rewarded, cause = your boss recognised your hard work, result = you have a higher salary and status,
2 handed in my notice = good thing because you took control of a situation, cause = you didn't like the work and felt under-valued, result = you feel ready for a new beginning
3 got a raise = good thing because it means more money, cause = you did something valuable for the company or you got another qualification, result = you have more money to spend
4 getting-on-the-job training = good thing because it will help you to do your job better, cause = the company has introduced a new system, result = you'll become efficient at what you do
5 got made redundant = bad thing because you don't have a job now, cause = the company reorganised and moved the department to another city or country, result = you have to look for another job / you are unemployed
6 getting the hang of things = good thing because it means you are learning, cause = something was difficult or complicated, result = you are getting better at doing it
7 struggling to cope = bad thing because there's a lot to do, result = you feel under pressure
8 a complete control freak = bad because you have no freedom, result = you can't take responsibility
9 finding it rewarding = good thing because you feel you are valued, result = you enjoy your work

10 stimulating, stretching myself = good thing because it's using all your abilities, result = feel good about yourself
11 really emotionally draining = bad thing because it's not allowing you to be yourself, result = you feel frustrated
12 pretty menial = bad because it's boring, result = you don't feel you are using your abilities.

Step 2 In pairs ask students to discuss if any of the sentences in exercise A have ever been true for them or any of their friends / family. Conduct brief feedback.

LISTENING

Aim
To develop listening for specific information.

Step 1 Tell students they are going to hear the first part of a conversation between two friends, Melissa and Richard. Tell them to read the questions in exercise A.

Step 2 Play the recording and then put students in pairs to compare answers before checking in open class.

Answers
1 He isn't very satisfied because it's so menial.
2 He spends most of his time running round making cups of tea and photocopying things.
3 He can't see himself staying there long-term.
4 He's bound to get a lot of offers if he decides to move.

🔊 9.1 Part 1
M = Melissa, R = Richard
M: So how're you finding your job? Is it going OK?
 R: Oh, it's all right, I suppose. It's not what I want to do long-term, though.
M: No? How come?
 R: Oh, it's just so menial! I'm not using any of the skills I learned at university – and my boss is just dreadful! I seem to spend most of my time

running round making him cups of tea and photocopying things and if I ask about doing other stuff, he just tells me to be patient and then starts going on about how he did the same when he started at the company.

M: Well, maybe it's true.

R: Oh, I don't know. I was talking to this girl who joined at the same time as me and she said she was learning loads in her department – being really stretched, apparently. It makes me think it's maybe more about me!

M: Oh, I am sorry! If it's that bad, maybe you should think about handing in your notice!

R: I don't know. I guess it might get better if I just give it a bit more time.

M: Well, you'd think so. I mean, it is a big company, isn't it?

R: Mmm, but maybe that's it, you see. Maybe it's a bit too big. Anyway, I can't see myself staying there long term.

M: No? Well, if you do decide to make a move, you're bound to get lots of offers.

R: I don't know about that, but it's nice of you to say so!

M: It's true!

Step 3 Tell students they are going to listen to the second part of the conversation and to take notes on what Richard and Melissa say about the words in the vocabulary box.

Answers

training = Melissa has been getting loads of on-the-job training

college = they've been letting her go to college one day a week to improve her skills

clients = she's been meeting them quite a bit

presentation = she gave her first big presentation last week

business trip = her first one is coming up next week

promotion = she's applying for promotion at the moment and she feels confident about it

employee = Richard says she's their star employee

firm = she'll be running the entire firm in five years' time

🔊 9.1 Part 2

R: Well, anyway. What about you! How's your job going?

M: Oh, you probably won't want to hear to this, but it's great, yeah. It's going really well.

R: Well, I'm glad at least one of us is happy, anyway!

M: Yeah, it's amazing. I've been getting loads of on-the-job training – and they've been letting me go into college one day a week as well, to improve my skills. It's been really stimulating. I've also been meeting clients quite a bit. Oh, and I gave my first big presentation last week.

R: Wow! ... sounds amazing. Did it go OK?

M: Yeah, it went brilliantly. I've got my first business trip coming up next month – to New York. And I'm applying for promotion at the moment too.

R: Really? Already? Do you think you'll get it?

M: Hopefully, yeah, but you never know, do you?

R: Oh, you're bound to. From the sound of it, you're their star employee. I can just see you in five years' time, running the entire firm.

M: Ha!

R: And if the worst comes to the worst, I'll end up knocking on the door of your office, begging you for a job!

Tip With a weaker class, you could exploit the audioscript on page 173 by getting students to read and listen and underline any of the things they say about the vocabulary items.

Step 4 Put students into pairs to discuss the questions in C. Monitor and help out with any language problems. Conduct brief feedback at the end.

LANGUAGE PATTERNS

Aim

To draw attention to some common patterns using *see*.

Step 1 Tell students to read the language pattern box and tell students that in English we can use *see* to mean *imagine*, check understanding by getting them to substitute *imagine* for *see* in the sentences.

Step 2 Ask students to translate the sentences into their own language. In a monolingual class, ask students to compare their translation. In a multilingual class, ask students to work in pairs and tell each other if *see* in all the sentences can be replaced with one word direct translation. Why / Why not?

Step 3 Ask students to cover their English translations and using their translation translate the sentences back into English. Then ask them to compare their translations in pairs against the book and discuss who had the least mistakes. Alternatively, if you prefer not to use translation ask students to notice the patterns. You could ask students for example sentences, If the sentences are wrong, ask students to correct them or correct them yourself.

GRAMMAR Conditionals with present tenses

Aim

To practise conditionals with present tenses.

Step 1 Tell students to read the explanation box and check understanding: *What is the condition?* (sentence 1 = Richard asks about doing other stuff, sentence 2 = Richards gives it a bit more time), *What is the result?* (sentence 1 = his boss tells him to be patient, sentence 2 = it might get better), *When is Richard talking?* (in the present), *Is it a real situation for him?* (Yes).

Step 2 Ask students individually to complete the sentences in exercise A with the words in the box. Students compare answers in pairs before checking in open class. Direct students to the grammar reference on page 148 if they still seem unsure.

Answers

1 fails, come	4 work out, give	7 sack, change
2 talk, feel	5 happens, get	8 end up, carry on
3 is, start	6 do, goes	

DEVELOPING CONVERSATIONS

Feelings about the future

Aim

To practise expressing feelings about the future.

Step 1 Tell students to read the explanation box and exercise A and check understanding. Which expression is more certain in sentences 1, 2 & 5? (1 = *bound to*, 2 = *Definitely*, 5 *I'm bound to*), Which is less sure? = 1 *doubt it*, 2 *might*, 5 *doubt it*. Which expression is more positive in sentences 3 and 4? (*Hopefully*), Which is less positive? (*Probably*).

Step 2 Tell students to look at the sentences and choose the correct response. Then in pairs students compare answers before checking in open class.

Answers

1 I doubt it	3 Probably not	5 I'm bound to
2 I might	4 Hopefully	

Step 3 Tell students to read the questions in exercise B and to make notes about their answers. Remind them to use the expressions from exercise A. Also to think of similar questions of their own. Give them time to prepare what they want to say.

Step 4 In pairs students discuss the questions. Conduct brief feedback at the end.

CONVERSATION PRACTICE

Aim

To provide conversation practice using the language practised in the unit so far.

Step 1 Tell students they are going to have similar conversations to the one they heard in *Listening*. Put students into two groups, A and B. Tell group A to imagine

they are working and their job is going really well and to think of at least three reasons why. Tell group B to imagine their job is going really badly and to think of at least three reasons why. Give them time to prepare what they want to say and get them to help each other in their groups.

Step 2 Put students in AB pairs and tell them they should role-play the conversation, greet each other and catch up with each other's news and they should try to use at least two conditional sentences with present tenses. Monitor for a correction slot at the end.

---

 pp. 66–67

 Next class Make photocopies of **9A** p. 144 and **9B** p. 145.

LISTENING

Aim

To develop listening skills for general and specific information.

Step 1 In pairs students look at the pictures and answer the questions in A. Conduct brief feedback.

Step 2 Tell students they are going to hear a news report about changes in the way a particular job is done and they should listen and see if their ideas in exercise A were right. Check understanding of *noughties* = the decade of 2000–2009. Play the recording and ask students to compare in pairs before checking in open class.

🔊 **9.2**

And finally, it's official: the paperboy is a dying breed. For the first time, there are more adults delivering newspapers in the United States than young people. The steady shift from youth carriers to adults over the last few years is down to a number of factors: newspapers want deliveries to take place in the mornings rather than afternoons after school hours and more adults – particularly retired people – are grabbing the opportunity to earn some extra income to supplement their salaries or pensions. There are also those who blame the economic boom of the early noughties – families could afford to buy more things for their kids, and so many kids settled for the comfort of a sofa and Playstation rather than take to the streets to earn pocket money. Many delivery companies say adults are more reliable and provide a better service, but there are those who are saddened by the changes. Bud Keynes, managing director of the Milwaukee Herald: 'Doing a paper route when I was 13 was my first experience of business. It taught me responsibility, how to manage my time and communicate with people. More than once, I got soaked or froze to death or got chased by dogs, but it

---

> was character building. Too many young people these days enter what is a very competitive job market lacking those basic business skills that you get from being a carrier.'

Step 3 Tell students to read the questions in exercise C and to discuss what they think in pairs. Play the recording again to check their answers. Check in open class.

Answers
1 newspapers want deliveries to take place in the morning, more adults – particularly retired people – are grabbing the opportunity to earn extra money, the economic boom of the early noughties where families can afford to buy things for the kids, so the kids settle for the comfort of the sofa and Playstation rather than take to the streets to earn money.
2 He thinks too many young people these days enter a competitive job market lacking basic business skills you can get from being a carrier – responsibility, how to manage time and communicate with people.

SPEAKING

Aim
To provide fluency practice of expressing opinions.

Step 1 Tell students to read the question in exercise A and give then time to think about what they want to say.

Step 2 Put students into groups of four or five and get them to discuss the questions. Monitor and correct any language problems. Conduct brief feedback at the end.

 9A see Teacher's notes p. 124.

READING

Aim
To develop reading for general and detailed information.

Step 1 Tell students to individually read the text about five people's first jobs and to decide who they think had the best first job. In groups of four or five they explain and discuss their choices. Conduct brief feedback in open class.

Step 2 Individually tell students to read the statements in exercise B and read the texts to answer the questions. Then they compare in pairs before checking in open class.

Answers
1 Eduardo = By the time I got home, I was dead and slept till one...
2 Eduardo = I started work at two in the afternoon ... and then worked solidly through til' five in the morning
3 Carla = For sure, people associate the army with war
4 Jock = I went part-time

5 Simon = I'm very conscious of be fair to staff at all levels
6 Carla = we get training for things like logistics
7 Simon = I was pushed around a bit
8 Eduardo = It sounded ideal ... Big mistake!
9 Jock = I'm not sure I'd have got through it (cancer) if I hadn't been working
10 Eduardo = my boss was a complete control freak
11 Carla = women are often better than men in these roles
12 Jock = I walk down a road that was named after me
13 Simon = I'm a manager myself now
14 Eun Suk = I need the money to help them (my parents) out while I'm studying

Step 3 Tell students to read the article again and find adjectives / verbs that go with the nouns in the vocabulary box. Check understanding of *rank* = official position. In pairs they compare before checking the answers in open class.

Answers
carrying trays, set foot, straight out of college, had cancer, had the choice, joined the army, see the practical benefits, achieve a high rank, serves as a valuable lesson, suck up to the boss

Step 4 Tell students to read the statements in exercise D. Then put students into groups to discuss their opinions. Conduct brief feedback.

GRAMMAR Conditionals with past tenses

Aim
To introduce and practise conditionals with past tenses.

Step 1 Write on the board *If Eduardo had asked about the job before, he mightn't have taken it* and *If Eduardo had the choice, he wouldn't do it again* and check understanding: Sentence 1 = *Did Eduardo ask about the job before?* (No.) *Did he take the job* (Yes.) *Was it a real situation?* (No.) Ask students to read the explanation box and identify the unreal situation (he didn't ask about the job) and if it speculates about a past situation (yes = *had asked*) and identify the consequence (*mightn't have taken it*) and if it refers to the past (yes). Sentence 2 = *Did Eduardo have the choice?* (No.) *Did he do it?* (Yes.) *Was it a real situation?* (No.) *What was the situation?* (He didn't have the choice.) *When is it referring to?* (The future.) *What's the consequence?* (He wouldn't do it again.) *When does it refer to?* (The future.)

Step 2 Tell students to complete the sentences by putting the verbs into the correct form without looking at the text. Then students compare in pairs, check against the article and explain to each other the use of different forms according to the rules. Check answers in open class.

Answers

1 work, won't be = real situation in the present with a future consequence
2 I'd have got through, hadn't been working = unreal consequence in the past with a past situation
3 gets, are wearing = real situation in the present with a present consequence
4 wouldn't do, had = present consequence of an unlikely situation in the present
5 wasn't, would never have gone = present consequence of an unreal situation in the past
6 hadn't got, might've left = past situation with an unreal consequence in the past.

Step 3 Individually students read the situations in 1–5 and write a conditional sentence for each one. Ask students to compare in pairs and decide who has the most interesting ideas. The whole class could vote on the best ideas.

Suggested answers

1 If she works hard she might get promoted quickly
2 If he went back to college, he could learn a new skill
3 I'll help you with the lessons, if you take me out for dinner once a week
4 If she hadn't gone on holiday, she wouldn't have met the love of her life

Step 4 Tell students to think of four events, situations or people that have had an impact on their lives. Give them time to make notes. Then put students into small groups to explain the events and remind them to use conditional sentences. Conduct brief feedback. Direct students to the grammar reference on page 148 if they still seem unsure.

  9B see Teacher's notes p. 124.

pp. 68–69

LISTENING

Aim
To develop listening skills for specific information.

Step 1 Put students in pairs to discuss the questions in A. Tell them not to worry if they don't know anything about the Bologna Process. They will hear about it in a moment. Conduct quick feedback in open class on their opinions.

Step 2 Tell students they are going to hear a presentation about the Bologna Process. They should listen and take notes. Play the recording and tell students to compare in pairs and decide whose notes are more useful and why.

9.3
If you haven't heard of the Bologna Process yet, then the odds are that you soon will. And no, before you ask, it's NOT a new way of cooking pasta! Instead, the Bologna Process is a voluntary initiative that is

changing the face of education across Europe – and that's starting to have a knock-on effect elsewhere as well.

What I'm going to try and do today is tell you a bit about the initiative before moving on to explore what it involves in more detail.

Named after the Italian city where the idea was first put forward, the Bologna Process aims to create a European 'higher education area' by making academic degree and quality control standards more compatible and easier to compare with one another.

Now, for many people across the EU, any mention of Europe-wide initiatives is terrifying! There have been countless ridiculous media scare stories about unelected bureaucrats in Brussels telling us what size bananas we are – and aren't – allowed to eat or about football supporters supposedly being forced to wear earplugs at matches due to crazy health and safety measures. Obviously, for some traditionalists, the idea of any kind of standardisation is too much for them to bear.

However, it seems to me that almost anything is better than the way things were. Under the old system, credits were sometimes awarded to students based simply on the number of hours they'd done. This led to some countries refusing to recognise qualifications from others. Under Bologna, credits will be based on learning outcomes – or what students have actually achieved – rather than length of study. There will also be greater emphasis placed on project work, practical experiments, research, presentations, and so on.

This will mean both students and academic staff can move around the Euro zone more easily, without always having to explain their qualifications! It should also mean that Europe becomes a more attractive destination for non-European students.

The main change happening is that most European countries are getting rid of the four- or five-year degree courses they used to offer and instead are starting to adopt a British and Irish style system of three-year degrees. These are then followed by two-year Master's degrees and three-year doctoral degrees – or PhDs.

Many countries have introduced radical reforms, changing not only degree and Master's courses, but introducing tuition fees, restructuring departments and allowing universities to have much greater autonomy, decentralising the curricula, allowing the creation of private universities, and so on.

Of course, these changes have not gone unchallenged – and what I want to do now is to consider the negative responses more fully. Public reaction has been particularly heated in Greece, where there have been massive demonstrations against Bologna, sit-ins and even riots. France has seen general strikes – and even the UK is worried that it will now lose its appeal, as it is no longer the only country to offer shorter degree courses!

Step 3 Tell students to read the sentences in D about the presentation and decide if they are true or false.

Step 4 Play the recording for students to check their ideas. In pairs they compare their ideas and look at the audioscript on page 174 to underline any words or expressions that helped them.

> **Answers**
> 1 T = it's starting to have a knock-on (*indirect effect of something*) effect elsewhere
> 2 F = supposedly being forced to wear earplugs
> 3 T = based simply on the number of hours you'd done
> 4 T = there will also be greater emphasis placed on project work, practical experiments, research, presentations and so on
> 5 F = they are getting rid of (*stop / abolish*) four- or five-year degrees and adopting the British and Irish system of three-year degrees
> 6 T = allowing universities to have much greater autonomy
> 7 T = in Greece there have been massive demonstrations, sit-ins (*demonstration where protesters literally sit on the ground*) and riots and France has seen general strikes (the whole country goes on strike)
> 8 F = the UK is worried that it will now lose its appeal, as it is no longer the only country to offer shorter degree courses

NATIVE SPEAKER ENGLISH *the odds*

Ask students to read the box and check they understand by asking What words could you replace *odds* with? (*chances / possibilities*.)

SPEAKING

Aim
To provide fluency practice of expressing their opinions.

Step 1 Tell students they are going to discuss their opinions about the Bologna Process and the changes it might involve. They should think about the implications for the areas in the box. Give them time to prepare their ideas and to look at the expressions of agreeing and disagreeing in Unit 8 *Vocabulary* page 57.

Step 2 Put students into groups of four or five to discuss their ideas and say whether they agree or disagree with their partner's opinions. Monitor and take notes on their use of language for a correction slot at the end.

VOCABULARY Starting presentations

Aim
To practise expressions when introducing presentations and explaining what you are going to talk about.

Step 1 Ask students to read the explanation box and get them to notice the expressions. Tell them they are useful ways to let your listeners know what you are going to talk about.

Step 2 Tell students to complete the sentences in exercise A with the verbs in italics. In pairs students compare their answers before checking in open class.

> **Answers**
> 1 a take, b tell, c talk, d summarise
> 2 e giving, f reviewing, g commenting, h outlining
> 3 i focus, j consider, k make, l highlight

Step 3 Tell students that the sentences in exercise A parts 1, 2 and 3 make the introductions to four different presentations. They should connect the sentences from 1, 2 and 3. Monitor and help out with any problems.

> **Answers**
> 1 a, g, k   2 b, e, i   3 c, h, j   4 d, f, l

Step 4 In pairs students take turns reading out each introduction.

Step 5 Ask students to work in pairs and discuss which of the four presentations they'd most / least like to hear and why and how much they know about each of the four topics. Conduct brief feedback.

SPEAKING

Aim
To practice giving a short presentation.

Step 1 In pairs students discuss the questions in exercise A. Conduct brief feedback in open class.

Step 2 Tell students to choose one of the topics in exercise B and to plan a five-minute presentation on the subject. They can use a dictionary to help them prepare if they need to. Remind them to begin by explaining what they are going to be talking about and refer to *Vocabulary* for a model.

Step 3 Put students into groups of four or five and tell them to take turns to give their presentations and while they are listening they should think of a question to ask the speaker after the presentation. Monitor and take notes on their use of language.

Step 4 Tell them to decide on the best presentation in each group and what made it so good. Then get a student from each group to feedback to the rest of the class. Finish with a correction slot.

10 SOCIALISING

UNIT OVERVIEW
The main aim of this unit is to enable students to **describe how people celebrate events, suggest different times / places to meet** and **start and end different kinds of conversations**. They have practice in dealing with **awkward social situations**. The main grammatical focus is the **future perfect** and **question tags** and **ways of making mistakes** and **talking about parties**.

 Next class Make photocopies of **10A** p. 146.

SPEAKING

Aim
To lead in to the topic of celebrations.

Step 1 Ask students to look at the celebrations in the box and check understanding and word stress: *Easter* = the week leading up to Christ's death and resurrection, *Eid ul Fitr* = the end of Ramadan, *Valentine's Day* = 14 February and the day of romance, *May Day* = 1 May and workers day, *Christmas* = the period in late December to celebrate Christ's birth. In open class ask students if they celebrate any of the celebrations in the box or any other special days that they celebrate and how do they celebrate them.

Step 2 Tell students to read the statements in exercise C and get them to guess the meaning of the words from the context or check in the *Vocabulary builder*. Individually ask students to think about which of the ways of celebrating appeal to them and why. Then tell each other in pairs.

Step 3 In new pairs students tell each other how they celebrated their last birthday or another special day. Conduct brief feedback in open class.

LISTENING

Aim
To develop listening for specific information.

Step 1 Tell students they are going to hear three friends talking about what to do on Friday. Tell them to listen for why they are going out to celebrate on Friday and to take notes on what they hear about the three places = Equinox, Rico's and Guanabara and what time they agree to meet up.

Step 2 Play the recording and ask students to compare answers in pairs. Check answers as a class.

Answers
1 they will have finished their exams
2 Equinox = it's a big disco on the main square in town, one girl really likes it but another doesn't like it, says she can't stand the music and it's full of horrible guys, Rico's = a restaurant, it's a bit of a rip-off, spent something like 60 euros last time, Guanabara = Brazilian place near the station, restaurant and they do salsa after 10 o'clock
3 8 o'clock.

🎧 10.1
N=Nina, L=Linda, V=Vita

N: So how much longer have you got?
L: Three more days. By four o'clock Friday we'll have finished every single one. I can't wait!
V: Me neither. The Physics one yesterday was a nightmare.
L: I know! I'm sure I failed it.
N: You must be sick of it all.
V: I am. If I revise much more my head's going to explode!
L: Just keep telling yourself: three more days, three more days.
N: So shall we go out and celebrate on Friday, then?
V: That sounds like an excellent idea.
L: Yeah, I'd be up for that as well. Do you have anywhere in mind?
N: I thought that Equinox might be fun.
L: Where's that?
N: Oh, don't you know it? It's the big disco on the main square in town. It's great.
V: If you like that kind of place! I have to say, it's not my kind of thing. I can't stand the music down there and besides - it's full of horrible guys.
N: Oh! I thought it was OK when I went there, but if you'd rather go somewhere else, that's fine by me.
L: Well, personally, I'd quite like to get something to eat at some point, if that's all right with you?
V: Yeah, that sounds good. Any thoughts on where?
L: Well, Rico's is always a good bet.
V: Oh, it's such a rip-off, that place. Last time I went there, I spent something like sixty euros. Can't we go somewhere cheaper?

N: How about that Brazilian place near the station?
V: Guanabara? Yeah, that'd be fine with me. Linda?
L: Yeah, whatever. I'm easy. They have music later on down there, don't they?
N: Yeah, they do salsa after ten.
V: It sounds ideal. So what time do you want to meet? Seven? Seven thirty?
N: I'm working till six and it'd be nice if I could go home first, so could we make it eight? I'll have had time to get changed and freshen up a bit by then.
V: Yeah, fine.
N: And I'll phone and book a table – just to be on the safe side.
L: OK. I'll ring a few other people and see if anyone else is up for it - and see you down there.
N: OK. Brilliant. Bye.
V: Bye.

Step 3 Tell students to complete the sentences from the conversation in exercise B from memory and that there are two or three words missing in each space. Compare in pairs and then play the recording again to check their answers.

Answers
1 shall we
2 up for that, in mind
3 be fun
4 can't stand, horrible guys
5 like, all right
6 good bet
7 I'm easy
8 make it.

NATIVE SPEAKER ENGLISH *Up for it*

Ask students to read the box and the sentences. Tell them it's a fixed expression we use a lot in informal English.

GRAMMAR The future perfect

Aim
To present and practise the future perfect.

Step 1 Tell students to read the explanation box and notice the language pattern = *will (won't)* + *have*+ past participle. Check understanding: *When is the person speaking?* (Now.) *When will the exams finish?* (By four o'clock on Friday.) Tell students that when we want to connect an action from now to some point in the future we use the future perfect.

Step 2 Get students to look at the words in the box and check understanding, *graduate* = finish university and get your degree. Then tell them individually to complete the sentences in exercise A with the words in the box and that

they need to use a negative form once. In pairs students compare answers before checking in open class.

Answers
1 will have been
2 will, have forgotten
3 will have tried
4 will have learnt
5 will have left
6 will have graduated
7 won't have finished

Direct students to the grammar reference on page 149 if they still seem unsure.

Step 3 Tell students to spend three minutes thinking about how the world will be different in 30 years. Get them to look at the two examples on the page for ideas and highlight the use of the future perfect, e.g. *they'll have found, I'll have started.*

Step 4 Put them in pairs to compare their ideas. Conduct brief feedback.

 10A see Teacher's notes p. 124.

DEVELOPING CONVERSATIONS
Arranging to meet

Aim
To introduce and practise arranging to meet.

Step 1 Get students to read the explanation box and tell them we use *Can / Could we make it* to sound more polite. Get them to notice that the pattern after the expression is usually a place or time.

Step 2 Tell students to complete the dialogues 1–6 by adding the suggestions in a–f. Check understanding: *awkward* = difficult. Students compare answers in pairs before checking in open class.

Answers					
1 d	2 f	3 b	4 e	5 a	6 c

Step 3 Get students to read the questions in exercise B and ask what are the possible endings = 1 x time and 2 x place. Tell students to write three possible endings, monitor and help out with any problems. Then in pairs tell them to take turns in suggesting where / when to meet and each time they should reject their partner's suggestions. Tell them to suggest an alternative using *Could we make it …?* and explain why. Conduct brief feedback by getting a selection of pairs to act out their dialogue for the rest of the class.

CONVERSATION PRACTICE

Aim
To provide conversation practice using the language learnt so far.

Step 1 Tell students to imagine that their course finishes on Friday. They are going to role-play a conversation similar to the one they heard in *Listening* and they want to arrange to go out and celebrate. Tell them to write down three places they would like to go and why they would be good. Give them time to prepare what they want to say.

Step 2 When students are ready, put them into groups of three and tell them they should arrange where to go and where / when to meet. They should reject some of their partner's ideas, explain why and make an alternative suggestion. Monitor and take notes on their use of language.

Step 3 Ask a couple of students to tell the class about what arrangements they made. Conduct a correction slot.

 pp. 72–73

READING

Aim
To develop reading for general and detailed information.

Step 1 Ask students to read the situations and look at the photographs and to think of what the problem might be and discuss in pairs. Conduct brief feedback.

Step 2 Tell students to individually read the text and find out what each of the five problems actually was and what the result was in each case. Then they compare in pairs before checking in open class.

> **Answers**
> 1 Problem = The woman didn't know Tim was married, result = she slapped him.
> 2 problem = the writer was moaning (*complaining*) about his tutor to a friend, result = the friend introduced him to Tracy Gray who must a be a relative of his tutor Dr Gray and was standing close to them.
> 3 problem= Gerald Ratner joked about the cheap quality of his products at a meeting, result = his customers didn't see the funny side of it, the share prices crashed and he had to resign.
> 4 problem = Richard Gere kissed the Indian actress on the cheek, result = he was threatened with arrest because public displays of affection are frowned upon (*not accepted*).
> 5 problem = Paul Keating put his arm around the back of the Queen when introducing her, result = it caused outrage in some British newspapers.

Step 3 Individually tell students to read the questions in exercise C and read the texts to answer the questions. Then they compare in pairs before checking in open class.

> **Answers**
> 1 put your foot in it = say or do the wrong thing and this upsets someone.
> 2 He was a victim of globalised 24-hour news coverage, he was at a semi-private meeting and a journalist happened to be there.
> 3 These days people in the public eye have to be very careful with what they say or do – they both made comments that were reported and lost them money or their jobs
> 4 he quite often puts his foot in it – if he were famous, it could undermine relationships between countries and even destroy business deals and careers.

LANGUAGE PATTERNS

Aim
To draw attention to common patterns with *even*.

Step 1 Ask students to look at the sentences in the language patterns box. Ask them what difference it makes to the sentences if the word *even* is left out (in the last sentence *even* cannot be left out). Elicit or tell students that we use *even* when we want to emphasise something and say that it surprises us. Point out that grammatically *even* comes after the verb *to be*, an auxiliary and a modal verb and before an ordinary verb.

Step 2 Ask students to translate the sentences into their own language. In a monolingual class, ask students to compare their translation. In a multilingual class, students work in pairs and tell each other if *even* in all the sentences can be replaced with one word direct translation.

Step 3 Ask students to cover their English translations and using their translation translate the sentences back into English. Then ask them to compare their translations in pairs against the book. Alternatively, if you prefer not to use translation ask students to notice the patterns.

VOCABULARY Making mistakes

Aim
To practise expressions when making mistakes.

Step 1 Get students to read the words in the vocabulary box and check understanding: *due* = expected to happen, *clue* = idea (in this context), *turned up* = arrive. Tell them to complete the sentences with the pairs of words in the box and that they might need to change the order of the words. In pairs they compare their answers before checking in open class.

Answers
1 due, pregnant	5 meant, see
2 crying, realised	6 foot, surprise
3 send, copying	7 politician, clue
4 turned up, dressed	8 stupid, live

Step 3 Tell students to read the statements again and decide which of them they think is the most serious. Then in pairs they explain their ideas and see if they agree. Monitor and help out with any language problems. Conduct brief feedback.

SPEAKING

Aim
To practise talking about making mistakes.

Step 1 Tell students to read the questions in exercise A and to take notes on what they think. Give them time to prepare their ideas.

Step 2 Put students into pairs and get them to discuss the questions. Monitor and help out with any language problems.

Step 3 Get a selection of students to tell the rest of the class of any funny moments when they or someone famous put their foot in it and what has caused outrage in their countries.

 pp. 74–75

 Next class Make photocopies of **10B** p. 147.

SPEAKING

Aim
To provide fluency practice talking about dealing with awkward situations.

Step 1 Tell students to read the situations in exercise A. Put students into groups and tell them to discuss the questions. Monitor their use of language.

Step 3 Get a student from each group to tell the rest of the class about the best reaction to the situations. Then finish with a correction slot.

LISTENING

Aim
To develop listening for general and specific information.

Step 1 Tell students they are going to hear five short conversations and they should listen and decide in which of the situations from *Speaking* each conversation takes place. Tell them one situation is not included. Play the recording and

then get students to compare in pairs before checking in open class. If necessary, play the recording again before checking.

Answers
1 situation 4	3 situation 2	5 situation 6
2 situation 1	4 situation 5	

10.2
Conversation 1
A: Sorry, but you couldn't pass me the salt, could you? Thank you. They look nice.
B: They are. They're lovely. Have you tried that aubergine dip? It's gorgeous.
A: Hmm. I have to say I'm not that keen on aubergines. There's something wrong with them as a vegetable.
B: You're joking! Aubergines - they're the king of vegetables! Although strictly speaking, they're a fruit, of course.
A: Mmm.
B: They're so versatile. You can fry them, grill them, have them mashed, stuffed, barbecued … .
A: Right.
B: Did you know that they used to use the skin as a dye? The Chinese apparently used to polish their teeth with it!
A: Sorry, I've just seen my friend Mercedes. I must just go and talk to her. I've been meaning to all evening.
Conversation 2
C: So how do you know Niall?
D: Who?
C: Er … the person whose party this is.
D: Oh right. Well, he's like the friend of a friend of my flatmate. I don't know why I'm here, really. I feel a bit left out. My flatmate dragged me along because she thought she wouldn't know anyone. Oh – that's her over there, with that blonde guy. I think I might just go. How do you know Niall anyway?
C: I'm his fiancée! You did know this is a party to celebrate our engagement, didn't you?
D: No, actually I didn't. Congratulations, though! It's a great party.
Conversation 3
E: I'm glad I'm not the only person who couldn't stand it any more.
F: Tell me about it! It was so stuffy in there, wasn't it? You could hardly breathe.
E: Yeah. They need some air conditioning or something.
F: The speaker wasn't exactly helping either, was he? I thought I was going to fall asleep at one point there.
E: Yeah. He's very dull, isn't he? I think I might just go and grab a coffee instead of going back in.
F: That sounds like a good idea. Do you mind if I join you?
Conversation 4
G: Is this the queue for the toilet?
H: I'm afraid so.
G: I love your top.
H: Oh, thanks.
G: It's quite unusual. Where did you get it?

H: I actually picked it up in a second-hand clothes stall. It was only five pounds.

G: Really? That's fantastic! I never really bother looking in places like that. I mean, there's a second-hand place near me, but the stuff in there always looks in pretty poor condition. That looks brand new, though.

H: I think it's quite old actually, but the stall I got it from is just fantastic – just really nice stuff.

G: Mind you, it's so difficult getting stuff in my size.

H: I can imagine. It must be hard. I've got a friend who's maybe your height and she's always moaning about it as well. That dress is lovely, though.

G: It's great, isn't it? I actually just found this place online. Oh look – it's your turn.

Conversation 5

I: Sorry. I couldn't help overhearing. Did you say Everton beat Chelsea?

J: Yeah.

I: What was the final score?

J: They thrashed them! Five-nil.

I: You're joking! I saw the beginning of the game, but then I had to go out.

J: Are you an Everton fan?

I: No – West Ham.

J: Oh dear! You can't be enjoying things much this year!

I: Ah, it's just a temporary loss of form. It won't last. We're just going through a bad patch at the moment. We'll be all right by the end of the season. We'll finish in the top half of the league.

J: You're optimistic! I can't see it myself.

I: Trust me! It'll all work out OK. Anyway, sorry, I didn't want to stop you chatting.

J: That's OK.

Step 2 Tell students to read the sentences in exercise B and check understanding of *stuffy* = no air in the room, *loss of form* = not playing as well as they usually do, *fiancée* = engaged to be married (female), *thrashed* = defeat an opponent in a game very easily. Then play the recording and tell students to decide in which conversation they hear the sentences.

Note In English we use *we* to talk about the football team we support and *you* for the opposing team e.g. *We're [West Ham] just going through a bad patch at the moment.*

Step 3 Tell students to compare their ideas with a partner and can they remember what each person was talking about. Then play the recording again and pause after each conversation to check their ideas in open class.

Answers
1 conversation 3 (the speaker was boring)
2 conversation 1 (the aubergine dip = thick cold sauce for putting on pieces of food before eating them)
3 conversation 3 (there was no air-conditioning)
4 conversation 5 (his team, West Ham, are not doing well at the moment)

5 conversation 1 (aubergines, you can cook them in many different ways)
6 conversation 2 (the girl at the party)
7 conversation 4 (her height)
8 conversation 2 (the flatmate who brought her to the party)
9 conversation 4 (the girl compliments someone in the queue)
10 conversation 5 (Everton beat Chelsea five-nil)

Step 4 Tell students to read the questions in exercise D and to discuss in pairs. Conduct brief feedback.

GRAMMAR Question tags

Aim
To present and practise question tags.

Step 1 Tell students to read the explanation box and check understanding: *Which sentences does the speaker ask for clarification?* (Sentence 1.) *Which sentences does the speaker ask for agreement?* (Sentences 2 and 3.) *Which sentence is a polite request?* (Sentence 4.)

Step 2 Tell students to look at sentences in the box and decide how the tags are formed. Then they check in pairs before checking in open class. Direct students to the grammar reference on page 149 if they still seem unsure.

Answers
If the statement is positive, the question tag is negative, e.g. sentences 1 and 2. If the statement is negative, the question tag is positive e.g. sentences 3 and 4.
The questions tag uses the auxiliary verb: sentence 1 = *don't they?* or the main verb = sentence 2 = *wasn't it?* sentence 3 = *was he?* and sentence 4 = *could you?*

Step 3 Tell students to read the dialogues and complete them by adding question tags in the appropriate places. Do the first one as an example in open class. In pairs students compare before checking in open class.

Answers
1 Miserable weather, isn't it? It's been like this for weeks, hasn't it?
2 You don't remember me, do you? It's Yuka, isn't it?
3 You haven't got a light, have you? You couldn't lend me a euro, could you?
4 You missed class on Monday, didn't you? The school was closed for the holiday, wasn't it? Well, to be honest the whole course is dissapointing, isn't it?
5 It's from Zara, isn't it? You wouldn't happen to know the address, would you? You know where the McDonalds is, don't you?

Step 4 Tell students to read the explanation box and check understanding: *When does our voice go up?* (When we are asking a real question, we don't know the answer.) *When does our voice go down?* (When we are just making a comment.)

Step 5 Tell students to listen to the dialogues from exercise B and mark whether the voice goes up or down on each tag. Play the recording and in pairs compare their answers. If necessary, play the recording again before checking in open class.

🔊 **10.43**

Conversation 1
A: Miserable weather, isn't it?
B: Yeah, awful. It's been like this for weeks, hasn't it?
A: I know. I can't remember when I last saw the sun. Can you?

Conversation 2
C: You don't remember me, do you?
D: It's Yuka, isn't it?
C: No. It's Naomi.

Conversation 3
E: Excuse me. You haven't got a light, have you?
F: Yeah. Here you go.
E: Thanks.
F: You couldn't lend me a euro, could you?
E: No, sorry.

Conversation 4
G: You missed the class on Monday, didn't you?
H: There wasn't one, was there? It was closed for the holiday, wasn't it?
G: No. Mind you, you didn't miss much. It was quite boring.
H: Well, to be honest the whole course is a bit disappointing, isn't it?

Conversation 5
I: I love that jacket. It's from Zara, isn't it?
J: No, I got it from a shop called Monsoon.
I: Really? You wouldn't happen to know the address, would you?
J: Sorry. I've forgotten the name of the road. You know the McDonald's, don't you? Well, it's the next road down on the left.

Step 6 Tell students to work in pairs and practise the five dialogues in exercise B. Remind them to make sure their voices go up or down in the right places.

Step 7 Tell students to spend three minutes thinking of questions to ask using the patterns in the speech bubbles. Then, put them in pairs to take turns asking their questions. Remind them to make sure their voices go up or down and that they can answer in any way they want. Conduct brief feedback.

Step 8 Tell students to write four comments about the weather, news, food or sport and to include question tags. When students are ready, put them in new pairs to say their comments to a partner with the correct intonation and their partner can make up a suitable reply. Monitor and help with intonation patterns.

 10B see Teacher's notes p. 124.

VOCABULARY Talking about parties

Aim
To practise guessing the meaning from context.

Step 1 Ask students to read the sentences in 1–8 and use the extra information to guess the meaning of the words in bold. Tell them they can use the *Vocabulary builder* to help them if they need to. In pairs students compare their answers. Check answers and word stress in open class.

Answers
1 *set up a marquee* = to erect a big tent for a party, *a fortune* = a lot of money, *chat me up* = to start a conversation because you want a romantic relationship, *get lost* = strong way of telling someone to go away, *the host* = the person who invites you to their party, *dragged me along* = to take someone with you unwillingly, *fancied* = was attracted to someone, *break it up* = stop it, *out of hand* = out of control, *left out* = not included, *threw a party* = gave a party, *burst into tears* = suddenly start crying, *turned up* = arrive unexpectedly, *went to waste* = wasn't used and had to be thrown away.

Step 2 Tell students to look at the sentences in exercise A. In pairs they discuss. Conduct brief feedback.

SPEAKING

Aim
To practise starting and ending conversations.

Step 1 Tell students to imagine they are at a party and that they are going to have brief conversations with other students about the subjects in exercise A. Tell them they have five minutes to plan how they will begin and end each conversation and what they will say. Elicit ways of starting and ending conversations. Remind them of *Listening* 10.3, e.g. in conversation 1 = *Sorry, you couldn't …* , elicit other examples, e.g. *So, how do you know X, Is this the queue for…, Have you been waiting long?*, and to end the conversation, e.g. in conversation 1 the speaker ends the conversation with = *Sorry, I've just seen my friend. I must just go and talk to her. I've been meaning to all evening.* Tell them we usually start with *sorry*, then say what it is we have to do and sometimes end with a leaving phrase, e.g. *Nice talking to you, I'll hopefully see you later.*

Step 2 Tell students to stand up and move around the room and when you clap your hands they should start a conversation with the person next to them, then after two minutes, you will clap you hands again and they should end the conversation and continue walking around the room until you clap your hands again. Do this for three or four conversations. Monitor for a correction slot.

11 TRANSPORT AND TRAVEL

UNIT OVERVIEW
The main aim of this unit is to enable students to **talk about problems with vehicles** and **good and bad drivers** and **renting a car**. They have practice in **describing the features of different kinds of vehicles**. The main grammatical focus is **uncountable nouns and emphatic structures** and **ways of expressing problems with vehicles and driving**.

SPEAKING

Aim
To lead in to the topic of different kinds of vehicles.

Step 1 Ask students to look at the pictures and decide what kind of vehicles they can see.

> **Suggested answers**
> *A sports car, hatchback* = car that has an extra door at the back that opens from the bottom, *large estate car* = long car with an extra door at the back and a lot of space between the back seats, *4 X 4 or SUV* = sport utility vehicle, *van* = used for transporting merchandise, *camper van* = has space to sleep

Step 2 Put students into pairs and tell them to discuss the questions. Monitor and help out with any language problems. Conduct brief feedback.

LISTENING 1

Aim
To develop listening for specific information.

Step 1 Tell students they are going to hear a conversation in a car rental office. Tell them to read the words in the box and check understanding of *automatic* = a car in which the gears change by themselves, *diesel* = heavy oil used instead of petrol, *unlimited mileage* = there is no limit to the amount of miles (or kilometres) you can drive while renting, *boot* = the part at the back of a vehicle where you can put luggage and other things. Then tell them to think about which of the things in the box are (a) really important, (b) quite important and (c) not very important when renting a car. In groups they compare their ideas. Conduct brief feedback in open class.

Step 2 Tell students to read the questions in exercise C and they should listen to the conversation and answer the questions. Play the recording and then put students

in pairs to compare answers and if necessary play the recording again before checking answers in open class.

> **Answers**
> 1 You can upgrade to the next range for just €2 a day
> 2 No, because they don't have much luggage and they want something smaller, more fuel efficient
> 3 GPS
> 4 Yes, it's quite cheap
> 5 They don't need to return it with a full tank and it's diesel, they should check the car as well as there are some scratches = *the paint has a mark on it*, dent = *a part of the car has been banged inwards*.

> 🔊 **11.1**
> **A = Assistant, C = Customer**
> A: Hi. How can I help you today?
> C: Hi. I reserved a car online. Here's my voucher and my driving licence.
> A: Yep. OK. Let's have a look. Right. We have your car ready, but we're running a special offer this week. You can upgrade to the next range for just two euros a day, so you could have an estate car if you like.
> C: It's OK. We don't have much luggage.
> A: Are you sure? It's a bit more powerful as well.
> C: No, I think something smaller – more fuel-efficient – is OK.
> A: Fine. You ordered GPS, yes?
> C: That's right.
> A: OK. Would you like our additional insurance cover for damage to tyres and windscreen?
> C: Isn't that already included in what I paid for online?
> A: No. I think it's in the small print - and this is only three euros extra a day.
> C: What are the chances of anything going wrong?
> A: Well, it's up to you, but better safe than sorry, isn't it?
> C: I suppose so. OK, then. It is quite cheap.
> A: Fine. Can I just have your credit card? That's for the insurance, the cost of the fuel and also your deposit on the car – which is returnable when you bring the car back.
> C: Right, so should I return the tank full?
> A: No, there's no need, but it is full now. It's diesel, by the way.

C: OK.

A: So could you just sign where I've marked with a cross? You may want to check the car as well before you leave. There are some scratches here and here and a small dent in the rear door.

C: OK. Great.

A: Have a good trip.

NATIVE SPEAKER ENGLISH

Better safe than sorry

Ask students to read the box and check they understand by asking, *Why is it better to be safe than sorry?* E.g. sentence 1 = could be anything that the speaker feels could go wrong. Tell them this sentence comes from *Listening* and ask if they remember why the speaker said it = *it's a good idea to take the additional insurance, in case anything goes wrong.*

VOCABULARY Problems with vehicles

Aim
To introduce expressions related to problems with vehicles.

Step 1 Ask students to look at the sentences in exercise A. Monitor and help out with any problems. In pairs they compare answers before checking in open class.

Answers

1 tyre	6 windscreen
2 engine	7 tank
3 wing	8 scratch
4 tyres	9 dent
5 battery	10 brakes

Step 2 Tell students to consider whether any of the things in exercise A have happened to cars they have been in and what happened. In pairs they tell each other. Conduct brief feedback.

LISTENING 2

Aim
To develop listening for specific information.

Step 1 Tell students they are going to hear John Farnham, the man who rented the car in *Listening* 1, calling the car rental office and that they should listen for what the problem is with the car and how he feels about the solution. Play the recording and then put students in pairs to compare answers before checking in open class.

Answers

1 he was driving and something flew up and cracked the windscreen

2 he's not very happy, it will take at least four hours before someone can come to fix it

Optional activity To make a link to *Listening*, you could ask students = *Did he do the right thing here by buying insurance?* (Yes.) *Do you think he was better to be safe than sorry?* (Yes.)

11.2
A = Assistant, C = Customer

C: Hello. Right Car Rentals.

A: Oh hello. I wonder if you can help me. My name's John Farnham. I was in this morning and picked up a car from you.

C: Oh hello, Mr. Farnham. How's it going?

A: Not that well, to be honest. I'm actually calling because we have a problem with the car. I was driving along the motorway and something flew up at the windscreen and cracked it.

C: Oh, I am sorry to hear that. How bad is it?

A: Quite bad. It's a very big crack. I'm uncomfortable driving with it like this.

C: OK. I totally understand. You'll need to ring our breakdown service. The number's written in the book that came with the car.

A: Oh, OK. I'll do that now. How long do you think they will be?

C: We guarantee they'll be with you within four hours.

A: Four hours? Is that really the best you can do?

C: Well, it's usually less. Still, at least you've got insurance!

DEVELOPING CONVERSATIONS

Expressing surprise or shock

Aim
To introduce and practise expressing shock.

Step 1 Get students to read the explanation box and check understanding. Drill the class with the strong stress.

Step 2 Tell students to write responses to each of the sentences in exercise A and that they should repeat the information that surprises them as a question and then add another comment or question. Monitor for stress and a higher voice. Then in pairs students compare answers before checking in open class.

Step 3 Tell students to practise reading the conversations with a partner and to take turns responding to the sentences in exercise A. Tell them their voice should be higher when they repeat the information. Tell them to try and continue the conversations for as long as they can. Monitor for stress. If necessary drill the stress again.

CONVERSATION PRACTICE

Aim
To give practice in using the language learnt so far.

Step 1 Tell students they are going to role-play a conversation between a car rental firm assistant and a customer. Put students into two groups = A and B. Tell group A to read File 19 on page 162 and group B to read File 3 on page 156. Give them time to prepare what they want to say and get them to help each other in their groups. Tell them to look at the audioscripts 11.1 and 11.2 on pp. 175–176 for useful language.

Step 2 When ready, put them in AB pairs to role-play the conversation. Monitor and help out as necessary.

Step 3 When students are ready, put them in new AB pairs and tell them they should role-play a telephone conversation about a problem with a rental car. Tell them to read the instructions in exercise C and to look through the audioscript 11.2 on pp. 175–176 for ideas. Tell them to make notes on what they want to say and when they are ready they act out the role-play. Monitor and take notes on their use of language for a correction slot.

 pp. 78–79

 Next class Make photocopies of **11A** p. 148.

READING

Aim
To develop reading for general and detailed information.

Step 1 Tell students they are going to read about three journeys. Get them to look at the photographs and identify each journey. Ask students what they know about each journey.

Note The 6,000-kilometre journey from Moscow to Beijing is known as the Trans-Siberian express, it starts in Moscow and finishes in Beijing and you can get off and explore for a couple of days and then get another train to continue your journey.

The 4,500-kilometre drive across the United States is known as Route 66, also called the Main street of America, it goes from Chicago to Los Angeles, it was built in 1925 and was officially removed in 1985 as the government changed the naming of the road system. It is still referred to as Route 66 by fans though.

The 800-kilometre walk from the south of France to Spain is known as the Camino de Santiago (St James' way). People usually start in the French Pyrenees and end in the Spanish city of Santiago de Compostela. They either walk, cycle or go on horses or donkeys.

Step 2 Tell students to read the questions in exercise A and discuss in pairs. Conduct brief feedback in open class.

Step 3 Tell students to read the questions in exercise B individually and read the texts to answer them, tell them that they will look at the words in bold later and not to worry about them now. Then they compare in pairs before checking in open class.

Step 4 Tell students to complete the sentences without reading the stories and check understanding of *bankrupt* = officially say you have no money and cannot pay your debts, *desolate* = completely empty with no people or pleasant scenery, *set off* = start a journey, *disrepair* = in a broken or damaged state. In pairs they compare and then check their answers against the expression in bold in the blogs. Check as a class.

Answers		
1 redundancy	4 untouched	7 word
2 put	5 heart	8 fallen
3 scenery	6 claustrophobic	9 faith

Step 5 Tell students to read the questions exercise E and to discuss them in pairs. Conduct brief feedback.

GRAMMAR Uncountable nouns

Aim
To present and practise uncountable nouns.

Step 1 Tell students to read the explanation box and to choose the correct form of the sentences from the three journeys. They can look back at the texts and check if they need to. In pairs they compare answers before checking in open class. Check understanding: *Which word is used with uncountable nouns much or many?* (much), *What other quantifiers are used?* (some, all) *What other quantifiers do you know?* (any, little, plenty, a good deal, etc), *Do uncountable nouns have a plural form?* (no).

Answers		
1 much research	2 information	3 equipment

Direct students to the grammar reference on page 150 if they still seem unsure.

Step 2 Get students to complete the sentences with one word in each space. Do the first one with them. Students compare answers in pairs before checking in open class.

Answers			
1 some	3 little	5 any	7 plenty
2 any	4 any	6 much	8 deal

Step 3 Get students to read the questions in exercise D and give them time to think about their answers. Monitor and help out with any language problems, especially with nouns and quantifiers. When they are ready put them in pairs to discuss the questions. Conduct brief feedback.

 11A see Teacher's notes p. 125.

 pp. 80–81

 Next class Make photocopies of **11B** p. 149.

VOCABULARY Driving

Aim
To present and practise expressions related to driving.

Step 1 Ask students if they can drive and if they can remember some of the problems they had when they first started driving, e.g. learning how to use all the controls and pedals. Get them to read the words in exercise A and check understanding and word stress: *flash* = shine a light for a short time, *swerve* = change direction suddenly when you are driving, *slam* = hit or push with a lot of force, *handbrake* = used to stop the car moving when it is parked, *lane* = parts of the road that are divided for cars to drive in, *indicate* = put a light on to show which direction your are going to move in, *points on your licence* = penalty points for breaking the law, e.g. speeding.

Step 2 Tell students to match the verbs 1–10 with the words they collocate with a–j. In pairs students compare their answers before checking in open class.

Answers	
1 c	6 j
2 d	7 h
3 e (c could also be possible here)	8 i
4 a	9 f
5 b	10 g

Step 3 Tell students to discuss why and / or where they would do the actions in exercise A. Check in pairs then check as a class.

Suggested answers
1 You might drive in the middle lane on the motorway because you want to overtake another vehicle
2 you want to tell another driver they have their lights on in the daytime
3 the car in front is going too slow
4 you have parked the car on a hill
5 you are about to move turn right or left
6 You have had an accident
7 the car in front braked suddenly
8 you were caught speeding by the police
9 you are on the motorway
10 an animal runs onto the road

LISTENING

Aim
To develop listening skills for specific information.

Step 1 Tell students they are going to hear two friends, Lily from Britain and Saghar from Iran, talking about driving experiences, they should listen and answer the questions. Play the recording and then get students to compare in pairs before checking in open class. If necessary, play the recording again before checking.

Answers
1 She's just got a parking ticket and the other day was speeding
2 £80 for both offences and three points on her driving licence
3 It was terrifying, There were six lanes and everyone was swerving in and out of the lanes, she got cut up (another car drives into your lane suddenly) a couple of times and had to brake, but then she got beeped at (sound the horn on the car)
4 You take your life in your hands driving there, people go so fast, but really close behind you and they don't use their brakes they just flash their lights, people ignore stop signs, shoot through red lights.

Tip If you have any students from Iran or who have been to Iran, ask them if they think this is a true portrayal of Iranian drivers.

🔊 **11.3**
S = Saghar, L = Lily
S: Lily. What's up? You look really fed up!
L: I just got a parking ticket!
S: Oh no! That's so annoying! Where were you parked?
L: Just round the corner. The thing that's really infuriating, though, is that it happened while I'd gone to look for change for the machine.
S: You're joking!
L: No! I parked my car and then I suddenly realised I only had notes. There was no-one around, so I went off to a shop to get change and when I got back ...
S: That's terrible. Didn't you see the traffic warden?
L: I did look, but they'd vanished. They can't have been there long. I think they must've run away to avoid any arguments.
S: Probably! Couldn't you appeal?
L: It's not worth it. In the end, it's basically my word against theirs.
S: I know. You'd never win that one. How much is the fine?
L: Eighty pounds! AND I got a speeding ticket the other day after I got flashed by a speed camera! That was another eighty – and three points on my licence.
S: Oh Lily! Poor you! They're so strict on these things.
L: But it's so over-the-top. I mean, I was only doing three or four miles over the speed limit. What annoys me is the fact that people who are essentially honest are being criminalised for these little things.
S: I know! And it's not as though people drive that fast here. You should go to Iran. You take your life in your hands driving there. People, they go so fast, but really close behind you and they don't use their brakes. They just flash their lights!
L: Ooh! It's horrible when people do that. I don't know about Iran, but I have to say, I drove through Paris last year and that was terrifying. There were like six lanes and everyone was swerving in and out of the lanes. I got cut up a couple of times and I had to brake, but then I got beeped at!

S: You see! That kind of thing doesn't happen so often here. People really are more polite here. The thing that amazed me when I first came here was the fact that people actually stopped for pedestrians at crossings. That hardly ever happens back home! You have to be really careful not to get knocked over.
L: It can't be that bad, can it? Drivers here can be very inconsiderate and I've had plenty of people swearing at me in London.
S: Believe me! It's nothing compared to Tehran. Sometimes there you're not even safe on the pavement! People ignore stop signs, shoot through red lights. Honestly, it's anarchy!

Step 2 Tell students to read the statements in exercise B and decide if they are true or false. Play the recording again to check their answers. Then in pairs they compare before checking in open class.

Answers

1 F	3 T	5 T	7 F
2 F	4 F	6 T	8 F

Optional activity For extra practice, ask students to correct the false statements, then they compare in pairs before checking in open class.

Answers
1 Lily had gone to look for change
2 The traffic warden had vanished
4 She got flashed by a speed camera
7 Saghar was surprised that people actually stopped for pedestrians at crossings
8 Lily says that drivers here can be very inconsiderate. She's had plenty of people swearing at her in London.

Step 4 Ask students to read the questions in exercise C and to discuss them in pairs. Monitor and correct any errors as they come up. Conduct brief feedback.

LANGUAGE PATTERNS

Aim
To draw attention to useful patterns with *be careful*.

Step 1 Get students to look at the sentences. Students should have no problem understanding the meaning, but may well have problems producing sentences like these. It is better that they simply notice that there are patterns but do not try to reproduce their own examples. However, there are three grammar patterns here: 1 *to be (really / very) careful (not) to* + verb; 2 *to be careful* + an adjective clause (*where, when, what* and *why*); 3 *be careful* + *-ing*.

Step 2 Ask students to translate the sentences into their own language. In a monolingual class ask students to compare their translation. In a multilingual class ask students to work in pairs and tell each other if the sentences were easy to translate into their language.

Step 3 Ask students to cover their English translations and using their translation translate the sentences back into English. Then ask them to compare their translations in pairs against the book. Alternatively, if you prefer not to use translation you can draw students' attention to the patterns.

GRAMMAR Emphatic structures

Aim
To present and practice emphatic structures.

Step 1 Tell students to read the two pairs of sentences from the listening and check understanding by asking *Which sentence in each pair emphasises how you feel?* (1 b, 2 a) *How do we know?* (the emotive adjective comes near the beginning: 1 b = horrible, 2 a = infuriates) and *Which sentences have a shorter subject for the verb?* (1 a = people, 2 b = The fact that). Tell them in English we can put our emotion at the front of the sentence to let the speaker know how we feel and to emphasise the point. Ask them if they can construct both pairs of sentences the same way in their own language.

Step 2 Tell students to look at the explanation box and to notice the patterns. Tell students to read the audioscript on page 176 and find two more examples of these patterns (any two of the following).

Answers
1 The thing that's really infuriating, though, is that it happened while I'd gone to look for change for the machine.
2 What annoys me is the fact that people who are essentially honest are being criminalised for these little things.
3 The thing that amazed me when I first came here was the fact that people actually stopped for pedestrians at crossings.

Direct students to the grammar reference on page 150 if they still seem unsure.

Step 3 Tell students to complete the sentences in exercise C with their own ideas. In pairs they compare before sharing their ideas in open class.

Suggested answers
1 that we aren't doing enough about global warming
2 that we don't know our neighbours
3 the way he never listens to what I say
4 the way people really helped me when I couldn't understand
5 when you introduce someone and you can't remember their name
6 the number of tourists in the summer

Step 4 Write *Travelling* on the board and elicit what students love, can't stand, get annoyed or worry about, e.g. *love* = you meet new people, *can't stand* = waiting around in airports, *get annoyed about* = it's hard to find a good cup of coffee, *worry about* = have I forgotten to pack something. Then write *Public transport* on the board and elicit what they think about *cost* = it's really cheap, *reliability* = the buses are quite frequent, *cleanliness* = it's worse at the weekend, *efficiency* = it's good value for money. Then tell students to take notes on their ideas about travelling and to think about cars, planes trains, etc. and the public transport in their city. They should also think about cost, reliability, cleanliness, etc. Monitor and help out with any language problems, especially with using emphatic structures and ideas.

Step 5 In groups students discuss. Monitor and take notes on their use of language they use for a correction slot at the end.

Optional activity If time, ask a student from each group to tell the rest of the class one thing they all agreed on and one thing they disagreed on, ask the other students what they think.

 11A see Teacher's notes p. 125.

SPEAKING

Aim
To provide fluency practice in expressing opinions about driving.

Step 1 Tell students to read the questionnaire and to check the *Vocabulary builder* for any words they are not sure of. They should answer the questionnaire for themselves – if they don't drive, they should answer for someone they know who drives.

Step 2 In pairs students discuss the questions and decide how good a driver their partner sounds. Conduct brief feedback on who is the best driver in each pair.

Step 3 Tell students to think of the best / worst driver they've ever driven with and why. Monitor and take notes on their use of language. Finish with a correction slot.

12 HEALTH AND MEDICINE

UNIT OVERVIEW

The main aim of this unit is to enable students to **talk about health problems in more detail and issues connected to health systems** and **pass on sympathetic messages**. They have practice in **telling jokes**. The main grammatical focus is *supposed to be, should, shouldn't* and **determiners** and ways of **expressing health problems** and **parts of the body and illnesses**.

 Next class Make photocopies of **12A** p. 150.

SPEAKING

Aim
To lead in to the topic of health problems.

Step 1 Ask students to look at the pictures of the hospital waiting room and name the problems the people have.

> **Suggested answers**
> 1 a pregnant woman
> 2 a drunk man with a big bump on his head
> 3 a woman who's been in a car accident, she's on crutches and has a black eye, scratches and bruises on her arm and a broken leg
> 4 an old man in a wheelchair with an oxygen mask
> 5 young, muscled-up guy holding his lower back in pain – probably a slipped disc
> 6 a man holding his stomach and looking very ill
> 7 a mother with a daughter who's having some allergic reaction – her face is swollen
> 8 a middle-aged woman with terrible flu

Step 2 Tell students to make a list of the order they'd treat the patients if they were a doctor. Put students into groups to discuss their lists. Conduct brief feedback.

VOCABULARY
Health problems

Aim
To practise expressions related to health problems.

Step 1 In pairs ask students to match the groups of words in 1–9 with the health problems in the vocabulary box and to make sure they can explain the connection between them. Conduct feedback and check word stress.

> **Suggested answers**
> 1 *eczema* = it's very itchy and makes you want to scratch it. The doctor can give you steroid cream. It's believed to be caused by stress and can start in childhood
> 2 *an allergy* = some people are allergic to nuts and their skin can swell up or they get a rash, other people sneeze a lot or have to throw up
> 3 *the flu* = it's usually an infection when you get a fever and a sore throat, your muscles are stiff and some people get an earache
> 4 *stress* = affects people in different ways, some get insomnia, or high blood pressure, others have dizzy spells and sometimes faint
> 5 *an accident* = you can have scratches, bumps and bruises and if you cut yourself you might need stitches or bandages to stop the infection
> 6 *a broken leg* = you might have an operation and have pins put in to keep the bone together. The pin is then removed; your leg could be in plaster and you'll need crutches to help you walk
> 7 *a cold* = you have a runny nose, sore throat and a cough, some people believe the best remedy is herbal
> 8 *asthma* = you often are short of breath and have a tight chest, especially when in contact with smoke and fumes, you need to carry an inhaler with you all the time
> 9 *upset stomach* = usually caused by a bug and you have to throw up and have diarrhoea and feel rough (a very informal way to say you don't feel well)

Step 2 Tell students that they are going to test each other in pairs or threes. One student should act or draw the words from 1–9 in exercise A and their partner(s) should say the health problem. You might like to give them a time limit of three minutes. Conduct brief feedback.

Listening

Aim
To develop listening for specific information.

Step 1 Tell students they are going to hear two telephone conversations and to answer the questions in A. Play the recording and get students to compare answers in pairs before checking in open class.

> **Answers**
> Conversation 1 = 1 They won't be coming later, 2 Kaatje fainted, she suddenly had a dizzy spell and passed out
> Conversation 2 = 1 They won't be going to the concert tonight, 2 Caitlin said Lachlan was feeling funny, he was a bit short of breath and then she noticed a rash, there were spots breaking out all round his mouth, his lips just started swelling up and he was really struggling to breathe.

🔊 **12.1**
Conversation 1
M = Michelle, J = Joop

M: Hello.

J: Oh, hi Michelle. It's me, Joop. Listen I'm just ringing to say we're not coming later. Kaatje isn't feeling very well.

M: Oh dear. What's up?

J: She actually fainted this morning while we were out.

M: You're joking!

J: No. We were in a shop and she suddenly had a dizzy spell and then she just passed out.

M: Oh no! Is she all right, now?

J: Yeah, she recovered quite quickly, but still she says sorry she'd rather stay here.

M: Don't be silly! Tell her there's no need to apologise and I understand.

J: Thanks. I will.

M: It's not this bug that's going round, is it? One of my colleagues had it recently and said it left him quite faint and stiff and achy.

J: I don't think so. She hasn't had a fever or cough. In fact, she's been complaining about dizzy spells for a while and she's lost weight. She has been under a lot of pressure at work recently as well.

M: That is a bit worrying. Has she been to see anyone?

J: No, not yet and we're supposed to be going away for a few days. I don't know whether we should stay here and get an appointment or leave it till we come back.

M: Well, maybe all she needs is a break.

J: Mmm. Maybe.

M: I know you're worried, but if it's only a few days ... Why don't you see how she is when you get back?

J: I guess.

M: Anyway, send her my love and tell her I'm thinking of her.

Conversation 2
C = Caitlin, N = Nina

N: Hello.

C: Hello. Nina? Hi. It's me, Caitlin.

N: Hi! Where are you? I was expecting you at six.

C: Yeah, sorry, but Lachlan's had some kind of reaction to something he ate. We're in Rome hospital.

N: You're joking! Is he all right?

C: Yes, yes. He's fine now. He's with the nurse and they're running some tests.

N: No! What happened?

C: Well, we were in the middle of lunch and he suddenly said he was feeling funny – that he was a bit short of breath – and then I noticed a rash. There were spots breaking out all round his mouth. Then his lips just started swelling up and he was really struggling to breathe.

N: That sounds terrifying. He IS all right now, though?

C: Yes, yes, honestly. We rushed him to the hospital – someone from the restaurant actually took us – and they dealt with him very quickly. He had an injection to reduce the swelling and oxygen to help him breathe.

N: Oh Caitlin. You sound so calm. It must've been awful.

C: Well, I wasn't at the time, but everyone's been so good to us. Anyway, listen, they're going to keep him in overnight – to be on the safe side.

N: Oh, right.

C: Sorry. I know we're supposed to be going to the concert tonight.

N: Don't be silly! Lachlan's health is much more important than a concert. When do you think you'll get here tomorrow?

C: It shouldn't be too late. The doctor's going to come at 9, so if he gives the all clear, we should be at yours by lunchtime.

N: OK. Well, listen. Give him a hug from me and don't worry about rushing to get here tomorrow.

Step 2 Tell students to listen again and decide if statements 1–8 in exercise B are true or false. Play the recording. Students compare answers in pairs before checking as a class.

> **Answers**
> | 1 F | 2 T | 3 F | 4 T | 5 T | 6 F | 7 F | 8 F |
> | --- | --- | --- | --- | --- | --- | --- | --- |

Speaking

Aim
To provide fluency practice.

Step 1 Tell students to read the questions in exercise A. Give them time to prepare. They discuss the questions. Conduct brief feedback.

DEVELOPING CONVERSATIONS

Passing on messages

Aim

To introduce and practise passing on messages.

Step 1 Tell students to read the explanation box and notice the pattern = use of imperatives + pronoun, e.g. *Tell her..., Send her...*.

Step 2 Tell students to put the sentences in exercise A in the correct order to make messages. Students compare answers in pairs before checking in open class.

> **Answers**
> 1 Give them my best regards.
> 2 Give her a big hug from me.
> 3 Give them my apologies for not coming.
> 4 Tell them I'm thinking of them and say hi.
> 5 Tell her not to worry and send her my love.
> 6 Tell him to take it easy and get better soon.
> 7 Tell him there's no need to apologise and to look after himself.
> 8 Give them my congratulations and tell them I can't wait to see the baby.

Step 3 Ask students if there are any messages in exercise A that they would feel uncomfortable saying, maybe because of the use of emotive language, e.g. *give her my love*. Ask them if they say the same thing in their language.

Step 4 Tell students they are going to take turns passing on different messages and to look at the examples in exercise C and exercise A for ideas. In pairs they drill each other. Tell them it's not a natural conversation, just pronunciation practice.

GRAMMAR *Supposed to be -ing* and *should*

Aim

To present and practise *supposed to be -ing* and *should* for future arrangements that have now changed.

Step 1 Tell students to read the explanation box and check understanding of *supposed to*: *Had they planned to go away?* (Yes.) *Has something happened to change their plans?* (Yes.) *How do we know their plans have changed?* (Use of *supposed to*.) Check understanding of *shouldn't / should*: *How does the person feel in both sentences?* (Positive.)

Step 2 Get students to complete the sentences with *should, shouldn't* or *be supposed to be -ing* and the verb in brackets. Students compare answers in pairs before checking as a class. Direct students to the grammar reference on page 151 if they still seem unsure.

> **Answers**
> 1 should be
> 2 'm supposed to be meeting
> 3 shouldn't hurt
> 4 's supposed to be having
> 5 shouldn't take
> 6 'm supposed to be going, should be

CONVERSATION PRACTICE

Aim

To provide conversation practice about health problems.

Step 1 Tell students they are going to role-play similar conversations to the ones in *Listening*. They should spend two minutes thinking about what they might say or ask.

Step 2 When students are ready, put students in AB pairs to role-play the conversation following the pattern shown. Then they change roles. Monitor their use of language for a correction slot at the end.

> **12A** see Teacher's notes p. 125.

> **pp. 84–85**

VOCABULARY Parts of the body and illnesses

Aim

To practise expressions related to the body and illnesses.

Step 1 Tell students to look at the picture and label it with the words from the vocabulary box. Check understanding by asking if they have any questions. Check in pairs.

Step 2 Tell students to look at the diseases and conditions in B and check they understand them (see answer box). Put them in groups to discuss before checking as a class.

> **Answers**
> AIDS = 1 affects the immune system, 2 transmission of body fluids
> Diabetes = 1 the blood system, 2 lack of sugar in the blood
> A stroke = 1 developing loss of the brain system, 2 a lack of blood supply
> Athlete's foot = 1 fungal infection of the skin usually the foot, 2 can be picked up by walking barefoot in public showers
> Alzheimer's = 1 the brain, 2 can be age related or caused by stress
> Parkinson's = 1 the nervous system, 2 insufficient formation and action of dopamine (a chemical in the brain)
> Tuberculosis = 1 lungs or central nervous system, 2 contagious and spread through the air when people who have it cough, sneeze or spit
> Arthritis = 1 damage to the joints, 2 trauma or infection of the joint or age

Hepatitis = 1 liver, 2 caused by a virus and can be caught in many different ways
3 / 4 = many possible: suggestions – 4 swine flu, cancer, B12 deficiency, Crohn's disease, IBS.

READING

Aim
To develop reading for general and detailed information.

Step 1 Tell students they are going to read a news article about health and humour and to discuss in pairs what effect laughter or a sense of humour might have on health.

Step 2 Tell students to read the article and answer the questions individually. Then they compare in pairs before checking in open class.

Step 3 Tell students to look at the aspects in exercise C and ask if they find any of them funny. Why? In groups they discuss their opinions. Conduct brief feedback in open class.

Note If students are struggling with the jokes, you might like to explain to them why they are funny: 1 = with each wish his rival gets double, so by donating his kidney, his rival will donate both and die, 2 = play on the pronunciation of *choking* and *joking*, 3 = her eyesight isn't bad – just her taste in wigs, 4 = if he sleeps in another room he won't keep himself awake, but obviously he can't be in two places, 5 = it gives the idea the nose is not attached to his body and is literally running around, 6 = after having therapy he still has the condition, but the therapist helped him get over his shame, 7 = he now doesn't have one day to live as the results came in yesterday.

Step 4 Tell students to read the jokes and give them a rating of 1–5 on how funny they found them (1 = very funny, 5 = not very funny) and put a question mark by any they don't understand. Then put students into groups to compare their ratings. Do they agree? Can anyone explain to them the jokes they didn't get? Conduct brief feedback.

Step 5 Tell students to complete sentences 1–10 in exercise F with the correct form of the words in bold. In pairs they compare before checking in open class.

Answers	
1 undergoing	6 tripped
2 came back	7 granted
3 terminal	8 snoring
4 outrage	9 get hold of
5 get rid of	10 donated

PRONUNCIATION
Sound chunking and stress

Aim
To practise sound chunking (groups of words) and stress.

Step 1 Tell students to read the explanation box and tell them that when we read out a lot of text we chunk words together according to meaning. Tell them we do this to keep the listener's attention.

Step 2 Tell students to read the joke and say it to themselves following the stress and pauses that are marked. Ask them to guess how the joke might end. Give them some time to think of a suitable ending and when ready to tell a partner and decide whose ending is better.

Step 3 Play the recording to listen for the actual ending. Ask then if they think their endings were better.

> 🔊 **12.2**
> A <u>man</u> goes to a <u>doctor</u> // and <u>says</u> // "Doc. // I <u>think</u> there's something <u>wrong</u> with me // <u>Every</u> time I <u>poke</u> myself // it <u>hurts</u>. // <u>Look!</u>" // And he starts poking himself. // He <u>pokes</u> himself in the <u>leg</u>. // "<u>Ouch</u>" // He <u>pokes</u> himself in the <u>ribs</u> // "<u>Aagh</u>" // He <u>pokes</u> himself in the <u>head</u> // and he literally // <u>screams</u> in agony // "<u>Aaaaagh!</u> // You <u>see</u> what I <u>mean</u> Doc?// You <u>see</u> how <u>bad</u> it is? // What's <u>happening</u> to me?"// And the <u>doctor</u> replies // "<u>Yes</u>, you seem to have broken your finger!"

SPEAKING

Aim
To provide fluency practice in telling jokes with the correct sound chunking and stress.

Step 1 Tell students they are going to tell a joke. Put students into three groups = A, B and C . Tell group A to look at File 10 on page 158, group B to look at File 5 on page 157 and group C to look at File 14 on page 159. Tell them to read the jokes and choose their favourite. Alternatively, they can find a joke they like on the Internet.

Step 2 Then tell them to spend five minutes working on their favourite joke. They should mark the words that are grouped together and the words that are stressed. Tell them to practise saying the joke to themselves in a whisper and to think of any actions they could use to emphasise what happens in the joke.

Step 3 Put students in ABC groups and tell them to take turns telling their jokes. Conduct brief feedback.

NATIVE SPEAKER ENGLISH *Chuck*

Ask students to read the box. Ask them to think of other things they could *chuck*, e.g. old clothes, a ball to someone.

 pp. 86–87

 Next class Make photocopies of **12B** p. 151.

GRAMMAR Determiners

Aim
To present and practise determiners.

Step 1 Write the following headings on the board and tell students to copy them into their notebooks: *singular nouns, plural nouns, plural countable nouns, plural uncountable nouns and all nouns*. Dictate the following determiners (word used before a noun to show which thing or things you are talking about): *a, these, each, those, both, all, my, another, few, this, some, no*, and tell students to put them in the correct category. In pairs they compare their answers before checking in open class. Tell students to read the explanation box and tell them to notice when we use *of* (when we have another determiner) and with pronouns, e.g. each of *my* (determiner) sisters, both of *them* (pronoun).

Answers
Singular nouns = *a, each, another, this*
plural nouns = *these, those, few*
plural countable nouns = *both*
plural uncountable nouns = *all, some*
all nouns = *my, no.*

Step 2 Get students to complete the quotes in exercise A with the words in the box. Check answers.

Answers

1 no	3 all	5 much
2 many	4 more	6 any, a little

Step 3 In pairs students discuss which quote they like best and why. Direct students to the grammar reference on page 151 if they still seem unsure.

Step 4 Tell students to read the statements in exercise C and choose the correct words in italics.

Answers

1 both	5 all, any	9 many
2 a few	6 no	10 other
3 many, other	7 less and less, the whole	
4 most	8 every	

Step 5 Tell students to tick (√) the sentences in exercise C that they think are true for their country and decide why the sentences they didn't tick aren't true. Ask them to compare their ideas in groups. Conduct brief feedback.

   12B see Teacher's notes p. 125.

LISTENING

Aim
To develop listening for general and specific information.

Step 1 Tell students to read the Fact File in exercise A and in pairs discuss the questions. Conduct brief feedback.

Step 2 Tell students they are going to listen to the introduction of the radio programme and to complete the notes in exercise B. Play the recording. Students compare in pairs before checking in open class.

Answers
1 medical staff moving from country to country
2 the reading of X-rays
3 6 million
4 100,000
5 Malaysia,
6 India
7 over $4 billion.

⏺ 12.3
P = Presenter, DF = Damien Frisch,
CL = Cindy Leong, CS = Charlotte Staples
P: The incredible boom in medical tourism over the last few years has been one of the more interesting side effects of globalisation. For quite some time already, we've been used to the idea of medical staff moving from country to country, while more recently many hospitals have also started outsourcing record-keeping and the reading of X-rays to developing countries in an attempt to cut costs. However, what's remarkably new is the ever-increasing numbers of patients from developed western countries who are opting to go abroad for treatment.

It's estimated that before too long over 6 million Americans and over 100,000 Britons will be travelling overseas for private medical or dental work - all done at knockdown prices. Countries such as Mexico, Jordan, Malaysia, India and Thailand all stand to benefit from a trade expected to be soon generate over $4 billion a year.

This question arises, however, as to whether this is a genuine win-win situation.

Step 3 Tell students to think of three good things and three bad things about medical tourism. They can look at the Fact File for ideas, if necessary. In groups they discuss their ideas.

Step 4 Tell them they are going to listen to the rest of the programme where three people, Damian, Cindy and Charlotte, give their opinions. They should take notes on any good / bad things about medical tourism they mention. Play the recording and then get students to compare in pairs before checking in open class.

Answers
Good = excellent dental work in Poland, Malaysia boasts some of the best doctors in the world and has a wide array = range of ultra-modern hospitals, Malaysia also offers all-inclusive packages for visitors, a portion of the profit go towards providing a basic level of healthcare for the poor, it can save money.

Bad = you are taking a risk, gambling with your health and your money, fraudulent claims and dishonest money-making schemes are commonplace and are on the increase, the regulatory environment in many places is not as rigorous as it should be, many treatments are still experimental, no after-care as patients return home.

🔊 12.3

Damian Frisch is a German lawyer specialising in medical negligence cases:

DF: 'I don't want to be accused of causing panic. I myself have had dental work done in Poland and it was excellent. However, anyone thinking of going abroad for treatment needs to know they are taking a risk. You have to be very careful and do extensive research before making a decision. Otherwise, you are gambling with your health as well as your money. Fraudulent claims and dishonest money-making schemes are commonplace and are on the increase – and the regulatory environment in many places is not as rigorous as it should be. In addition to this, many treatments are still experimental and all too often there is no after-care as patients return to their home countries. My advice would be it's better to be safe than sorry – and if something sounds too good to be true, then it probably is.'

CL: Cindy Leong, the CEO of a hospital in Kuala Lumpur that's particularly popular with foreigners, acknowledges that there are some opportunistic practitioners, but that this should not detract from the reality of the change that is happening. "The old stereotypes of Asia as some kind of impoverished Third World are now very outdated. We boast some of the best doctors in the world and have a wide array of ultra-modern hospitals. On top of that, a few of the operations we offer now are so hi-tech that they are actually only found in Malaysia!'

In addition, we offer all-inclusive packages for visitors: we can arrange visas and flights, offer a range of special menus, look after patients' companions, even book holiday resorts for post-surgery recuperation – and all at very reasonable prices. At the same time, of course, 90% of our patients are still local – and they all benefit from our innovations. Furthermore, we ensure that a portion of our profits go towards providing at least a basic level of health care for the poor, so everyone stands to benefit.'

P: Certainly, that's how **Charlotte Staples**, a bank clerk from Rotherham, England, feels:

CS: 'I had a hip replacement operation in Jordan last year and I can't speak highly enough of the place. I'd been on the waiting list in England for almost a year and I reached the point where I was becoming a very impatient patient! If I'd gone private here, it would've cost me something in the region of £10,000. As it was, I got my flight, a ten-day stay in hospital, a pioneering new surgical technique *and* a two-week holiday

afterwards for just over £5,000. Sun, sand surgery *and* savings!'

Step 5 Tell students to read the statements a–f in exercise E and decide if they apply to Damian, Cindy or Charlotte – they can choose more than one person. Play the recording. Students compare in pairs before checking in open class.

Answers	
a Damian and Charlotte	d Damian and Cindy
b Cindy	e Charlotte
c Damian	f Cindy and Charlotte

Step 6 Tell students to read the questions in exercise F and to think about their answers. Conduct brief feedback.

LANGUAGE PATTERNS

Aim
To draw students' attention to some common patterns using *anyone* in general open questions and statements.

Step 1 Tell students that we can use *Anyone ...* in English when we want to ask a general open question to a group of people or make a statement about a group of people.

Step 2 Ask students to translate the sentences into their own language. In a monolingual class, ask students to compare their translation. In a multilingual classes, ask students to work in pairs and tell each other if *anyone* in all the sentences can be replaced with one word direct translation.

Step 3 Ask students to cover their English translations and using their translation translate the sentences back into English. Then ask them to compare their translations in pairs against the book. Alternatively, if you prefer not to use translation ask students to notice the patterns.

SPEAKING

Aim
To provide fluency practice.

Step 1 Tell students they are going to conduct a class survey about health and to read the survey sheet in exercise A and to add four extra things they would like to find out about, e.g. 1 *Why do you hate having injections?*

Step 2 Tell students to ask their questions to as many students as they can and to take notes on the answers.

Step 3 Tell students to write a short report detailing the findings of their survey. In pairs they compare their findings. Conduct brief feedback and finish with a correction slot.

LEARNER TRAINING

Aim
To raise students' awareness about the importance of learning vocabulary or grammar.

Step 1 Tell students to individually think about whether they believe vocabulary or grammar is more important to study, or are they both equally important? Give them a couple of minutes to think about their opinions. Monitor and help out with any ideas.

Step 2 Put students into groups to discuss their opinions and tell them to explain their ideas. You might like to do a brief class discussion, then, still in their groups, ask students to read the statistics about grammar and to discuss the questions in exercise B.

Step 3 Conduct feedback by eliciting students' ideas and writing them on the board.

GAME, CONVERSATION PRACTICE, ACT OR DRAW & QUIZ

For aims and suggested procedure, see Review 01, pp. 32–35.

Answers
1 When a company **restructures**, it changes the management and the way the organisation is run.
2 Cleaning the streets and filling shelves in a supermarket are two types of **menial** jobs, usually they are not **stimulating**.
3 General and captain are two different **ranks** in the army.
4 Someone might **suck up** to the boss because they want to be favoured or get a promotion.
5 If something is an **outrage**, you feel angry and upset.
6 A living room, a bedroom can be **cosy**, it's nice because it's comfortable and welcoming.
7 A politician might **resign** because they accepted a bribe, the opposition is increasing their power, they are getting old, etc.
8 If a room is very **stuffy**, you can open the windows or door to let some air in.
9 **Chat** is a friendly conversation; **chat up** is when you are attracted to someone and you talk to them.
10 If a party **gets out of hand**, people might be very drunk and noisy, there might be a problem and people start arguing.

11 Oil, petrol, diesel can all be used as **fuel**.
12 You need to **indicate** when you want to turn right or left.
13 You **embark** from a port, station or airport.
14 You usually get **blisters** on your feet because your shoes are new or too tight.
15 You can rest in bed, go on a relaxing holiday, go to a spa, etc. to **recuperate**.

COLLOCATIONS

For aims and suggested procedure, see Review 01, pp. 32–35.

PRONUNCIATION
Word stress

Aim
To revise and practise word stress.

Step 1 Get students to read the explanation box. Then tell them in pairs to decide where they think the main stress is in each of the compound nouns.

Step 2 Play the recording and get students to check their answers. The play the recording again and get them to repeat the words with the correct stress.

> 🔊 **R3.1 and Answers**
> Au-to-<u>ma</u>-tic (4 syllables)
> claus-tro-<u>pho</u>-bic (4 syllables)
> con-<u>tag</u>-ious (3 syllables)
> <u>de</u>-so-late (3 syllables)
> <u>fraud</u>-u-lent (3 syllables)
> <u>glo</u>-ba-lised (3 syllables)
> in-<u>fur</u>-i-a-ting (5 syllables)
> <u>ir</u>-ri-tab-le (4 syllables)
> <u>me</u>-ni-al (3 syllables)
> pi-o-<u>neer</u>-ing (4 syllables)
> re-<u>mark</u>-ab-le (4 syllables)
> <u>ri</u>-go-rous (3 syllables)
> <u>sp</u>-ir-it-ual (4 syllables)
> <u>stim</u>-u-lat-ing (4 syllables)
> <u>ter</u>-mi-nal (3 syllables)
> un-der-<u>val</u>-ued (4 syllables)
> un-pat-ri-<u>o</u>-tic (5 syllables)
> <u>ver</u>-sa-tile (3 syllables)

Step 3 Put students into pairs and tell them to think of one thing each of the adjectives can describe.

Suggested answers
automatic car / response   claustrophobic
room   contagious disease   desolate place /
landscape   fraudulent person   globalised economy /
market   infuriating person   irritable person
menial job   pioneering technology / event
remarkable person / place   rigorous training
spiritual place / person   stimulating idea   terminal
illness   undervalued person/ asset / job
unpatriotic person / behaviour   versatile food / actor

Step 3 Give students a moment to memorise the adjectives, then put two pairs together: Group A and Group B. Tell As to close their books and tell Bs to test them by explaining each adjective, without saying the actual word. As should try to remember the correct adjective. Then they swap.

DICTATION

For aims and suggested procedure, see Review 01, pp. 32–35.

♻ R3.2
Do extensive research before making a decision. Otherwise, you are gambling with your health as well as your money. Fraudulent claims and dishonest money-making schemes are commonplace and are on the increase – and the regulatory environment in many places is not as rigorous as it should be.

 pp. 90–91

LISTENING

Aim
For aims and suggested procedure for the rest of the Review, see Review 01 pp. 32—35. The audio is ♻ R3.2.

Exercise A answers
1 c	2 d	3 f	4 e	5 b

Exercise B answers
1 d	2 b	3 f	4 c	5 a

GRAMMAR

Exercise A answers
1 supposed	4 been	7 no	10 have
2 much	5 What	8 hasn't	11 some
3 hadn't	6 is	9 could	12 should

Exercise B answers
1 shouldn't be home
2 I'm supposed to be going out
3 annoys me is / annoys me about her is
4 'nt have crashed if he hadn't have been driving
5 been offered a job, I wouldn't be

LANGUAGE PATTERNS

Answers
1 see myself staying
2 not to spill
3 when crossing the road
4 see yourself doing
5 correct
6 bad, but this was even worse!
7 correct
8 Anyone planning on

PREPOSITIONS

Answers
1 against	3 of	5 by	7 in	9 on
2 on	4 in	6 against	8 to	

COLLOCATIONS

Answers
1 effect	3 fortune	5 spell	7 remark	9 breath
2 organ	4 surgery	6 brakes	8 faith	10 chest

FORMING WORDS

Answers
1 retirement	6 untouched
2 qualifications	7 engagement
3 insurance	8 disrepair
4 misunderstood	9 redundancy
5 implementation	10 summarise

PHRASAL VERBS

Answers
1 freshen up	4 turned up	7 frowned on
2 work out	5 take out	8 break out
3 live up to	6 passed out	

VOCABULARY

Answers
1 rewarding	4 stretching	7 overheats
2 draining	5 raise	8 windscreen
3 promoted	6 scratches	

13 LIFE EVENTS

UNIT OVERVIEW
The main aim of this unit is to enable students to **describe major life events in more detail, discuss gossip and news about people** and **complain about annoying habits**. They have practice in **reporting facts they are not 100% sure of**. The main grammatical focus is **the past perfect simple / continuous** and *be always -ing*, *wish* and *would* and ways of **expressing life events like birth, marriage and death**.

Next class Make photocopies of **13A** p. 152.

VOCABULARY
Life events

Aim
To introduce expressions related to life events.

Step 1 Ask students to look at the situations in exercise A and to think of an example for each of them. Check understanding: *pass away* = a polite way to say *die*. Give them some time to think about the associations. In pairs tell each other what they know about each story and if they have anything in common. Conduct brief feedback.

Alternatively If you are short on time you could get students to just talk about four or six of the items.

Step 2 Tell students to match the sentences in exercise B to the events in exercise A and that three of the sentences have no matching event. Check understanding: *fed up with* = not very happy with something or someone, *rough patch* = a difficult period, *fancied* = liked a person a lot, *a run* = a period of time when things go well or badly for you. In pairs they compare answers before checking in open class.

Answers
1 someone being sent to jail
2 someone dropping out of university
3 someone giving birth
4 someone being sacked
5 someone passing away
6 someone changing careers
7 a couple splitting up
8 a couple getting together
9 someone being kicked out of somewhere

Step 3 Tell students to complete the collocations with nouns from exercise B. In pairs they compare their answers before checking in open class. In a multilingual class, ask students to translate the collocations in their

own language and then without looking at the originals, translate back into English. In a monolingual class, get students in pairs or threes to compare their translations and their English translations. What similarities do they notice? Alternatively, if you prefer not to use translation ask students to practise writing their own sentences using the collocations.

Answers
a a bribe
b a job
c labour
d continued to
e counsellor
f patch
g a day call it a day = *say something is over*
h her
i run
j cup

Step 5 In new pairs students compare their original examples from exercise A and explain what led up to each event and what followed, they should try to use some of the language from exercises B and C. Conduct brief feedback.

GRAMMAR
Past perfect simple and continuous

Aim
To practise past perfect simple and continuous.

Step 1 Tell students to read the explanation box and check understanding of the sentences: Did he drop out of university? (Yes.) Why did he drop out of university? (He'd been struggling.) Which action happened first? (He had been struggling.) Was this a single action or an event that happened over a period of time? (Over a period of time.) Tell them we use the past perfect continuous when we want to emphasis an ongoing event up to a point in the past. How do we form the past perfect continuous? (*had + been + verb-ing.* Then ask, *Why did he decide to drop out?* (He'd had enough.) *Which action happened first?* (He'd had enough.) Tell them we use the past perfect simple when we want to emphasise a single, completed event before another in the past. How do we form the past perfect simple? (*Had* + past participle.)

Step 2 Get students to look at *Vocabulary* exercise B and underline five examples of the past perfect simple and circle four examples of the past perfect continuous and to think about the way they are used. Students compare answers in pairs before checking in open class.

> **Answers**
> Past perfect simple = had insulted him, he'd then overreacted, they'd been through a rough patch, he'd fancied her, had been on a terrible run, they'd only won
> Past perfect continuous = he'd been taking bribes, he'd been struggling, she'd been having treatment, he'd been thinking

Direct students to the grammar reference on page 152 if they still seem unsure.

Step 3 Tell students to read the sentences in exercise B and to think of a response using the past perfect simple or continuous. Check in pairs then as a class.

> **Suggested answers**
> 1 His doctor had told him to do more exercise
> 2 She'd invested it badly and lost it all
> 3 They'd fallen in love with the place on their last holiday
> 4 I'd been helping out voluntarily at the zoo since I was at school
> 5 He'd been having trouble with his knee all season
> 6 We'd been thinking about moving to a bigger place for ages

> **13A** see Teacher's notes p. 126.

LISTENING

Aim
To develop listening for general and specific information.

Step 1 Tell students they are going to hear two conversations where the speakers gossip (talk about other people or things that are not important) and for each conversation to answer the questions in A. Play the recording. In pairs students compare answers and if necessary play the recording again before checking answers in open class.

> **Answers**
> Conversation 1 = 1 The girl was just flicking through an interview about Taylor Fox, 2 That's she's married to Scott Blake and that he isn't as nice as he seems.
> Conversation 2 = 1 The girl starts the conversation talking about Ollie in general, 2 That Ollie has left his job, He has a new girlfriend and is moving to Finland,

🔊 **13.1**
Conversation 1
A: Are you reading that interview with Taylor Fox?
B: No, not really. I was just flicking through. Why?
A: Oh, I just thought it was interesting. Did you know she's got two adopted kids from Malawi?
B: I did, actually. From what I heard, she couldn't have kids of her own.
A: No. As I understand it, she'd already had a son with Scott Blake.
B: She's married to Scott Blake?
A: *Was*! They got divorced a while back. She's with Cody Lescott now.
B: Of course! I was going to say. So how come she split up with Scott Blake? He seems really nice.
A: That's the image, but it turns out he's a bit of a jerk. He'd been leading a bit of a double life – he was very popular with the ladies and she decided she just couldn't trust him! That's why they called it a day.
B: You're joking! He comes across as so clean-cut and pleasant.
A: Well, apparently not. It seems – how shall I put it – that he likes to spread the love a lot!
B: I see. Well, she's better off without him, then.
A: Absolutely. You should read the interview. She had quite an interesting upbringing. She just sounds very down-to-earth.
Conversation 2
C: Have you seen Ollie recently?
D: No, not for ages. Have you?
C: Yeah, I saw him last week. We went for a drink.
D: Right. How is he?
C: Oh, he's good. Really good, actually. You know he left his job at Byfix?
D: No! Really? I was told he was doing well there.
C: He was, he was. But he'd actually been thinking about leaving for a while – basically ever since he started going out with Leila.
C: Who's Leila?
D: When was the last time you saw him?
C: It must've been about a year ago. As far as I know, he wasn't seeing anyone then.
C: Hmm maybe. Well, anyway, she's Finnish. They met on holiday. She lives in Helsinki. They were commuting between here and there more or less every two weeks, but in the end, he decided to quit his job and move there.
D: You're joking!
C: No. Apparently, she's got a really good job there so they can both afford to live off her salary.
D: So he's just going to be a househusband, then!
C: Yeah, well, he said he'd sent CVs to a couple of companies, but if that came to nothing he was going to retrain as an English teacher.
D: Really? Well, that's a change for the better!

SPEAKING

Aim
To provide fluency practice.

Step 1 Tell students to read the questions in exercise A. Give them time to prepare their ideas.

Step 2 Put students into groups of four or five to discuss their ideas and say whether they agree or disagree with their partner's opinions. Monitor and finish with a correction slot.

DEVELOPING CONVERSATIONS
Showing uncertainty

Aim
To introduce and practise showing uncertainty.

Step 1 Tell students to read the explanation box. Check understanding: Does the speaker feel 100% sure she has a good job? (No), How do we know? (*Apparently*).

Step 2 Tell students to complete the phrases in the dialogues with one word in each space and that the first letter will help. Then in pairs students compare answers before checking in open class.

Answers		
1 far	3 from	5 told
2 As	4 apparently	6 according.

Step 3 Tell students they are going to have a conversation like the one in exercise A, about an imaginary man called Bill. They should invent 'facts' about where he has moved to, why, what it's like and who he is living with. Remind then to use the expressions from exercise A. Give them time to prepare their ideas. Help with any problems using the target language.

Step 4 In pairs students take it in turns to have the conversation and to begin using the prompts in exercise B. Monitor and correct where necessary. Conduct brief feedback.

CONVERSATION PRACTICE

Aim
To provide conversation practice.

Step 1 Tell students they are going to have similar conversations to the one they heard in *Listening*. Tell them to think about someone they know or a celebrity and some news they've heard or some new fact they discovered about them recently. Give them time to prepare.

Step 2 When students are ready put them in new pairs to take turns starting the conversation with, *Did you know / hear about X ...?* They should try to keep the conversation

going for three minutes by asking questions or adding extra bits of information. Monitor and take notes on their use of language for a correction slot at the end.

 pp. 94–95

 Next class Make photocopies of **13B** p. 153.

SPEAKING

Aim
To provide fluency practice in complaining about annoying habits.

Step 1 Tell students they are going to talk about arguing and annoying habits. Check understanding of *confrontation* = argue angrily. Get them to read the questions in exercise A and give them some time to think about what they want to say. Then put students into groups of four or five to discuss their ideas. Conduct brief feedback in open class.

GRAMMAR *Be always –ing / wish* and *would*

Aim
To present and practise *be always –ing / wish* and *would*.

Step 1 Tell students to read the explanation box and check understanding: How often does the person argue / compliment? (sentence 1 & 2 = very often) Tell them that we can use *always, forever* and *constantly* to emphasise someone's habits and we put it between the verb *be* and the *ing* form, e.g. I'm *constantly / always / forever* arguing with people. Then check understanding with *I wish + would*: Does he listen carefully? (No.) Do I want him to? (Yes.) Does she smoke inside? (Yes.) Do I want her to? (No.) Tell them we use *wish + would* when want people to behave differently and that we use *would* when the person doesn't normally do it and we want them to and we use *wouldn't* when the person normally does it but we don't want them to do it.

Step 2 Get students to look at the first example in exercise A and notice how to combine the comments and ideas. Check understanding: *suck up to* = to be nice to someone in authority so that they will treat you well. Tell them to combine 2–7. Students compare answers in pairs before checking in open class.

Answers
2 I wish he would shut up and let others speak sometimes.
3 I wish he would talk about something else apart from studying.
4 He's always buying me roses and saying he loves me.
5 I wish she would lighten up a bit and have a laugh a bit more.

6 I wish you wouldn't take everything I say as a personal attack.
7 My dad's always letting her get her own way.

Direct students to the grammar reference on page 152 if they still seem unsure.

Step 3 Tell students to write two-line comments similar to those in exercise A about the characteristics in the vocabulary box. In pairs they compare their answers before doing brief feedback in open class.

Suggested answers
1 He's so stubborn, I wish he'd listen to me more when I give him advice.
2 She's so competitive, she's always playing to win.
3 He's so laid-back, I wish he would get more involved and get angry sometimes.
4 He's so moody, I wish he wouldn't change his attitude every time we tell him something.
5 He's so disruptive, it's hard to learn anything when he's in the class.
6 I'm so vain, I'm always looking at myself in mirrors to check I look OK.
7 She's so generous, she's always doing things for others without thinking of herself.
8 She's so polite, I wish she would say what she really thinks sometimes though.

Step 4 Put students in pairs to discuss the questions in C. Monitor and help out with any problems with the target language. Conduct brief feedback in open class.

 13B see Teacher's notes p. 126.

READING

Aim
To develop reading for general and detailed information.

Step 1 Tell students to individually read the introduction to the Wiki and to answer the questions in exercise A. In groups of four or five they discuss their opinions.

Step 2 Individually tell students to read the rest of the Wiki and to match the headings in exercise B to each paragraph and that there is one extra heading they will not need. Then they compare in pairs before checking in open class.

Answers
1 b   2 d   3 a   4 h   5 g   6 i   7 f   8 e

Step 3 Tell students to read the article again and find sentences in the Wiki that have the same meaning as 1–8 in exercise C. Tell them to try to guess the meaning from the context and the words around it. In pairs they compare before checking the answers in open class.

Answers
1 in paragraph 3, Resorting to personal abuse will then only make matters worse
2 in paragraph 8, When you get in touch, don't go over old ground again
3 in paragraph 3, Saying *always* or *never* is likely to immediately make people defensive
4 in paragraph 6, Don't get stuck defending an unreasonable position just for the sake of not losing face
5 in paragraph 1, Setting children boundaries and standing up for yourself is sometimes necessary
6 in paragraph 2, Don't raise your voice
7 in paragraph 4, try to put off sensitive topics of conversation till later on in the day
8 in paragraph 5, When it comes down to it, differences in gender, generation, character or nationality may produce a different perspective to yours and one that is equally valid

---

Tip With a weaker class, you could tell them which paragraphs the statements can be found in.

Step 4 Tell students to read the questions in exercise D and give them a moment to think about what they want to say. Then put students in pairs to discuss their opinions. Then they rewrite the Wiki based on their ideas in the discussion – tell them to remove things they don't agree with or change them so they agree and to add at least one idea of their own.

Alternatively You could get them to rewrite the Wiki for homework and then start the next class with students showing each other their new Wikis.

Optional extension Tell students to look back at the Wiki page and find words that collocate with the adjectives and nouns in exercise A and B. In pairs they compare answers before checking in open class.

Answers
sensitive topics of conversation, tackle sensitive or controversial matters, underlying message, the sake of not losing face, steer through these confrontations, worried about redundancy, have a falling-out, discussion will turn into an irrational shouting match, provide warning signs, accept any such offers you receive with good grace

---

 pp. 96–97

SPEAKING

Aim
To provide fluency practice in discussing life events.

Step 1 Tell students to put the life events in exercise A into the order they think they most usually happen. You could elicit the first (birth) and last (your death). Check understanding, *coming of age* = when you officially reach legal age (different in each country), *naming ceremony* = when you are given your name publicly and legally. Put students in pairs to compare their ideas.

> **Suggested answers**
> your birth, naming ceremony, coming of age, learning to drive, leaving home, getting a job, buying or renting a flat / house, engagement, wedding, starting a family, retirement, your death

Step 2 Tell them to think about the questions in C, then put them into groups of four or five to discuss their ideas and say whether they agree or disagree with their partner's opinions. Monitor for a correction slot at the end.

VOCABULARY Birth, marriage and death

Aim
To present and practise expressions related to birth, marriage and death.

Step 1 Tell students to read the short text in exercise A, to use the *Vocabulary builder* for words they are not sure of and to translate the words in bold into their language. If possible put them in monolingual pairs to compare answers before checking in open class.

> **Answers**
> 1 *straightforward birth* = simple and not problematic birth
> 2 *went into labour* = the moment the baby starts coming out
> 3 *rushed to the maternity ward* = taken quickly to the department in hospital for births
> 4 *in labour* = the period of giving birth
> 5 *maternity leave* = time off work after the birth
> 6 *expecting another baby* = pregnant
> 7 *had her first scan* = non-invasive medical ultrasound to check what's inside the body
> 8 *it's due* = when the baby is expected

Step 2 Tell students to read the questions in exercise B and to discuss their ideas in pairs. Conduct brief feedback.

Step 3 Tell students to read the words in the vocabulary box and decide which of the nouns are connected to weddings and which to funerals. In pairs they compare answers before checking in open class.

> **Answers**
> Weddings = best man, bride, groom, town hall, reception, honeymoon
> Funerals = mourners, cemetery, grave, coffin, condolences, ashes

Step 4 Tell students to complete the sentences with nouns from exercise C. In pairs they compare before checking in open class.

> **Answers**
> 1 town hall   4 reception   7 ashes
> 2 mourners   5 grave   8 bride
> 3 condolences   6 honeymoon

Step 5 Ask students to read the questions in exercise E and to prepare what they want to say. Then put them into pairs to discuss their opinions. Conduct brief feedback.

LISTENING

Aim
To develop listening for general and specific information.

Step 1 Tell students they are going to hear four people talking about significant life events and they will hear all the words in exercise A. In pairs they should discuss which life event each group might be connected to and how. Do brief feedback in open class.

> **Answers**
> 1 coming-of-age ceremony   3 retirement
> 2 funeral   4 getting married

Step 2 Play the recording and then get students to take notes on the connections with the words in exercise A. In pairs they compare before checking in open class.

> **Answers**
> 1 the second Monday of every January = Seijin No Hi, the Japanese Coming-of-Age Day, 20 = everyone who is 20 that year is invited to a special ceremony and is the age when you become a legal adult, many thousands of pounds = the cost of the traditional Japanese outfits the girls wear
> 2 three to seven days = how long a wedding can last in Morocco, dawn = the bride changes again and the couple disappear for a while
> 3 65 = retirement age for men in Chile, 60 = retirement age for women, 75% = their pension is 75% of their final year's salary
> 4 90 = grandmother died at the age of 90 last year, over 3000 = number of mourners at her funeral, five blossoms = they represent the things you want to happen in your life.

> 🔊 **13.2**
> 1: The second Monday of every January is called *Seijin No Hi* – Coming-of-Age Day – here in Japan. Everyone who turns 20 that year is invited to attend a special ceremony. Twenty is the age you become a legal adult there. People gather at a city hall, a stadium, or wherever their city decides to hold the ceremony. The girls usually wear traditional Japanese outfits, which can cost many thousands of pounds, and guys wear either suits or *hakamas*, which are kind of like *kimonos* for guys. There then follow lengthy congratulations speeches from the mayor and other

dignitaries, after which everyone goes out and meets old school friends and parties!

2: Traditionally, Moroccan marriages were arranged, but nowadays people choose their own partners. Our parents still have the power of veto, though. Weddings join two families together, so parents are important. Our weddings are elaborate affairs and can last from three to seven days. First, each family has a big party in their own home, and then the groom proceeds to the home of his bride, accompanied by his guests, all singing and dancing and beating drums (or honking their horns!). The bride and groom are then lifted onto the shoulders of the crowd and paraded among their guests. Later, the bride changes into a traditional outfit and the party continues. Around dawn, she changes again, and the couple disappear to a hotel for a while. Parties and feasting continue throughout the week, though, as the newlyweds visit friends and relatives.

3: Retirement age here in my country is 65 for men and 60 for women. We're not legally obliged to stop working then, but we can if we want to, which is always good to know. I actually took early retirement – after my wife talked me into it! To begin with, I found it .... well, not exactly traumatic, but difficult, shall we say. It certainly took me quite a while to get used to having so much free time on my hands, but now I've finally started getting the hang of it. I get a decent annual pension – about 75% of my final year's salary – so I can't complain. My wife and I both still have our health, which is the most important thing, and we have three grandchildren now as well, who we adore.

4: My grandmother died last year at the age of 90. There were over 3,000 mourners at her funeral; everyone was crying and wailing and lots of people wanted to touch her because she died such a good death. People felt that touching her could bring good luck. My grandmother had what we in China call 'a five-blossoms death'. The five blossoms represent things you want to happen in your life. The five blossoms are marriage, having a son, being respected, having a grandson who loves you, and dying in your sleep after a long life. This is the best way to die.

Step 3 Tell students to discuss the questions in exercise C in pairs. Play the recording again to check their answers.

Answers

1 a at a city hall, a stadium, or wherever their city decides to hold the ceremony

1 b The girls usually wear traditional Japanese outfits and guys wear either suits or *hakamas*, which are kind of like *kimonos* for guys, there are lengthy congratulations speeches from the mayor and other dignitaries, after which everyone goes out and meets old school friends and parties

---

2 a traditionally, Moroccan marriages were arranged, but nowadays people choose their own partners, parents still have the power of veto, though

2 b He is accompanied by his guests who are all singing and dancing and beating drums or honking their horns

3 a he found it not traumatic, but difficult and it took him quite a while to get used to having so much free time on his hands

3 b His wife and he both still have their health, which is the most important thing, and they have three grandchildren now as well, who they adore

4 a everyone was crying and wailing and lots of people wanted to touch his grandmother because she died such a good death. People felt that touching her could bring good luck

4 b marriage, having a son, being respected, having a grandson who loves you, and dying in your sleep after a long life

---

LANGUAGE PATTERNS

Aim
To draw students' attention to some common patterns using *throughout*.

Step 1 Get students to read the language pattern box and tell students that in English we can use *throughout* to mean in every part of a place or during the whole of a period of time or an event.

Step 2 Ask students to translate the sentences into their own language. In a monolingual class, ask students to compare their translation. In a multilingual class, ask students to work in pairs and tell each other if *throughout* in all the sentences can be replaced with one word direct translation.

Step 3 Ask students to use their translation to translate the sentences back into English. Then ask them to compare their translations in pairs against the book. Alternatively, if you prefer not to use translation ask students to notice the patterns.

SPEAKING

Aim
To provide fluency practice in talking about life events.

Step 1 Tell students to read the questions in exercise A and to make notes on their ideas.

Step 2 Put students into groups of four or five and tell them to discuss the questions. Monitor their use of language. Finish with a correction slot.

14 BANKS AND MONEY

UNIT OVERVIEW

The main aim of this unit is to enable students to **talk about dealing with banks** and **express regrets** and **apologise and explain problems in formal settings**. They have practice in **using descriptive literary language**. The main grammatical focus is **passives and *wish*** and ways of talking about **banks and money**.

 Next class Make photocopies of **14A** p. 154.

VOCABULARY Banks and money

Aim
To practise expressions related to banks and money.

Step 1 Tell students to add the nouns in the vocabulary box to the group of words they combine with in 1–8. In pairs they compare answers before checking in open class.

> **Answers**
>
> | | | |
> |---|---|---|
> | 1 account | 4 debt | 7 loan |
> | 2 cash | 5 currency | 8 overdraft |
> | 3 credit | 6 money | |

Step 2 Tell students to discuss the questions in exercise B in pairs. Check as a class.

> **Suggested answers**
> *cash-flow problems* = companies that owe them money haven't paid, or the company itself hasn't paid the money it owes, *offered credit* = if your bank account is continually in good shape, *collapsed currency* = Iceland in 2008, Zimbabwe, *good with money* = save and spend within their limits, *bad* = always overspending, *money laundering*: why = criminals try to disguise the origins of the money they have gained through illegal activities, how = change the accounts to make it look like the money has come from somewhere else, *borrowing from a loan shark* = very high interest rates and they may threaten your family if you don't pay

LISTENING

Aim
To develop listening for general and specific information.

Step 1 Tell students they are going to hear two conversations and to answer the questions in A. Play the recording. Students compare answers in pairs before checking in open class.

> **Answers**
> Conversation 1 = 1 She wants to open a bank account, 2 she doesn't have proof of her current address nor proof of income, 3 she is given a three-month trial period on a current account, which costs £10 a month, if she decides to stay with the bank it will be refunded
> Conversation 2 = 1 He wants to buy £500 worth of Venezuelan currency, 2 The bank is completely out of bolivars, 3 He buys US dollars instead

🔊 14.1
Conversation 1
A: Hi. I'd like to open a bank account, please.
B: Certainly. Do you have some form of identification?
A: Yes, I've got my passport with me. Is that OK?
B: Yes, that's fine, but we also need proof of your current address. Do you have a utility bill – a gas bill or electricity bill or anything - with you?
A: No, I don't, I'm afraid. You see, I'm not directly paying bills at the moment. I'm living in a shared house, a student house, and I just pay a fixed amount every month.
B: OK. Well, do you have any proof of income or a National Insurance number at all?
A: No. This is crazy! I'm a student. I'm not working. I have my passport, my driving licence from back home, three cheques I want to deposit and this letter from my uni.
B: Oh, can I just have a quick look at that? Ah OK, I see. Right, well this should be fine. What kind of account were you after?
A: Just a normal current account.
B: OK. Well, what we can do is give you a three-month trial period on a current account, which will cost you ten pounds a month, and if you do decide to stay with us after that, the thirty pounds will be refunded.
A: This is extortion, really, but what choice do I have?
B: OK. Well, if you can just fill out these forms ….
Conversation 2
C: Hi. I'm flying to Caracas and I need to get some hold of some Venezuelan currency. I'm not sure what it's called, I'm afraid.

D: No problem. I'll just check for you. Yes, there we are. It's the bolivar. How much are you after?

C: About five hundred pounds worth, please.

D: OK. That shouldn't be a problem. Let's see. Oh, I'm awfully sorry, sir, but I'm afraid we're actually completely out of bolivar.

C: Oh, OK.

D: I wouldn't have thought we usually hold that much, anyway, but it looks as if it's all been bought.

C: Ah, that's annoying.

D: I'm terribly sorry. Would US dollars do? As I understand it, they're often accepted instead of the local currency. Otherwise, I'm sure you can just change money once you arrive or make a withdrawal from a cash point there.

C: In theory, yes, but I've been caught out before thinking that. Maybe I'll get some dollars just to be on the safe side.

D: Of course. How much would you like?

C: I'll take three hundred, please.

D: OK. That'll be two hundred and six pounds seventy-five pence.

C: Really? What's the exchange rate?

D: We're currently selling at 1.48 to the pound and then there's 2% commission on all transactions.

C: Right. Well, that's the way it goes, I suppose. Can I pay by Visa?

D: Yeah, of course. Just pop the card in there. OK. And just enter your PIN number. Great. Thanks.

Step 2 Tell students to complete the sentences in exercise B and to check in pairs. Play the recording and check answers.

Answers

1 a identification   b proof   c fixed   d trial
  e extortion
2 a shouldn't   b out   c side   d exchange
  e commission

Step 3 In pairs ask students to discuss the questions in C. Conduct brief feedback.

NATIVE SPEAKER ENGLISH *After*

Ask students to read the box and check they understand by asking, What words could you replace *after* with? (*looking for* or *trying to find*). Is this formal or informal? (Informal.)

DEVELOPING CONVERSATIONS
Apologising and offering explanations

Aim
To practise apologising and offering explanations.

Step 1 Get students to read the explanation box and check understanding. *How does the speaker emphasise*

the apology? = uses *really / terribly / awfully* or auxiliary *do* between the subject and the verb. *How do they offer an explanation?* 1 = but I'm afraid … , 2 = this is taking so long. Tell them we use this language in formal setting, usually in business and that we usually stress the emphasis.

Step 2 Tell students to put the words in A in the correct order. In pairs they compare answers before playing the recording to check. Play the recording again and get them to practise the pronunciation.

⏺ 14.2

1 I'll look into the matter at once.
2 The computers are being very slow today.
3 There must've been some kind of mix-up.
4 I'm afraid our system is down at the moment.
5 I'm afraid there's absolutely nothing we can do.
6 I'm afraid I'm not authorised to make that decision.
7 I'll have a word with my manager and see what I can do.

Step 3 Tell students to look at the statements in exercise C and get them to think of how they can apologise and offer an explanation / solution. Put them in pairs to practise.

GRAMMAR
Passives

Aim
To present and practise passives.

Step 1 Tell students to look at the two sentences from *Listening*, then answer the questions. Check understanding: Sentence 1 = *Who will give the money back?* (Don't know.) *Is the process of getting the 30 pounds back important?* (Yes.) Sentence 2 = *Who has bought all the money?* (Don't know.) *Is it important?* (No.) Direct students to the grammar reference on page 153 if they still seem unsure.

Answers

Forms = 1 *will be* + past participle, 2 *has been* + past participle

Why = 1 & 2 The agent is unknown or not important, the process is important.

Step 2 Tell students to complete the sentences with the correct passive form of the verbs in brackets. In pairs students compare answers before checking in open class.

Answers

1 is being updated
2 is sent

---

3 has repeatedly been exceeded
4 had already been transferred
5 was rejected
6 hasn't been signed
7 was forwarded
8 was sent
9 will be contacted, has been made

Note For answer 7 *has been forwarded* is also possible (not common, but not wrong). The best answer is *was forwarded*.

CONVERSATION PRACTICE

Aim
To provide conversation practice.

Step 1 Tell students they are going to role-play six short conversations similar to the ones in *Listening*. Put students into groups A and B. Tell group A to read File 7 page on 157 and group B to read File 19 on page 161. Give them time to prepare what they want to say and get them to help each other in their groups.

Step 2 When students are ready, put them in AB pairs to have their role-play. Monitor for a correction slot.

 14A see Teacher's notes p. 126.

 pp. 100–101

 Next class Make photocopies of **14B** p. 157.

SPEAKING

Aim
To provide fluency practice talking about money.

Step 1 Tell students to read the traditional Chinese sayings connected to money and check understanding of *march* = a walk in which people walk together at the same speed, like soldiers. Tell them to decide what each one means and how far they agree. Check ideas as a class.

Suggested answers
1 Be careful what you wish and think about is it going to make the situation better or worse
2 a big goal starts with small steps
3 you should keep exploring new things
4 even when all is lost, beauty is still important
5 without the right materials, no matter how good you are, you may not succeed
6 shows the importance of team work
7 learning is more important than money
8 Don't be greedy, one person can only use so much, so you shouldn't try and take more than you need
9 we should make good use of our time

Step 2 In pairs students discuss their ideas and talk about any similar sayings in their language. Conduct brief feedback.

READING

Aim
To develop reading for general and detailed information.

Step 1 Tell students they are going to read a Chinese folktale about attitudes to work and wealth. Tell them to read the first part of the tale and to answer the questions in pairs. Conduct brief feedback in open class.

Step 2 Tell them they are going to listen to the end of the story and compare what was similar and what was different to their predictions. Play the recording and in pairs they compare answers before checking in open class.

> **14.3**
> The husband bought bricks and hired builders. Before too long, the pile of silver was almost exhausted, but their mansion remained unfinished. The husband decided to see if the moneybag would produce more silver, so without his wife's knowledge, he opened the bag for a second time that day. Instantly, another lump of silver rolled out. He opened it a third time and received a third lump.
>
> He thought to himself, 'If I go on like this, I can get the house finished in no time!'. He quite forgot the old man's warning. However, when he opened the bag a fourth time, it was completely empty. This time not a scrap of silver fell out of it. It was just an old cloth bag. When he turned to look at his unfinished house, that was gone as well. There before him was his old thatched hut.
>
> The woodcutter fell to his knees in despair, crying 'How I wish I'd never opened that bag. Now everything is lost'. His wife came over to comfort him, saying, 'Not all is lost. We still have each other. Let's go back to the mountain and cut firewood like we did before. That's a more dependable way of earning a living'.
>
> And from that day on, that's exactly what they did.

Step 3 Tell students to replace the words in italics in exercise C with the more descriptive synonyms used in the first part of the tale. Tell them that this is more descriptive and is used to engage the reader. In pairs they compare before checking in open class.

Answers
1 sensed (paragraph 2)
2 descended (paragraph 3)
3 peering (paragraph 4)
4 chuckled (paragraph 6)
5 ushered (paragraph 7)
6 glistening (paragraph 7)
7 crammed (paragraph 8)
8 clinging (paragraph 8)

Step 4 Tell students to read the topics in the vocabulary box and put them in groups to discuss the questions in D. Conduct brief feedback.

> **Answers**
> poverty = they live in a tiny hut and survive by selling and chopping wood, greed = the husband wanted more, dignity = when they lost everything his wife said they had each other and that was more important
>
> The story expresses the value of being happy with what you have and not to be overcome with greed, the moral is be careful what you wish for
>
> Jack and the beanstalk is a similar story.

GRAMMAR *Wish*

Aim
To present and practise *wish* for things that can't be changed and regrets about past situations.

Step 1 Tell students to read the box and check understanding of sentence 1. *What did he have to do?* (Cut two bundles of wood each day.) *Does he want to?* (No.) *Is it a current situation?* (Yes.) *Can he change the situation?* (No.) *What's the tense of the verb after wish?* (Past simple.) Tell them when we use *wish* to refer to a *present situation* that can't be changed we use *wish + past simple.* Sentence 2 = *Did he open the bag?* (Yes.) *Does he think this was a bad idea?* (Yes.) *When did this happen?* (In the past.) *What's the tense after wish?* (Past perfect.) So, when we regret a *past situation*, we use *wish + past perfect.*

Step 2 Get students to choose the correct option in B. Students compare answers in pairs then as a class.

> **Answers**
> 1 hadn't taken out (past regret)
> 2 didn't have to (current situation that can't be changed)
> 3 'd stuck (past regret)
> 4 he'd been better (past regret)
> 5 could pay (current situation)
> 6 you'd said (past regret)
> 7 was (current situation)
> 8 I'd never started (past regret).

Step 3 Tell students to look back at sentences 1–8 in B and decide what actually happened and / or what the situation is now. In pairs they compare opinions before checking in open class. Direct students to the grammar reference on page 153 if they still seem unsure.

> **Suggested answers**
> 1 the person took out a loan to pay for something, now they regret the decision
> 2 the person has to tell someone some bad news and doesn't want to but would feel bad if they didn't

3 the person is in a new job that they don't like and now thinks it would have been better to stay in the old job
4 the person had not saved any money and spent most of it and now doesn't have enough to buy a house
5 the person wants to pay back what they owe, but doesn't have enough money to do it now
6 the person embarrassed themselves by congratulating a friend on being pregnant when actually she wasn't
7 the person knows their friend is not happy with their job but doesn't know what to say to make it better
8 the person started redecorating their flat but the walls were in such a bad condition that they spent more time repairing them than just painting them

Step 4 Tell students they should think of five, fun, wishes, and in pairs they tell each other their wishes and their partner should say how the wish goes / went wrong.

 14B see Teacher's notes p. 126.

📖 **pp. 102–103**

SPEAKING

Aim
To provide further speaking practice in expressing opinions about money.

Step 1 Tell students to read the questions in exercise A. Then in pairs to discuss them. Conduct brief feedback.

VOCABULARY *Metaphor*

Aim
To present and practise talking about using metaphor.

Step 1 Tell students to read the explanation box and check understanding: In sentence 1 did he really *invest* money? (Yes.) In the second sentence did he literally *invest time and effort?* (No.) Is *invest* used to emphasise it has a similar quality? (Yes.) Tell them that we often use words or expressions related to money to emphasise it has a similar quality to its literal meaning and we call this metaphor. Ask them if they do the same thing in their language.

Step 2 Tell students to complete each pair of sentences in A with one of the words with box. In pairs students compare their answers before checking in open class. Ask them if one word in their language can be used in both pairs of sentences.

> **Answers**
> 1 a earn (literal) 1 b earned (metaphor)
> 2 a waste (literal) 2 b waste (metaphor)
> 3 a bet (literal) 3b bet (metaphor)
> 4 a gamble (literal) 4 b gambling (metaphor)
> 5 a odds (literal), 5 b odds (metaphor)

6 a lottery (literal) 6 b lottery (metaphor)
7 a jackpot (literal) 7 b jackpot (metaphor)
8 a stakes (literal) 8 b stake (metaphor)

LISTENING

Aim
To develop listening skills for specific information.

Step 1 Tell students they are going hear to two speakers present their arguments in a debate. Get them to read the Fact File and discuss the questions in pairs. Conduct brief feedback.

Step 2 In groups tell students to think of reasons someone might give for banning a lottery and the group with the most reasons is the winner, set a time limit of three minutes.

Step 3 Tell students to listen to the first person, Zak, and see if any of the reasons they thought of are mentioned. In their groups they compare before checking in open class.

14.4
Part 1: Zak
Here's an offer: if you give me one dollar each week, I promise to give you $2.6 million at some point in the future. There's just one catch, when I say 'at some point in the future', I mean at any point within the next quarter of a million years! Tempted? I bet you aren't. So why is it that so many people gamble on lotteries when the odds are nearly 1 in 14 million? Probably because the whole marketing of lotteries downplays the odds against winning and emphasises the dream, the ease of getting money, and the 'good causes' that are funded by the profits lotteries make. But I don't see subsidising things like opera and Olympic sportsmen as a good cause. And it's not good when profits simply go to the government or the company that runs the lottery.

Not only does the advertising of lotteries tend to obscure this tiny chance, it also sends this subtle message - people don't need to work hard or get a good education to become wealthy; all you have to do is choose six numbers and your dreams will come true. And then also consider what those dreams are. Are they for a better society and health care? Peace and understanding? No! It's a mansion and a Ferrari for me! These are values – anti-educational, money-driven and selfish – that go against society. No doubt Stacy will argue that in fact it's all innocent fun and that the stakes are small, but not only do lotteries damage society in this way, they also bring pain to individuals. Take these words from John, a gambling addict from Sydney, for example: "I sometimes gambled away my whole pay cheque and had nothing left with which to pay the mortgage or feed the family. In the end, I'd bet on anything - horse races, rugby, roulette, even what the weather would be like - but it all started with lottery tickets. I wish I'd never seen one."

There's more at stake than we imagine. Gambling destroys people's lives and nine times out of ten it starts with lotteries. They're a tax on the poor and benefit the rich and they undermine social values. They really should be banned.

Part 2: Stacy
Well, that really was a sad story that Zak finished with there, wasn't it? Sad – but, sadly for him, also rather misleading in this particular debate. Of course, compulsive gambling is not something that we should approve of. It not only causes pain to the gambler, but also hurts their family and friends. However, addictive behaviour can take many forms: if it wasn't gambling, it might well be drugs or shopping or work. Banning lotteries won't reduce addictive behaviour – even if it were true that nine out of ten gambling addictions started with the lottery. By the way, I'd be interested to hear the source of that figure – dubiousstatistics.com, I'd imagine. But just for a moment, say it was true, nine out of ten gambling addicts start with lotteries, should we also consider banning cigarettes on the basis that heroin addicts started by smoking? Or prohibit credit cards because some people go on to be shopaholics and run up huge debts? No. In the end, I actually agree with Zak – we should take responsibility for our future wealth. It's just that where he suggests we do that by banning the lottery and investing in education, I believe that people should do it by learning self-control.

Which brings me to his point that the lottery somehow goes against hard work and education. With the greatest respect - that's complete rubbish! People don't spend money on the lottery instead of studying and working hard – it's on top of it. Similarly, lottery dreams don't replace friendship, they add to it. The real equivalent of spending money on a lottery ticket is buying, say, an ice cream. Neither are necessary for living – they provide pleasure. Let's face it, gambling in one form or another has featured in human society since time began because it's fun! The only difference is that, unlike ice cream, the lottery ticket, however remote the chance is, might just possibly bring you the additional benefit of riches.

From that standpoint, it's a sound investment. Now Zak may not find lotteries exciting or wish that he had a Ferrari, but I do – and I can't see that there is anything anti-social in that or anything worth banning.

Step 3 Tell students to read exercise C and explain the points Zak was making. Play the recording again to check their answers. Check answers.

Answers
1 that the money you give him will be the same money you get back
2 it downplays the odds against winning and emphasises the dream
3 giving money to opera and Olympic sportsmen is something the government or public companies should be doing

4 it's a dream to think you can get rich by choosing numbers
5 that people's dreams are selfish and not for the benefit of society
6 it can become an addiction and ruin your life

Step 4 Tell students to think about the questions in E while they listen again. In pairs they compare ideas.

Step 5 Tell students to listen and take notes on Stacy's reply to Zak. Play the recording. Let students compare their answers in pairs first, then in small groups. Then tell them to check what they understood of Stacy's argument against the audioscript of on page 180.

Answers
Stacey's argument: Addictive behaviour can take many forms and if it wasn't gambling, it might well be drugs or shopping or work, banning lotteries won't reduce addictive behaviour. People don't spend money on the lottery instead of studying and working hard – it's on top of it, gambling in one form or another has featured in human society since time began because it's fun!

Step 6 In the same groups ask them to discuss the questions in H. Conduct brief feedback in open class.

LANGUAGE PATTERNS

Aim
To draw attention to useful patterns with *not only*.

Step 1 Get students to look at the sentences in the box. Tell them we use the expression *not only* to emphasise that although one thing is true, something else is also true.

Step 2 Ask students to translate the sentences into their own language. In a monolingual class, ask students to compare their translation. In a multilingual class, ask students to work in pairs and tell each other if the sentences were easy to translate into their language.

Step 3 Ask students to cover their English translations and using their translation translate the sentences back into English. Then ask them to compare their translations in pairs against the book. Alternatively, if you prefer not to use translation, ask students to notice the patterns.

PRONUNCIATION Numbers

Aim
To present and practise pronunciation of numbers.

Step 1 Get students to look at the sentences in the box and to notice the different ways of saying numbers.

Step 2 Tell students to look at the numbers in exercise A and to think of two different ways to say them.

Monitor and help out with the alternatives. Then play the recording again and get students to repeat the numbers.

🔊 14.5
1 three point seven million, three million seven hundred thousand
2 fifteen hundred, one and a half thousand
3 nought point nought two, two hundredths
4 two thirds, two out of three
5 forty percent, two fifths
6 minus ten degrees, ten below zero

Step 4 Tell students they are going to listen to some statistics and to write down the numbers they hear. Play the recording and get students to compare in pairs. (Answers underlined in audioscript.)

🔊 14.6
1 The exact odds of winning the lottery are 1 in 13,983,816 when there are 49 numbers to choose from.
2 In Italy, food accounts for just under one fifth of a family's budget.
3 In the UK last year, 1.4 million people paid over £500 in bank charges - for example, exceeding overdraft limits.
4 On average, families spend just 0.015% of their income on books.
5 Over three quarters of all women worry about how they'll pay off credit card bills and loans - far more than men.
6 Only about 1 in 10 men know their current level of debt.

Step 5 Ask students if they remember the complete statistics, e.g. what the numbers refer to. In pairs they try to remember. If necessary, play the recording again before checking in open class. (For answers refer to audioscript 14.6.)

SPEAKING

Aim
To provide fluency practice by having a debate.

Step 1 Tell students they are going to have a debate and to read the topics in exercise A. Put students into groups of four or five and tell them to decide which of the topics they want to debate or to propose their own topic.

Step 2 Tell them to divide their group into two teams. One team should think of reasons to defend the statement in the topic they've chosen and the other team should think of reasons to counter it. Tell them to look at the audioscript on pp. 179–180 for techniques and expressions they want to use.

Step 3 Tell each team to nominate a speaker. Put two groups together and then get them to take turns to have their debate. The other group will give them marks out of ten – they could mark them on the clarity of their arguments, their use of target language and the number of their arguments, and decide the winner.

15 FOOD

UNIT OVERVIEW

The main aim of this unit is to enable students to **explain how to cook things, name different kinds of food, link ideas more clearly** and **give approximate meanings.** They have practice in **naming different kinds of foods**. The main grammatical focus is **reporting verbs** and **revision of linking words** and ways of **expressing food and cooking, prefixes** and **food in the news**.

 Next class Make photocopies of **15A** p. 156.

VOCABULARY Food and cooking

Aim
To introduce expressions related to food and cooking.

Step 1 Ask students to look at the questions in exercise A. Tell them to look at the pictures in File 23 on page 163 and discuss the questions in pairs. Conduct brief feedback in open class.

Step 2 In groups ask students to put as many things as possible from the pictures in the categories, tell them not to look at the pictures while they do this. Conduct feedback in open class.

> **Suggested answers**
> Fruits / nuts = almond and pear cake, fruit cake
> fish / seafood = Spanish seafood stew, fish with herb sauce, ceviche fish stew vegetables / salads = ratatouille pulses / beans = herbs / spices = Creole chicken stew.

Step 3 Tell students to complete the sentences in exercise C with the words in the vocabulary box. Tell them not to worry about the words in bold for the moment.

> **Answers**
> 1 peaches 6 courgettes
> 2 trout 7 almonds
> 3 chickpeas 8 parsley
> 4 chocolate 9 coconut
> 5 grapefruit 10 mixture

Step 4 Tell students in pairs to take it in turns to act or draw the words in bold in exercise C – their partner should guess the word. You could model first, e.g. you draw or act it out and students have to guess.

LISTENING

Aim
To develop listening for specific information.

Step 1 Tell students they are going to hear a conversation where a German woman comments on a dish and how it's made. They should listen and answer the questions in A. Play the recording and get students to compare answers in pairs before checking in open class.

> **Answers**
> 1 lemon grass, pumpkin, red lentils, a large onion, a couple of cloves of garlic and ginger, oil, a whole chilli pepper, coconut milk, chicken stock, parsley, pinch of salt
> 2 pumpkin and lentil soup, we know it's soup because it all gets blended at the end

> 🔊 **15.1**
> A: Mmmm, this is gorgeous!
> B: Thanks.
> A: What's in it? It's got a bit of a lemony taste.
> B: Yeah, that's the lemon grass.
> A: Lemon grass?
> B: Yeah, it's this ... actually I don't know what you call it – a herb or spice. It looks sort of like a spring onion, you know. It's like a greyish-white stick. Anyway, you drop it in the sauce while it's cooking and it gives it a kind of citrusy flavour.
> A: You don't eat it then.
> B: No. It's got a kind of woody texture - it's pretty tough – so you just pick it out at the end.
> A: Right - and the orangey colour ... is that from carrots?
> B: No. It's pumpkin and red lentils.
> A: Pumpkin?
> B: You know, like a big orange squash - like a melon or something - but rounder and the flesh is harder.
> A: Oh yeah, of course. Pumpkin – I know this word.
> B: Yeah, so you use that or sometimes I use sweet potato instead.

A: Right. So how do you make it?
B: Oh, it's dead easy. You get a large onion and a couple of cloves of garlic and ginger and you chop them all really finely. I actually sometimes use a food processor. Then you put some o il in a pan and heat it up and you just chuck the stuff in the oil with a couple of bits of lemon grass and I sometimes put in a whole chilli as well – just to spice things up a bit – you know, like to flavour the oil.
A: Right.
B: And then you cook it quite quickly, but you have to keep stirring 'cos you don't want it to burn. Otherwise, it can be a bit bitter.
A: OK.
B: Then you throw in the pumpkin. I should've said you have to cut it up into cubes.
A: How big?
B: I don't know – about an inch – a couple of centimetres? It doesn't matter that much – you blend it all in the end.
A: I meant how big should the pumpkin be.
B: Oh sorry! Yeah, I don't know. They vary so much in size. Biggish, I guess, but not like the huge ones.
A: OK, and then what? You just add water and boil it?
B: Yeah, more or less. You add lentils - roughly a cupful – and a tin of coconut milk.
A: Oh right. Coconut milk.
B: Yeah, actually I often use less, because I find it a bit much otherwise. And then I add about litre or so of chicken stock and as you say bring it to the boil and then once it's boiling, you reduce the heat and leave it for 15 minutes or so – till the pumpkin's soft, anyway – and then just blend it till it's smooth.
A: So when do you take out the lemon grass?
B: Oh right, yeah. Sorry. Basically after it's simmered – at the end. It sort of floats to the surface. You just get it out with a spoon.
A: And the green herbs?
B: Well, you can use different things. I usually sprinkle a bit of chopped parsley, but basil's nice as well. And obviously a pinch or two of salt, although personally I got out of the habit of using too much because my dad's got a heart condition and he can't have too much.
A: Right. Well, it's great.
B: Yeah, I like it. Actually I sometimes do it as a sauce – just everything in reduced quantities – and I cook pieces of cod or chicken in it.
A: Mmm. Sounds great.

Step 2 Tell students to discuss in pairs what they remember about how the dish was made. Play the recording and tell students to take notes. Then they compare their notes in groups before checking in open class.

Answers
You get a large onion and a couple of cloves of garlic and ginger and you chop them all really finely – she sometimes uses a food processor. Then put some oil in a pan and heat it up and you just chuck the stuff in the oil with a couple of bits of lemon grass and she sometimes puts in a whole chilli just to spice things up a bit. Then you cook it quite quickly, but you have to keep stirring 'cos you don't want it to burn. Then you throw in the pumpkin cut up into cubes. You add lentils, roughly a cupful and a tin of coconut milk. And then add about litre or so of chicken stock and bring it to the boil and then once it's boiling, reduce the heat and leave it for fifteen minutes or so, till the pumpkin's soft. Take out the lemon grass and blend it till it's smooth. Sprinkle a bit of chopped parsley, but basil's nice as well and a pinch or two of salt.

Step 3 Tell students to read the questions in exercise D. Put them into groups of four or five to discuss the questions. Monitor and take notes on their use of language. Conduct feedback in open class and finish with a brief correction slot.

NATIVE SPEAKER ENGLISH *dead easy*

Ask students to read the box and check they understand by asking, What word could you replace *dead* with? *(Very.)* Ask, What could be *dead easy*? (Riding a bike, making a cup of tea.) What could be *dead boring*? (A book, TV programme.)

DEVELOPING CONVERSATIONS
Vague language

Aim
To introduce and practise using vague language.

Step 1 Get students to read the explanation box and check understanding: *Does biggish mean it's big or more or less big?* (more or less big).

Step 2 Tell students to make the sentences less exact by adding the forms in brackets in the correct place. Do the first one together. Students compare answers in pairs before checking in open class.

Answers
1 You bake it in the oven for roughly 20 minutes.
2 I generally sprinkle some herbs on top and about two teaspoons of crushed pistachios.
3 If you add a squeeze of orange, it gives it a kind of sweet finish, which is really nice.
4 The colour put me off at first. It was kind of greenish blue, but it tasted great.

5 It has an odd oily texture and a weird eggy smell.
6 You need a largish pan, because you add two litres or so of fish stock.
7 If it's a smallish chicken and isn't stuffed, then it should only take 40 minutes or so to roast.
8 It's like a potato, but it's rounder and it's got purpleish skin and the flesh is kind of orange.

Step 3 Tell students to read the example in exercise B and elicit which words show that it's not exact (*biggish, yellowish, kind of*). Ask them to think of different foods and how would they describe them using the less exact language. Give them time to prepare. In pairs they take turns using vague language to describe different food for their partner to guess.

GRAMMAR Linking words

Aim
To present and practise linking words.

Step 1 Tell students to read the explanation box and check understanding: What linking words do we use with order and time? (*and, until, once, when, then, while, during*, etc.) What linking words do we use with result and reason / purpose? (*as, so, to*) What linking words do we use with condition? (*if, in case, provided*).

Step 2 Tell students to read the recipe in exercise A and to choose the correct linker. Students compare answers in pairs before checking in open class.

Answers		
1 and	6 although	11 provided
2 when	7 while	12 if
3 Then	8 otherwise	13 Then
4 as	9 Once	14 for
5 so	10 until	15 to

Direct students to the grammar reference on page 154 if they still seem unsure.

 15A see Teacher's notes p. 126.

CONVERSATION PRACTICE

Aim
To provide conversation practice using the language related to food and cooking.

Step 1 Tell students in pairs to choose a dish that they would like to eat from File 22 on page 165 and to discuss how they would make it. Before they start, get them to look back at *Vocabulary Food and cooking* on p. 104 for useful language.

Step 2 Tell them they are going to have conversations similar to the ones in *Listening* and put them in different pairs. Tell them to start by saying *Mmm! This is delicious!*

What's in it? Their partner should ask questions about the taste and about how to make the dish and to check details. Monitor for a correction slot at the end.

 pp. 106–107

READING

Aim
To develop reading skills for general and detailed information.

Step 1 Tell students they are going to read an article called 'Con-fusion food'. Tell them to look at the words in the vocabulary box and check understanding and word stress: *make* a *scene* = a noisy argument or strong show of feelings in a public place, *trademark* = a name or design that belongs to one organisation and is used on its products. Tell them that all the words feature in the rest of the story and in pairs they should try to guess what happens next and what the author then goes on to talk about.

Step 2 Tell them to read the article and find out if they were right. In new pairs they explain what the article said using the words in exercise A. Conduct brief feedback.

Step 3 Tell students to read the explanation box and check understanding: What words do we use to mark opinions? (*seems, think, probably*). Individually tell students to read the statements in exercise D and decide if they are facts or opinions. Then they discuss in pairs how they reached their decisions before checking in open class.

Answers
1 fact: a story from the author's past
2 opinion: he'd created a scene
3 fact: a study found that 10% of fish and chip shops in Britain were selling haddock and pollack rather than cod
4 opinion: the Italians, it seems
5 fact: Italy has passed a law
6 fact: Italians are not the only ones trying to protect their culinary heritage from globalisation. The Thai government [R1] while the Japanese have done something similar
7 fact: the explosion of interest in Japanese food
8 opinion: stop this tide of foreign fusions? Probably not
9 opinion: depending on who you believe, it originated in either China or Syria
10 opinion: it's simply annoying

Step 4 Tell students to complete the collocation in exercise E with the words in bold from the article in pairs. If they are not sure they can check meaning in the *Vocabulary builder*. Check answers in open class.

Answers

1 explosion	6 issue
2 flared up	7 subtle
3 full-blown	8 tide
4 muttering	9 uphold
5 settle	

Optional extension Ask students to discuss in groups: *Do you have any favourite brands of food? Why? And have you ever had food from your country abroad? What were they like?*

VOCABULARY Prefixes

Aim
To introduce and practise prefixes.

Step 1 Ask students to read the explanation box and check understanding: *dissatisfied* = not satisfied, *semi-cooked* = not cooked completely, *over-done* = cooked too much.

Step 2 Tell students to complete the definitions in 1–12 with the prefixes in the vocabulary box. In pairs they compare answers before checking in open class.

Answers

1 multi	3 mis	5 over	7 dis	9 re	11 pro
2 ex	4 out	6 non	8 pre	10 semi	12 super

Step 3 Tell students to think of another example for each prefix, e.g. *multi-national* and put it into a sentence, e.g. *There are a lot of multi-national companies in my part of town.* In pairs they challenge each other by taking it in turns to say a prefix and the other has to give their example. Conduct brief feedback in open class.

SPEAKING

Aim
To provide fluency practice in talking about how they would react in difficult situations.

Step 1 Tell students to look at the situations in exercise A and check understanding: *cooked rare* = under-cooked. Tell them to think of what they would do in each of the situations. Give them some time to prepare their ideas.

Step 2 Put students into groups of four or five to discuss their ideas. Monitor and take notes for an error correction slot at the end.

 pp. 108–109

 Next class Make photocopies of **15B** p. 157.

VOCABULARY Food in the news

Aim
To present and practise expressions related to food in the news.

Step 1 Ask students if they have read or heard any news stories related to food recently. Tell students to read the vocabulary boxes and check understanding: *staple* = a basic type of food that people eat or use very regularly, *GM* = foods that contain products whose genes have been changed (GM stands for genetically modified), *hygiene* = keeping things clean in order to prevent illnesses.

Step 2 Tell students to complete the newspaper headlines with the words in the vocabulary boxes, tell them the words in the first box are for sentences 1–5 and the second box for 6–10. In pairs they compare before checking in open class.

Answers

a production	f allergies
b staple	g waste
c GM	h supplies
d poisoning	i hygiene
e advertising	j shortages

Step 3 Tell students to underline any new collocations in 1–10. In pairs they compare before checking in open class.

Suggested answers

a faces challenge	f Fear of
b urged not to	g now exceeds
c should replace	h in bid to
d following outbreak of	i prove to be
e call for ban on	j facing food shortages.

Step 4 Tell students to think about what happens in each of the ten newspaper stories in exercise A and which stories would they be interested in reading and why. Give them some time to prepare their ideas. In pairs they discuss. Conduct brief feedback in open class.

LISTENING

Aim
To develop listening for general and specific information.

Step 1 Tell students they are going to hear four pieces of news about food. They should listen and match each news story with one of the headlines from *Vocabulary* exercise A. Play the recording and then get students to compare in pairs and discuss how they made their decision before checking in open class.

Answers

1 headline 9 = A man in Johannesburg has been arrested, accused of defrauding restaurants, he

was found out when two waiters had a chance conversation about him.

2 headline 3 = A leading scientist blames the food crisis in Africa on the rise of organic farming and criticised NGOs and the United Nations for backing traditional farming techniques.

3 headline 5 = A leading consumer protection group is calling for a ban on junk food advertising saying it causes obesity.

4 headline 7 = Researchers found that more than half the good food thrown out is bought and then simply left unused, each day 1.3 million unopened yoghurt pots, 5,500 whole chickens and 440,000 ready meals are simply discarded.

15.2

1 One of Johannesburg's most persistent – and successful – fraudsters has finally been arrested and is due to appear in court today accused of defrauding restaurants, a charge which carries a maximum penalty of nine months in prison and a 100,000 rand fine. For over a year, Wouter Gunning, aged 54, had been eating out on a regular basis in many of the city's most exclusive restaurants – and all completely free of charge. It's alleged that as he neared the end of his meals, Gunning would habitually introduce a cockroach into his food – safe in the knowledge that high-end establishments would be so sensitive to the damage that any negative publicity could do that they would invariably waive any charge.

Remarkably, the scam only came to light following a chance conversation between two waiters from different restaurants. Mr. Gunning denies all charges against him and will be pleading not guilty on the basis of temporary insanity.

2 In a keynote speech today a leading scientist will blame the food crises in Africa on the rise of organic farming in developed countries as well as the widespread rejection of agricultural technology in general – and of GM crops in particular.

Sir David King claims anti-scientific attitudes towards modern agriculture are being exported to Africa and are holding back a green revolution that could dramatically improve the continent's food supply.

In the past, Mr. King has criticised NGOs and the United Nations for backing traditional farming techniques, which he believes will never be able to provide enough food for the continent's growing population. In today's speech, he'll suggest that genetically modified crops could help Africa mirror the substantial increases in crop production seen in India and China, an idea bound to encounter fierce opposition across the European Union, where GM foods are still heavily restricted.

3 A leading consumer protection group is today calling for a total ban on junk food advertising on television between 6am and 9pm in a bid to tackle rising rates of obesity among children. The group, CHOICE, would also like to see a ban on the use of celebrities, cartoon characters and free gifts to induce under-sixteens to eat fast food.

At present, one in four Australian children is overweight or obese and experts have warned that the proportion could rise to 60% in the next 30 years unless urgent action is taken. The inspiration behind the new campaign lies in Scandinavia. Finland, Denmark and Sweden have all prohibited commercial sponsorship of children's programmes, and all have seen a subsequent drop in obesity rates.

4 New findings published today show that the cost of wasted food to UK households now exceeds £10 billion a year. The average household throws out £420 of good food per year, while the average family with children squanders £610.

Researchers also found that more than half the good food thrown out is bought and then simply left unused. Each day 1.3 million unopened yoghurt pots, 5,500 whole chickens and 440,000 ready meals are simply discarded.

In response to the report, the environment minister expressed her dismay:

'These findings are shocking – and at a time when global food shortages are in the headlines this kind of wastefulness becomes even more appalling. This is costing consumers three times over. Not only are they paying hard-earned money for food they're not eating, there's also the cost of dealing with the waste this creates. And then there are the climate change costs of growing, processing, packaging, transporting, and refrigerating food – just for it all to end up in the rubbish bin.'

Step 2 Tell students to read the questions in exercise C and to listen again and answer the questions. In pairs they compare answers before checking in open class.

Answers
1a he would habitually introduce a cockroach into his food, safe in the knowledge that high-end establishments would be so sensitive to the damage that any negative publicity could do that they would invariably waive any charge
1b he denies all charges and is pleading insanity
2a the rise of organic farming in developed countries as well as the widespread rejection of agricultural technology in general and of GM crops in particular
2b he thinks genetically modified crops could help Africa mirror the substantial increases in crop production seen in India and China, an idea which will encounter fierce opposition across the European Union, where GM foods are still heavily restricted
3a It's a leading consumer protection group and they want to see a ban on junk food advertising between 6–9 pm and a ban on the use of celebrities, cartoon characters and free gifts to induce under-16s to eat fast food

3b they have prohibited commercial sponsorship of children's programmes and have seen a subsequent drop in obesity rates
4a £10 billion a year
4b they are paying hard-earned money for food they're not eating and the cost of dealing with the waste this creates, there are also the climate change costs of growing, processing, packaging, transporting and refrigerating food

Step 3 Get students to read the questions in exercise D and give them time to think about what they want to say. In pairs they discuss the questions. Monitor and take notes for a correction slot at the end.

LANGUAGE PATTERNS

Aim
To draw attention to some common patterns using *basis*.

Step 1 Get students to read the language pattern box and to notice the pattern with *basis*. Tell them we use this pattern in English when we want to talk about a particular system or method used for doing or organising something or the regularity that something happens. Ask them, Which expressions talk about how often something happens? = *on a regular / weekly basis*. Which expressions talk about a particular system or method? = *on the basis of, no basis in, first-served basis.*

Step 2 Ask students to translate the sentences into their own language. In a monolingual class, ask students to compare their translation. In a multilingual class, ask students to work in pairs and tell each other if the sentences were easy to translate into their language.

Step 3 Ask students to cover their English translations and using their translation translate the sentences back into English. Then ask them to compare their translations in pairs against the book. Alternatively, if you prefer not to use translation ask students to notice the patterns.

GRAMMAR Reporting verbs

Aim
To present and practise reporting verbs.

Step 1 Tell students to read the explanation box and get them to identify the reporting verbs in the example sentence = *will blame, he'll suggest*. Check understanding: *What will he blame?* (The food crises in Africa on the rise of organic farming in economically developed countries.) *What will he suggest?* (That genetically modified crops could help Africa.) Tell them that we often summarise the main ideas after reporting verbs and that the patterns that follow these verbs vary, usually the verb has a dependent preposition e.g. *blame something <u>on</u>*.

Step 2 Tell students to read the statements in exercise A and to choose the correct verb in each sentence. Students compare answers in pairs before checking in open class.

Answers

1 criticised, urged (to)	5 confessed (to)
2 announced	6 accused (of), deny
3 claims, calling for	7 reassure
4 warning, encouraging (to)	8 offered (to), insisted (on)

Direct students to the grammar reference on page 154 if they still seem unsure.

Step 3 Tell students to read the sentences in exercise C and complete by putting the verbs in brackets into the correct form and that they also might need to add prepositions. In pairs they compare answers before checking in open class.

Answers

1 to try	3 for making	5 not to waste
2 to stealing	4 of not doing	6 on ordering

Step 4 Tell students to read the questions in exercise D and elicit a couple of examples for the first two questions. Give them time to think of what they want to say.

Step 5 In groups students discuss the questions ideas and see if they agree. Monitor and take notes for a correction slot. Conduct brief feedback on anything unusual they spoke about, then finish with a correction slot.

 15B see Teacher's notes p. 127.

SPEAKING

Aim
To provide fluency practice in expressing their opinions about food-related news stories.

Step 1 Tell students they are going to make a podcast (a multimedia file that can be recorded and listened to on the Internet or MP3 player) about a food-related news story. In pairs they should think of a story, this could be one of the stories from *Vocabulary* exercise A or a different story they have heard. Tell them to prepare their short podcast and to try and use as much language from the unit as possible. Monitor and help out with any language problems.

Step 2 Tell students to present their podcast to another pair and to decide who told the most interesting story. When they have finished tell them they will have to report their decision to the rest of the class and to think of which reporting verbs they will use, give them some time to do this. Get a selection of students to report back to the class. Finish with a correction slot.

16 BUSINESS

UNIT OVERVIEW
The main aim of this unit is to enable students to **talk about markets, companies and products more fluently, be more polite in business contexts** and **explain why you are phoning.** They have practice in **pronouncing email addresses and websites.** The main grammatical focus is the **future continuous** and expressing **necessity and ability** and ways of **building up a business** and **business collocations.**

SPEAKING

Aim
To lead in to the topic.

Step 1 Tell students to read the questions in exercise A. Put them into groups to discuss. Conduct brief feedback.

VOCABULARY
Reasons for phoning

Aim
To practise expressions related to reasons for phoning.

Step 1 Ask students to look at the sentences in exercise A. Tell them in telephone English we have fixed phrases to say what we want. Tell them to notice *I'm (just) phoning / calling to* + reason.

Step 2 Tell students to match the sentence starters in 1–5 to the endings in a-e and the starters in 6–10 to the endings in f–j. Students check answers in pairs, then as a class.

> **Answers**
> 1 a   3 e   5 b   7 i   9 f
> 2 c   4 d   6 g   8 j   10 h

Step 3 Tell students in pairs to discuss who they think is calling whom in each of the sentences in exercise A and why they made each call. Conduct brief feedback.

Step 4 Tell students in the same pairs to think of one other possible ending for each of the sentence starters in exercise A. Check possible answers in open class.

> **Suggested answers**
> 1 *I'm phoning to chase up* an order I placed last month.
> 2 *I'm just phoning to remind you* that the meeting has been moved to tomorrow.
> 3 *I'm phoning to try to arrange* an appointment.
> 4 *I'm just phoning to pass on* my account details.
> 5 *I'm just phoning to check* the availability of an item.

6 *I'm just calling to let you know* that your order has arrived.
7 *I'm just calling to enquire* about any job vacancies.
8 *I'm just calling to confirm* that Mr. Jackson will be attending the meeting.
9 *I'm just calling to apologise for* the delay in sending out your order.
10 *I'm just calling to see* whether you received my email.

LISTENING

Aim
To develop listening for specific information.

Step 1 Tell students they are going to hear two business-related conversations and to listen to the first conversation and answer the questions in A. Play the recording and get students to compare answers in pairs then as a class.

> **Answers**
> 1 to arrange a good time for a video conference
> 2 to have the meeting next week
> 3 if he could wait until the week after that, she'll be visiting Spain for the trade fair so she could fit in a day with him then
> 4 they pencil in Tuesday the 24th anytime after 10, but they will confirm details by email

> 🔊 **16.1**
> **Conversation 1**
> **I = Ian, C = Claudia**
> C: Hello. Claudia Hellmann speaking.
> I: Oh, hi, Claudia. This is Ian calling, from Madrid.
> C: Oh hi, Ian. How're things?
> I: Pretty good, thanks. A bit hectic – as usual for this time of the year – but, you know, hectic is good. Anyway, listen, I'm just calling, really, to try to arrange a good time for a video conference. I think we need to talk through the sales strategy ahead of the coming season and it'd be good if the two of us could get together with Piotr in Warsaw and Eudora in Greece to throw some ideas around.

C: Yeah, that sounds good. When were you thinking of?
I: Well, to be honest, the sooner, the better. Would next week work for you?
C: It's possible, yeah, but is there any way you could wait until the week after that? I'll be visiting Spain for the trade fair so I could fit in a day with you then.
I: Oh, that'd be perfect, yeah. Face-to-face is always better. What day would work best for you?
C: The Tuesday would be good for me. That's the 24th.
I: OK, great. I can make any time after 10.
C: Brilliant. We can confirm the details by email.
I: OK. I'll pencil it in and I'll see you then.

Step 2 Tell students to listen to the second conversation and complete the note. Play the recording and get students to compare answers in pairs before checking as a class.

Answers
Order no = EIA-290–3969; date placed = the 29th of August; client's name = Fabio Baldassari; e-mail address = baldassari underscore (_) f at (@) meccanica dot (.) com (baldassari_f@meccanica.com); action = the agent has just put the order through and it'll be going out today by special delivery so it should be with him first thing tomorrow, at no extra charge.

♫ 16.2
Conversation 2
C: **Hello, customer services.**
F: Hi. I wonder if you can help me. I'm phoning to chase up an order I placed with your company some time ago – and that I still haven't received.
C: I'm sorry to hear that. Let's see what we can do. Would you happen to have the order number there?
F: Yeah, I do. It's EIA-290-3969.
C: Right. I'm just checking that now and I can't actually see any record of the transaction. When was the order placed?
F: The 29th of August, so that's over a month ago now. It should be under my name – Fabio Baldassari.
C: Ah, OK. I've got it now. I'm afraid there must've been some kind of mix-up in the system because it doesn't appear to have been sent out yet. I do apologise. I'll get that off to you ASAP.
F: OK. Well, at least that explains that, then!
C: Again I'm really sorry about that again, Mr. Baldassari.
F: It's OK. These things happen.
C: Thanks for being so understanding. I've just put that through and it'll be going out today by special delivery so it should be with you first thing tomorrow. That's at no extra charge, of course.

F: Great. Thanks. Would you mind just emailing me confirmation of that?
C: No, of course not. Can I just take your email address?
F: Sure. It's Baldassari – that's B-A-L-D-A-Double S-A-R-I underscore f at meccanica dot com. That's meccanica with a double c.
C: Got it. OK. I'll send that through in a minute.

DEVELOPING CONVERSATIONS
Using *would* to be polite

Aim
To introduce and practise using *would* to be polite.

Step 1 Get students to read the explanation box and notice the pattern: *would* + infinitive without *to*, e.g. *would be*.

Step 2 Get students to look at the audioscript for 16.1 and 16.2 on pp. 181–182 and find two more examples in each conversation where *would* is used to be polite. Students compare answers in pairs before checking in open class.

Answers
conversation 1 = Would next week work for you? Oh, that'd be perfect, What day would work best for you? The Tuesday would be good for me
conversation 2 = Would you happen to have the order number there? Would you mind just emailing me confirmation of that?

Step 3 Tell students to rewrite the sentences in exercise B using *would* and the words in brackets. In pairs they compare answers before checking in open class.

Answers
1 Would Friday be good for you at all?
2 Would you be able to make the 29th at all?
3 Would you happen to have the address there?
4 Would you mind just spelling the street name?
5 I was wondering if you would like to come with us?
6 Would it be possible for you to email me over the details?
7 Any day next week would suit me
8 If you don't mind, I'd rather not.

Step 4 Tell students to arrange a time and a place for a meeting and that they should reject at least two suggestions. They should use polite expressions including *would*. Tell them that when we reject we usually give a reason and start with *but*. Give them time to think of some suggestions. In small groups of four or five tell them to accept or reject the suggestions. Conduct brief feedback.

PRONUNCIATION
Email addresses and websites

Aim
To give practice in saying email addresses and websites.

Step 1 Tell students to read the symbols in exercise A and in pairs decide how to say them. Play the recording to check.

Note We normally say *full stop* but when talking about email addresses and websites we use *dot*.

> 🔊 **16.3**
> 1 at   3 underscore   5 dash
> 2 forward slash 4 dot

Step 2 Tell students they are going to hear some email addresses and websites, and they should write them down. Play the recording. In pairs they compare answers before checking in open class – ask students to tell you the answers and you write them on the board.

> 🔊 **16.4**
> 1 postmaster at claes geller brink – that's c-l-a-e-s-g-e-double l-e-r-br-i-n-k dot com
> 2 www dot study tefl – that's t-e-f-l, dot co dot u-k
> 3 zip dot oh nine eight dot k-d at mail dot r-u
> 4 do or die, that's all one word, underscore ninety-nine at sez-nam –that's s-e-z-n-am dot c-z
> 5 u-c-y-l-j-e-double-h – that's double the word and then h – not double h – at u-c-l dot a-c dot u-k
> 6 h-t-t-p colon and then two forward slashes, w-w-w dot xoomer [pron: ksuma] – that's x-double o-m-e-r dot alice forward slash sweet floral albion – that's all one word – forward slash capital s capital f capital a dot h-t-m

Step 3 Tell students they are going to swap email addresses (if they don't feel comfortable doing this you could tell them to invent one) and to think of five websites they use and would like to recommend. When they are ready put them into groups of four or five to swap email addresses and recommend their five websites. Tell them to explain why. Conduct brief feedback.

GRAMMAR The future continuous

Aim
To present and practise the future continuous.

Step 1 Tell students to read the explanation box and check understanding of future continuous: *Did they arrange to visit Spain?* (Yes.) When will they be visiting Spain? (In the future.) Does it have a consequence on the meeting? (Yes.) How do we form it? (*will be / going to be* + a verb in the *-ing* form.)

Step 2 Tell students to complete the sentences by adding the verbs from the box in the future continuous form. In pairs

students compare answers before checking in open class. Direct students to the grammar reference on page 155 if they still seem unsure.

> **Answers**
> 1 I'll be taking / I'm going to be talking
> 2 I'll be working / I'm going to be working
> 3 We'll be taking on/ We're going to be taking on
> 4 I'll be talking / I'm going to be talking
> 5 We'll be opening / We're going to be opening
> 6 will be going out / is going to go out

Step 3 Tell students to read the endings in exercise B and match them to the sentences in 1–6. In pairs students compare answers before checking in open class.

> **Answers**
> 1 a   2 c   3 f   4 b   5 d   6 e

CONVERSATION PRACTICE

Aim
To practise making business phone calls.

Step 1 Tell students they are going to role-play four business-related conversations. In pairs they choose four of the sentences from *Vocabulary* exercise A and use these to begin each conversation.

Step 2 Tell them to decide which roles each of them will take in each of the four conversations then to role-play the conversations. Monitor for a correction slot at the end.

 pp. 112–113

VOCABULARY Building up a business

Aim
To practise expressions related to building up a business.

Step 1 Tell students to complete the story with the words in the vocabulary box. Check answers.

> **Answers**
> 1 set up   5 profit   9 bid
> 2 raised   6 ploughed   10 turnover
> 3 loss   7 floated
> 4 broke even   8 competition

Step 2 Tell students to discuss the questions in exercise B in pairs. Monitor for a correction slot at the end.

READING

Aim
To develop reading for general and detailed information.

Step 1 Tell students they are going to read a news article about the traits (characteristics) of successful people. Tell students to read the article then to read the statements and to give themselves a score of 1, 2 or 3 for each characteristic.

Step 2 Individually tell students to add up their score (out of 30) and in pairs compare their scores and explain their decisions. Then get them to discuss the questions in B.

Step 3 Tell students to look at the vocabulary box and see if they can remember the nouns that the words were used with in the article. In pairs they compare their answers and read the text again to check. Check as a class.

> **Answers**
> push themselves to the limit; set high standards; have a wide circle of friends; maintain relationships; be on the look-out for new ideas; accept responsibility for your actions; stay one step ahead of the crowd; maintain your cool; act on impulse; seize an opportunity

Step 4 Tell students to read the biography of Jan Telensky and consider the significance of the places / things in the box to his story. In pairs they compare how the places / things in exercise D are connected. Check answers in open class.

> **Answers**
> Proprad = a Slovakian town, home to AquaCity; underground lake = by exploiting the geothermal properties of the lake the resort is able to provide renewable energy for the whole area; Prague = Telensky was born there in 1948; school = his teachers told him he would only ever be good for blue-collar work (manual work for an hourly wage); evening classes = he tried to better himself by taking classes in maths, Russian, physics and biology; England = he moved there in 1969; menial jobs = doing this he improved his linguistic skills and saved enough money to buy a delicatessen; delicatessen = he built the business up and eventually sold it for £200,000; property = he ploughed the profit into this and built up a substantial portfolio; secretarial training institute = took a part-time job and climbed the corporate ladder and became UK sales manager

Step 6 Tell students to read the questions in exercise E and discuss them in pairs. Conduct brief feedback in open class.

Language patterns

Aim
To draw attention to some common patterns using *with*.

Step 1 Draw students' attention the fact that the text shows sentences with *with*. Tell them we use *with* in many different ways in English.

Step 2 In a multilingual class, ask students to translate the sentences into their own language and then without looking at the originals, translate back into English. What similarities / differences do they notice? In a monolingual class, tell students in pairs or threes to compare their translations and their English translations. Alternatively, if you prefer not to use translation ask students to notice the pattern and practise writing their own sentences.

Speaking

Aim
To provide fluency practice in talking about successful and wealthy people.

Step 1 Tell students to read the questions in exercise A. Give them a couple of minutes to think of what they want to say and then in small groups they discuss their opinions. Monitor for a correction slot at the end.

 Next class Make photocopies of **16A** p. 158 and **16B** p. 159

pp. 114–115

Speaking

Aim
To provide fluency practice of expressing opinions.

Step 1 Tell students to read the short extract from a magazine guide. Then to read and discuss the questions in pairs. Conduct brief feedback.

 16A see Teacher's notes p. 127.

Listening

Aim
To develop listening for general and specific information.

Step 1 Tell students they are going to hear a radio report about a reality TV programme in Afghanistan. Tell them to listen to the programme and answer the questions in D. Play the recording and then get students to compare in pairs before checking in open class. If necessary, play the recording again before checking.

> **Answers**
> 1 *Fikr wa Talsh* = Dream and achieve and is loosely based on business programmes such as Dragon's Den.
> 2 It is not only about education and development but also entertainment, TV has greater significance there because of the economic situation and the complex and changing nature of the society.
> 3 There are just two cash prizes and the proposed businesses also directly reflect the rather different needs of the Afghan economy.

⚡16.5
P = Presenter, KT = Kevin Thomas
P: *Dragon's Den* is soon to enter a new series with would-be entrepreneurs trying to **raise money** by pitching their ideas to five self-made millionaires who provide capital and business expertise **in return for** a stake in their companies. The show, which originates from a Japanese programme called *The Money Tigers*, has become an enormous success, with many other countries adopting similar formats. One of those countries, which may surprise some people, is Afghanistan. Kevin Thomas reports.

KT: In a country which has been devastated by war and where the average income is just $1,000 a year, starting up a company is a risky business. Yet if Afghanistan, which still **heavily depends on** foreign aid, is ever going to sustain itself, then it's a risk more investors are going to have to take, according to Damien Evans, a development economist:

'Small and **medium-sized businesses** are easily the biggest employers and if employment there is going to rise as it needs to, then it's these kinds of businesses which will have to be encouraged, developed and expanded. The problem at the moment is not just instability, but **a lack of skills** such as financial planning and marketing strategies among business people. These are still relatively new concepts for many people here.'

Which is where *Fikr wa Talash* comes in. 'Dream and Achieve', as the programme is translated in English, is loosely based on business programmes such as *Dragon's Den*. The show aims to provide just that sort of basic business education as struggling entrepreneurs present their businesses and plans for expansion, which then come **under scrutiny** from local experts. Unlike the British version though, there are just two cash prizes and the proposed businesses also **directly reflect** the rather different needs of the Afghan economy. Investors in Britain have backed things such as software that allows you to create a personalised doll with the face of your choice, a men's style magazine aimed at the super-rich, and a website that searches the Internet and alerts users to special offers for online gambling. In contrast, the Afghan programme included proposals to **set up a dairy** and a jam-making factory.

The winner was Faisulhaq Moshkani, a father of nine who had been running a plastic recycling plant in Kandahar until high **fuel costs** ultimately forced him to close down. The first prize of $20,000 has enabled him to build a mini-hydroelectric plant to power a new factory. The benefit for the country is that it'll soon be able to produce its own plastic rather than having to import it all from abroad.

But *Dream and Achieve* is not simply about education and development, it's also entertainment. It is one of numerous reality TV shows which have found success in the country, including the **hugely popular** singing contest *Afghan Star*. TV producer Farzad Amini:

'**Reality TV** is popular all round the world because it's **overwhelmingly positive**. It gives ordinary people a chance to succeed and this brings hope to the viewers. Afghans are no different, but perhaps TV has **greater significance** here because of our economic situation and the complex and changing nature of our society.'

Second place in *Dream and Achieve* went to a 25-year-old mother of five. Just ten years ago, as a woman, she wouldn't have been able to work, let alone run a business. Another character featured was an ex-warlord who had rejected violence in favour of milk production. Not the kind of background you'd find people having on the British programme and sure signs of a complex and changing society.

P: That was Kevin Thomas reporting.

Step 2 Tell students to read the statements in exercise B and decide if they are true or false. Play the recording. Students compare in pairs before checking in open class.

Answers
1 F   2 T   3 F   4 T   5 F   6 T   7 F   8 T

Optional activity For additional practise tell students to correct the false statements in B.

Answers
1 The show was originates from a Japanese programme called *The Money Tigers*.
3 Small and medium-sized businesses are easily the biggest employers.
5 He has built a mini-hydroelectric plant.
7 It is one of numerous reality TV shows.

Step 3 Tell students to discuss the questions in exercise D in groups. Conduct brief feedback.

Step 4 Tell students to read the explanation box and elicit examples of collocations so far in the unit, e.g. *set up, act on impulse*. Tell them to record new expressions with the full collocation, this will help them use them correctly in the future.

Step 5 Tell students to look at the audioscript 16.4 on page 182 and to match the collocations in bold to the combinations in exercise E. Tell them to find one more example of each kind of collocation. In pairs they compare before checking in open class.

Answers
(Note: extra examples in brackets)
1 greater significance (enormous success)
2 raise money (pitching ideas)
3 directly reflect (heavily depends)
4 overwhelmingly positive (hugely popular)
5 fuel costs (cash prizes)

6 a lack of skills (the kind of background)
7 set up a dairy
8 under scrutiny (all around the world)

NATIVE SPEAKER ENGLISH *let alone*

Ask students to read the box and check they understand: sentence 2 = *Does the person think it was impossible for the person to run?* (Yes.) *Why?* (It was already difficult for the person to walk.) Ask them to think of other examples.

GRAMMAR

Expressing necessity and ability

Aim
To practise ways of expressing necessity and ability.

Step 1 Tell students to read the explanation box and check understanding: e.g. *It's a risk more investors are going to have to take.* Ask students why *must* is not possible. (Because it is in the future so we use *are going to.*) *It'll soon be able to produce its own plastic.* Why is *can* not possible? (Because it is in the future so we use *It'll soon.*) When do we use *enable / allow / let somebody do something?* (To show something makes another thing possible.) *When do we use* force / make someone to do something? (To show something is an obligation.)

Step 2 Tell students to read the sentences in exercise A and to replace the incorrect uses in *italics*.

Answers
1 The device allows you to share files without you having to rely on a computer.
2 If the loan is approved, it will enable us to / allow us to / let us buy more stock and take advantage of the interest we've generated.
3 The negative feedback that we got forced us to / made us look at the design again.
4 This deal means I'll finally be able to give up my day job and focus entirely on the business.
5 We have been able to keep ahead of our competitors over the last few years by developing new products.
6 We were forced to cut costs to allow us to compete.
7 Thanks to all the effort everyone put in, in the end we will be able to fulfil all our orders before Christmas. Well done!
8 If we'd done more market research before launching the first model, we would not have been forced to redesign it so soon.

Direct students to the grammar reference on page 155 if they still seem unsure.

Step 3 Tell students to look at the sentences in exercise B and to think of things related to the ideas. In pairs they discuss. Conduct brief feedback.

VOCABULARY Business collocations

Aim
To introduce and practise collocations in business.

Step 1 Ask students to read the vocabulary box. Tell them to decide which word from the box completes each set of collocations in exercise A. In pairs they compare answers before checking in open class.

Answers			
1 market	3 order	5 product	7 business
2 stock	4 sales	6 area	8 company

Step 2 Tell students to underline any collocations that are new for them. In pairs they compare and discuss.

Step 3 Tell students in the same pairs to discuss which of the collocations in exercise A they think have already been mentioned in this unit. Check answers in open class.

Answers
chase up an order = *Vocabulary* Reasons for phoning, p.110, set up our own company = *Vocabulary* Building a business on page 112, for the following area = *Reading* text on page 113 paragraph 1, built up the business = *Reading* text on page 113 paragraph 3, Market research, fulfil all our orders, developing new products = *Grammar* exercise A on page 115.

Note Sales manager = *Reading* text, page 113 and sales figure *Grammar* The future continuous, page 111 are the only collocations used in the unit so far for *sales*.

SPEAKING

Aim
To provide fluency practice in persuasion.

Step 1 Put students into groups of four and in each group form two pairs: A and B. Tell pair A to look at the list of products and services in File 13 on page 159 and pair B to look at File 18 on page 161. Tell them they are going to try and persuade the other pair to invest in their products. With their partner they should spend five minutes discussing what they are going to say.

Step 2 Tell them to take turns to pitch (to sell something by saying how good it is) to the other pair and see how many deals they can make. Finish with a correction slot.

 16B see Teacher's notes p. 127.

LEARNER TRAINING

Aim
To raise students' awareness in developing their listening skills.

Step 1 Tell students to read the text about listening skills and in groups to discuss how true they think it is and give examples from their own experience. Monitor and help out with any ideas. Conduct brief feedback at the end in open class.

Step 2 Tell students individually to read the ways of improving their ability to hear / listen in exercise B and to give each one a mark out of five: 1 = not very good and 5 = great. Give them a couple of minutes to do this. Then put students into groups to discuss their decisions and say why. Conduct brief feedback in open class on which were the best ways of improving their listening ability.

GAME, CONVERSATION PRACTICE, ACT OR DRAW & QUIZ

For aims and suggested procedure, see Review 01, pp. 32–35.

Answers
1 **drop out** = you stop going to school or university before the end of the course; **kick out** = you are forced to leave somewhere because your behaviour was bad.
2 Someone might give you a **bribe** if they want you to do something which is illegal.
3 If a child is **affectionate** they might hug you, kiss you or say they love you a lot.
4 You get **ashes** when someone has been cremated, you might scatter them in a favourite place or keep them in a special place.
5 You would find a **ward** in a hospital, e.g. a maternity ward, a psychiatric ward, a geriatric ward.
6 If you go into **overdraft**, your spend more money than is in your bank account.
7 Drug dealers might **launder** money to hide the fact that the money was made illegally or to avoid paying taxes.
8 **The odds** are low.
9 People can be **driven** by ambition, greed, desire, etc.
10 You **remove** the peel, skin or bones before eating.
11 You would **make a scene** or a **fuss** if you get angry or upset in a public place and attract attention to yourself or the situation.
12 An investigation, fight or scandal can be **full-blown**.
13 You might **stockpile** food because there is a shortage.
14 You would **chase up** a payment if your cash-flow was bad, or it was overdue.
15 **Turnover** = the value of goods or services a company has sold; **profit** = the amount of money a company makes after the costs have been subtracted from the turnover.

COLLOCATIONS

For aims and suggested procedure, see Review 01, pp. 32–35.

PRONUNCIATION

The same or different?

Aim
To revise and practise differences in vowel sounds.

Step 1 Tell students to work in pairs and decide if the underlined sounds in each pairs of words in exercise A are pronounced in the same way or differently.

Step 2 Play the recording R4.1 and tell students to check their answers. Then play the recording again and tell them to practise saying the words.

Answers

1 same	6 same	11 same	16 same
2 different	7 different	12 same	17 different
3 same	8 same	13 different	18 same
4 same	9 different	14 same	
5 same	10 same	15 same	

DICTATION

For aims and suggested procedure, see Review 01, pp.32–35.

♪ R4.2
Italy has also passed a law which establishes the official ingredients, method, shape and size of pizza. The dough, which has to use natural yeast, must be worked and shaped with the hands and then baked on the floor of a wood-fired oven.

 pp. 118–119

LISTENING

Aim

For aims and suggested procedure for the rest o the Review, see Review 01 pp. 32–35. The audio is 🎵 R4.3.

Exercise A answers				
1 f	2 a	3 b	4 d	5 c
Exercise B answers				
1 e	2 f	3 d	4 b	5 a

GRAMMAR

Exercise A answers

1 ...... is still being serviced.
2 ...... is going to be built
3 ...... wish he wouldn't / didn't smoke ......
4 ...... urged us to go.
5 ...... I hadn't got married ......
6 ...... confessed to having taken the ......
7 ...... enabled us to expand
8 Despite having followed / following the recipe carefully ......
9 During dinner they had ......
10 ...... having to work ......

Exercise B answers

1 correct
2 ...... wish I spoke English ......
3 ...... turnover providing there's ......
4 ...... it hadn't been signed
5 ...... Grace reminded me ......
6 My salary is paid ......
7 ...... made me eat my ......
8 correct

Direct students to the grammar reference on page 155 if they find this difficult.

LANGUAGE PATTERNS

Answers	
1 With	5 the
2 until / till	6 being
3 does	7 regular
4 well	8 throughout

PREPOSITIONS

Answers				
1 against	3 on	5 on	7 in	9 to
2 with	4 for	6 with	8 of	10 on

FORMING WORDS

Answers	
1 lengthy	6 authorise
2 defensive	7 addictive
3 publicity	8 corruption
4 negotiations	9 disruption
5 strengthen	10 irrational

PHRASAL VERBS

Answers	
1 flicked throgh	5 move on
2 knocked out	6 put off
3 fell out	7 taken over
4 write off	8 pass on

COLLOCATIONS

Answers
1 company
2 ground
3 cash
4 grave
5 boundary
   (Note: check spelling of plurals = boundaries)
6 voice
7 transaction
8 leave

VOCABULARY

Answers	
1 profit	5 launch
2 gap	6 aimed
3 rejected	7 turnover
4 mortgage	8 stake

AN INTRODUCTION TO WRITING IN *OUTCOMES*

In this section we will look at two broad reasons for writing in a foreign language: to practise and play, and for the real world. We explain what we mean by them and how they may differ in teaching, tasks and feedback.

Practice and play The first reason for writing in a foreign language is simply to practise new language, experiment and learn more English. Writing may have significant benefits for students learning English. In contrast to speaking, students have time to plan what they want to say; they can look words up in a dictionary, they can check and re-write grammar and they may be more able to notice how English works. That might then give benefits in terms of their overall competence in English.

Writing for the purpose of practice and play does not depend on any particular genre or standard organisation in writing; it could be short sentences, paragraphs, dialogues, etc.; it could be about anything the student wants or it could be on a theme the teacher chooses; it could be random connections of sentences – true or imagined. Some grammar and vocabulary tasks in the Student's book are of this nature, with students having to complete sentences using their own ideas. Below are some more tasks. The ideas focus on revising language, but it doesn't have to be so. Here are some ideas your students could try:

- Write a diary about your day, trying to include new words or structures that you've learnt.
- Write five to ten lines of English every day about anything you like.
- Write every day / week about a story in the news you saw or read about.
- Write a poem or story using a new word you've learnt.
- Write a conversation based on one you had with someone during the class.
- Write an imagined conversation with someone you know based on a topic you've studied.
- Write an imagined conversation that takes place in a particular place.

As these kinds of writing tasks are unconnected to any particular genre, they require no 'teaching' or preparation, and can be set at any time. In terms of feedback, you may want to simply write a personal response to what the student wrote such as, *This really made me laugh* or *That's interesting*. Alternatively, you could engage in a dialogue with the student by asking them genuine questions, which they answer in writing. You may want to correct aspects of the key structure or words that they practised, or use common errors from different students as a way to re-teach language in class. However, we feel correction should be kept to a minimum

with these kinds of texts. The aim is not assessment, it is to encourage students, to engage with them and get them to play with language.

For the real world The second broad reason for writing is that students need to write a specific kind of text for an assessment or for a 'real life' task such as sending an email. These texts are generic in some way. They often have specific vocabulary (including large chunks or expressions) or grammar connected with them. They also have rules about the way they are presented, how they are paragraphed and ordered and other aspects of discourse. The problem for foreign learners of English is that these rules of discourse might be different in their languages. Unlike speaking, where listeners might accept errors because they can see other things to help interpret the message, with writing a reader may misunderstand a message or even be offended when the rules or conventions of a genre are broken. For this reason, students need careful preparation for writing such texts, and feedback should be more thorough.

The writing units in the Student's book aim to provide this careful preparation. They are based on genres commonly tested in international exams such as PET, FCE and IELTS, or on functional writing tasks we may perform at work or when studying in an English-speaking context.

WHAT'S IN *OUTCOMES* WRITING UNITS?

Each double-page spread teaches a different style of writing. You can follow them in any order or do them after every two units in the main Student's book. The units contain:

Speaking The units aim to be interactive. Speaking activities provide a warmer, relate to the topic, discuss the text types or may be part of planning for writing.

Writing The writing sections present model texts. While there may be some basic comprehension questions around these, the main focus is noticing useful language for the genre and how the texts are organised.

Key words This section focuses on words / expressions which link sentences and clauses and give texts coherence. They follow a similar pattern to grammar exercises, with a short explanation or guided questions and a controlled practice.

Vocabulary and grammar There are often short grammar or vocabulary sections if there is a close relation to the text type. Note there's *no* link to the grammar reference or *Vocabulary builder*.

Practice This is a task for students to write a similar kind of text to the one they looked at in **Writing** and try to incorporate some of the other language they have learnt in the unit. This section can be set as homework or be done in class. Doing the practice in class can be interactive, particularly if using a 'process writing' approach.

Process writing
Process writing approaches focus on the fact that good writers often go through several stages to produce a good piece of writing. They may:

- brainstorm ideas
- write a plan
- write a draft
- discuss their draft with someone
- write a second draft
- put it through a spell-checker
- have corrections made by someone
- write the final draft

Obviously, we don't always go through these stages when we write, but in the case of our students, having different stages and allowing for more than one draft gives more opportunity for teaching and learning. In fact, brainstorming and planning stages are often included in **Practice** or at some other stage of the lesson. However, there is no reason why any of the stages above shouldn't be done in pairs in class. Another way you might want to incorporate a process approach is to give the **Practice** task for homework *before* they do the actual writing lesson. They then re-write their work in light of what they learn.

Marking and feedback
There are a number of options available to teachers to mark and give feedback on students' writing.

Using symbols You can mark essays using symbols above the inappropriate word or grammar. Here are some examples:

- t = wrong tense
- wf = wrong word form (e.g. noun not adjective)
- col = wrong collocation (e.g. the noun is the right meaning but doesn't go with the verb)
- voc = you have the wrong word (it makes no sense here)
- prep = you need a different preposition
- pl = plural is wrong or should be plural
- sp = wrong spelling
- wo = the word order is wrong
- art = the article is wrong or absent

The idea of doing this is to make students notice their errors and try to find answers. You could do this as a pair activity in class. It may help them to become more aware of their common errors and edit their own work more carefully. The difficulty is that mistakes don't fit neatly into categories and students may still get the language wrong. You should mark the text again.

Re-formulation You may simply want to cross out and re-write things that are 'wrong' in the text. This may have the

advantage of teaching students the correct language (though note they may still be unclear *why* it was wrong). It may also be time-consuming for you and demoralising for students if they see lots of crossing out.

In this case – and indeed with all cases of teacher feedback – you need to strike a balance. At Upper-Intermediate, you will expect a reasonable degree of accuracy. Students should also be able to deal with a variety of text types, employing informal and formal registers. Students should also be able to structure their writing and use language appropriate to their readers.

Content and structure When you mark the texts you could ignore 'grammar' and individual vocabulary mistakes and focus only on whether the writing answers the question and is organised well. You simply write comments on the writing or at the end. This is often quicker for you, the teacher.

Marking this way trains students to appreciate the importance of these aspects of writing over basic 'accuracy'. Readers in fact will often ignore mistakes if the overall structure of the text is clear and the content is relevant, logical and / or interesting.

However, students will want to know if their writing is correct unless you clearly warn them beforehand that you'll only deal with content and structure.

Peer correction Students can also give feedback. Get them to read each other's writing and evaluate the texts and / or suggest changes. To do this they really need a 'mark scheme', this could be a list of statements they tick or adapt such as:

- *I enjoyed this.*
- *I wanted to know more about...*
- *I didn't understand the bit about... .*
- *You used some words / grammar I didn't know how to use.*

Another way is to give them marking criteria from an established source such as the FCE exam. Check they're not too difficult for your students.

The advantage of peer correction is that it's interactive and based on genuine readers' responses. It's also easy on the teacher! However, it is not so good for dealing with language, apart from general statements, as students may not trust each other's judgement – often with good reason! However, it is a useful stage and may save you time by reducing mistakes or inconsistencies before you come to mark the texts.

WRITING AND PORTFOLIOS

Whichever way you choose to correct the students' texts, we suggest you get students to re-write them. This would guarantee that the students focus on their errors and produce an improved text which they could then keep in a portfolio. Portfolios of work are recommended by the CEF and can provide evidence of students' progress and level.

UNIT AIMS

There are eight writing units in total. The aims of these units are to give additional writing practice and to introduce students to the kinds of texts they might need, or want to write in real life. They focus on developing fluent, coherent writing. It is suggested that you use these units towards the end of every two units of the *Student's book* as extra material, especially when you feel your students would benefit from the change of focus that writing activities provide. It is also recommended that you follow the steps suggested in the *Student's book*, although of course other variations are possible. You could either set the final writing task (*Practice*) in class and get students to mark / correct each other's work, or you could set it as a test or for homework.

01 GIVING ADVICE

GRAMMAR Advice and recommendations

Tip

Make sure students know the form after each expression = *I'd go / You should / You could* + infinitive without *to* and *You're best / You're better off* + verb-*ing*.

WRITING

Exercise B answers

Paragraph 1 As far as places to see are concerned, ...
Paragraph 2 If you want to escape the crowds, ...
Paragraph 3 While you're here, ...
Paragraph 4 Apart from the festival, ...
Paragraph 5 In terms of eating out, ...
Paragraph 6 Anyway, if there is anything else ......

KEY WORDS FOR WRITING *otherwise, other than, apart from*

Answers

1 Otherwise	5 both correct: Apart from /
2 apart than that	Other than
3 Other than	6 otherwise
4 Otherwise	7 Other than that

02 LETTERS OF COMPLAINT

WRITING

Exercise B answers

1 Regarding	6 matters
2 fact	7 did
3 as	8 further
4 to	9 regarding
5 was	10 charge

Exercise C suggested answers

I am writing to complain, it was not exactly as advertised, According to ......, I rang to complain ......, The main advert is misleading ......, To make matters worse ......, As compensation for ......, I feel I should ......

KEY WORDS FOR WRITING

According to

Exercise A answers

1 according to the forecast
2 According to the opposition
3 According to the flyer
4 According to your brochure
5 according to my brother
6 According to consumer laws

GRAMMAR Passives and reporting

Exercise A answers
1 I was informed that delivery would take two weeks
2 I was told that I should have looked more carefully and was then directed to the details on the website.
3 I was told I would still have to write if I wanted to take the matter further.

Exercise B answers
2 was promised a
3 was stated on
4 was told to
5 was only offered
6 was asked to arrive
7 was advertised as

03 A LEAFLET / POSTER

WRITING A leaflet / poster

Exercise A answers
1 d   2 f   3 b   4 e   5 a   6 c

VOCABULARY

Intensifying adjectives and adverbs

Exercise A answers
1 b   3 a   5 g   7 h
2 d   4 c   6 f   8 e

KEY WORDS FOR WRITING

whenever, wherever, however, etc.

Exercise A answers
1 whenever
2 However
3 whatever
4 Wherever
5 Whoever
6 however
7 Whatever
8 Whoever, whatever

Tip
Make sure students know when to use the key words (*whenever* with time, *whoever* with people, *however* with the way we do something and *whatever* with objects or things).

GRAMMAR Ellipsis

Exercise A answers
Are you feeling out of shape?
You can always rest and *you can always* chat.
I've gone to lunch, *I'll be* back at 2*pm*.

Exercise B answers
1 Planning to work abroad? This is your chance.
2 Worried about speaking in public? Get nervous in front of an audience or forget your words? Our course could help.
3 Never been to a gym before? We'll show you how the gym machines work and give you support while you're training.
4 Having a great time, wish you were here. Hope everything if fine with you. Karen.
5 Sara can't come this evening, but she'll be at the meeting tomorrow.
6 Had to go out, be back 8. Dinner in the oven. Love you.

04 STORIES

VOCABULARY

Describing disasters

Exercise A answers
1 an earthquake
2 a flood
3 a forest fire
4 a tsunami
5 a volcano erupting
6 a tornado

WRITING A travel blog story

Exercise A answers
1 On the island of Java, near Mount Semeru.
2 They were climbing the volcano when there was a minor earthquake and then the volcano erupted.
3 He felt scared / it was scary
4 They were relaxed about everything, They've seen it all before.

Exercise B answers
1 breeze   3 delayed   5 slopes   7 blocked
2 journey   4 active   6 minor   8 cleared

KEY WORDS FOR WRITING

like , unlike

Exercise A answers
1 b   2 c   3 a   4 g   5 h   6 f   7 e   8 d

05 PERSONAL STATEMENTS

WRITING

Exercise A suggested answers
Other areas he could include = future plans, extra skills
relevant to the course, e.g. computer skills, language ability.
The best order = 1 reasons for doing the course,
2 education and qualifications, 3 extra skills,
4 experience, 5 personal qualities, 6 future plans.

Exercise B answers
1 competitive edge   4 transferable skills
2 invaluable insight   5 valuable contribution
3 solid grounding   6 active interest

VOCABULARY Describing yourself

Exercise A answers
1 a   2 d   3 b   4 e   5 c

Exercise B answers
6 j   7 f   8 g   9 i   10 h

KEY WORDS FOR WRITING

Adding information

Exercise A answers
1 In addition   4 What's more
2 both correct   5 both correct, also
3 both correct   6 In addition to this, also

06 REPORTS

WRITING

Exercise B answers
1 minority   5 mentioned   9 rated
2 respondents   6 favourably   10 factor
3 majority   7 vast   11 widely
4 Examples   8 interviewed   12 long

GRAMMAR be to

Exercise A answers
1 If the government is to win the next election, they
   need to / must change their policies now.

2 We need to / must / have to improve our marketing,
   if we are to boost sales.
3 If we are to reduce crime, we need to /must / have to
   increase the number of police.
4 The company needs to reduce its debts if it doesn't
   want to go bankrupt.
5 The council needs to build more cycle lanes if it wants
   to encourage more people to cycle to work.
6 If we are to discourage waste, the government must
   / has to introduce a tax on the amount of rubbish
   people throw away.

KEY WORDS FOR WRITING

while, despite, however, even though

Exercise A answers
1 However
2 while, even though, despite
3 while, even though
4 despite
5 while, even though = after the first clause,
   despite = before,
   however = after

Exercise B answers
1 While / Even though
2 even though
3 However / Despite this
4 despite

07 ARGUING YOUR CASE

GRAMMAR Articles

Exercise A answers
1 *Zoos* protect endangered animals.
2 correct
3 I saw a TV programme the other day about the zoo in
   Singapore and it sounds like *an amazing place*.
4 The zoo in my town is home to *a very rare kind* of
   panda. That's the main attraction.
5 The fact that fewer and fewer people are visiting zoos
   these days does pose *a big problem*.
6 *Without funding*, what will happen to all the animals
   housed in such institutions?
7 correct

WRITING

Exercise A answers
1 The writer agrees with the idea of zoos (paragraphs 1, 2, 3 & 4 all make a strong case for zoos, especially in helping endangered species).

Exercise B answers

1	a	3	an	5	nothing	7	the	9	the
2	nothing	4	the	6	nothing	8	the / a	10	the

KEY WORDS FOR WRITING Indicating and dismissing weak arguments

Exercise A answers
1 *They are seen as* being a kind of prison for animals ......
2 *should supposedly be* left in the wild to roam ......
3 *It is also believed that* zoos somehow legitimize ......

Exercise B answers

1	sometimes	3	believed	5	seen
2	supposedly	4	claimed	6	common

08 FORMAL AND INFORMAL EMAILS

WRITING

Exercise A answers
1 It is formal writing and she doesn't know the person she is writing to
2 Mandarin Chinese
3 She has studied it before, but only at beginner level
4 what courses they are offering between January and June next year; the prices; what kind of excursions and cultural activities the centre offers; is it possible to invite friends along on the excursions; if they can forward any information about accommodation in the Manchester area
5 formal ending, she doesn't know the person

VOCABULARY
Formal and informal language

Exercise A answers
enquire = ask
currently = at the moment
would be looking to = want to
previously = before
I would be most grateful = it'd be great
Furthermore = on top of that
excursions = trips
I wonder if it would be possible for you to forward me = can you send me look forward to hearing = hope to hear

Exercise B answers
1 Thank you, matter
2 We are looking to, vacancies
3 We regret, to inform
4 Should you require, further
5 trust, prove, an inconvenience
6 I wonder if it would be possible for you, most recent
7 In the event of any delay, contact you, as soon as possible
8 dissatisfied, purchase, we would, provide
9 believe, a number, rectified
10 appreciate, ascertain, receive

Exercise C answers

1	I hope	7	pain
2	trips	8	chance
3	send	9	let
4	asked	10	find
5	top	11	sort
6	great	12	cheers

TEACHER'S NOTES

1A Who wants graffiti!

Aim
To practice using polite language of disagreement.

Before class
Make enough copies so you can divide the roles up evenly into groups of four. Use role cards 1, 2 and 4 with a smaller group.

In class
A Begin by asking students what they think about graffiti and if there is any in their neighbourhood.
B Put students in groups of four. Give out the role cards and ask each student to read their role silently. Check they understand.
C Tell each student with role card 1 to begin by telling the others what they think. Monitor and encourage students to use structures developing conversation and polite disagreement. e.g. *Graffiti is not really my kind of thing, but I don't think it's that bad! In fact, I think it makes the building..., I think we should...* etc.
D Keep moving round the groups so you can check they are working within the time limit.
E When students have finished ask them to tell you their decision. Find out how many groups decided the same thing.

1B Guess the word

Aim
To revise adverbs, adjectives and vocabulary.

Before class
Make enough copies of student A for half the class and enough copies of student B for the other half.

In class
A Give students two minutes write down as many adjectives and adverbs as they can from Unit 1 of the Student's book.
B Divide students into As and Bs. Tell them you will give them a piece of paper and they have to match the adjective or adverb to its definition. Hand out the definitions and monitor.
C When they are ready put them in AB pairs and tell them to test each other by reading out the definition. Stress that they cannot give the word to their partners, can give but clues if necessary.

Answers				
Students A				
1 c	2 d	3 e	4 a	5 b

Students B				
1 d	2 e	3 a	4 b	5 c

2A Call my bluff

Aim
To practise non-defining relative clauses.

Before class
Make enough copies so each group of three has one (A or B).

In class
A Introduce the idea of guessing the correct word / definition by doing an example on the board, e.g.
1 *Secateurs, which is a noun, is a place.*
2 *A secateur is a small room used for drying meat.*
3 *Secateurs is a type of garden tool, which looks like scissors and is used for cutting plants.* **(Answer = 3)**
B Put students in groups of three. Explain that they are going to read some other definitions of different words and decide which ones are correct. Give half the class A and half B.
C When they've finished go round to check their answers.
4 If time, get groups A and B to work together. Group A says the word, reads the definitions and group B have to guess the correct definition, then vice versa.

Answers			
Set A:	1 a	2 b	3 c
Set B:	1 b	2 a	3 c

2B Where am I going?

Aim
To practise talking about a future plan.

Before class
Make one copy for each student.

In class
A Introduce the theme by brainstorming any famous carnivals or festivals they know and like.
B Hand out the photocopy and tell students to read the information and pick one holiday they'd like to go on.
C Tell students that they can only go on their holiday if they persuade four others to go with them.
D Give students time to prepare their ideas. Then, tell them to walk around trying to get others to join them.

3A WORD SEARCH

Aim
To further practice language for describing purpose.

Before class
Make one copy for each pair of students.

In class
A Tell students they are going to do a word search.

B Divide the class into pairs. Tell students to first read the definition and guess the word, then find it in the word search.

D To make it more fun, make it a race with a time limit. Tell them one item appears twice and they can find it for extra points.

Answers

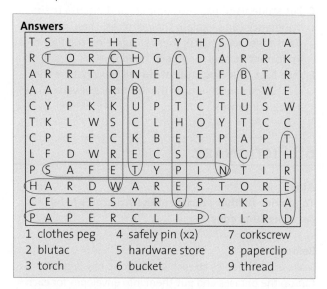

1 clothes peg	4 safely pin (x2)	7 corkscrew
2 blutac	5 hardware store	8 paperclip
3 torch	6 bucket	9 thread

3B I WONDER IF YOU COULD HELP ME?

Aim
To revise indirect questions / polite questions.

Before class
Make one copy for each pair of students.

In class
A Write on the board *Can you help me? I wonder if you could help me*, ask students what the difference in effect is between them.

B Put students in pairs and tell them to match the answers to the questions to complete the conversation. Check their answers quickly.

C Tell them they are going to practise this indirect language in some mini role-plays in a shop.
Hand out A and B cards. They should take it in turns to be the customer, 'C' and the shop assistant, 'SA'. Encourage them to be extra polite.

D Monitor and take notes on the use of indirect questions.

4A ODD PHRASE OUT

Aim
To give further practice of *so* and *such*.

Before class
Make one copy for each group of three.

In class
A Put students into groups of three and explain that this activity is a variation on the game Odd Word Out. Students have to guess the category and then find and underline the phase which doesn't match.

B Hand out the photocopies and ask students to start.

C Check students' answers and tell them to explain why each phrase doesn't fit the category.

D Ask students to find one topic from Units 1–3 and to write four phrases. They should use at least one *so* and one *such* for each. One of the phrases should be an odd one out. They should not name the category. When they are ready, they pass their paper over to another group who guess the category and underline the phrase which doesn't fit.

Answers to activity 1:
1 Politics: will lay the seeds of educational reform;
2 Economics: the leader of the party was so corrupt ...;
3 the Environment: new air freshener is so good that... .

4B WHAT'S YOUR OPINION?

Aim
To practise talking about social issues.

Before class
Make one copy for each student.

In class
A Tell students you want them to speak as much as possible in this activity by expanding their views on the topics.

B Tell students individually to read the statements and decide what their opinion is and why.

C Put students in pairs and tell them to pick three topics, then talk about them as long as they can.

5A RUNNING THE MARATHON

Aim
To practise using modals via communicative speaking practice.

Before class
Make enough copies so that each student has a part A, B or C.

In class
A Tell students that they are each going to get part of a story about running a marathon, and they have to tell each other about it.
B Put students into groups of three. Give each student the corresponding information (student 1 = Marta, student 2 = Abel, student 3 = The result)
C Tell students to read the information and then to tell each other about it, in order A then B then C.
D Tell them you want them to give their opinions about Marta and Abel. Ask them to discuss what they think happens. Put some questions on the board to get them started and indicate the structures you want them to use: e.g. *What should Abel have done? What could Marta do? What should(n't) Marta have done?*, etc.
E Then give out part C and get them to discuss what they think of the ending, e.g. *What should(n't) the author have done? How could the author have ended the story?*

5B QUESTIONS ABOUT ME

Aim
To practise the present perfect and present perfect continuous.

Before class
Make one copy for each student.

In class
A Introduce the activity by asking students to tell you two things they've been doing in the last few days.
B Hand out the photocopy and tell students to answer the questions individually.
C When finished, put students in pairs to take turns asking and answering the questions.
D Extend the activity by asking the pairs to create two more questions using the same structures (one in present perfect and the other in present perfect continuous).
E Put students in new pairs to ask and answer the new questions.

6A THE BEST HOLIDAY

Aim
To provide further practice of modifiers and vocabulary from the unit.

Before class
Make one copy for each student.

In class
A Introduce the topic by asking students what they think are important factors for a perfect holiday, and tell them they are going to talk about it.
B Hand out the photocopy and tell students to individually decide which on the list are the four most important factors to them for a good holiday.
C Put students in pairs to compare and discuss their preferences and explain their choices. Then, put two pairs together and ask them to agree on the four most important factors for a good holiday.
E Feed back by asking students to tell you what are the most important things on the list and see if you can get a class consensus.

6B PICTIONARY

Aim
To provide further practice of the structures *to have / get something done.*

Before class
Make enough copies so each small group has one set.
Cut up the phrases and put them into envelopes for each group.

In class
A Put students into small groups. Tell students they're going to play a game of pictionary.
B Tell students to take turns to pick a sentence and draw pictures related to the phrase until his / her classmates guess the sentence. Remind them that they're not allowed to say anything while they do this. The person who guesses correctly gets one point. Get all students to do the same until all the phrases have been done.
C Monitor while they're doing this for correct use of the language structures for a correction slot at the end.

7A STORIES ABOUT TOILETS

Aim
To give further practice of narrative tenses.

Before class
Make one copy for each pair of students. Cut the photocopy in half then stick them on the walls. Number each story and each pair so students B are clear about what they have to look at and read.

In class
A Tell the class they are going to read a story from Turkey or Uruguay, briefly ask them what they know about these countries.

B Put students in AB pairs and allocate half the class the story from Uruguay and half the class the story from Turkey. Student A is the writer and student B is the reader.

C Tell students B to find their story on the wall, read and remember sentences then go back to student A and dictate it. They don't have to remember the whole story, just the general idea. Tell students A to listen and write what they hear.

D When the pairs finish give them the copy from the wall to compare and use as a way of autonomous correction.

E Put two pairs together and tell them to tell their stories to each other from memory.

7B INFORMATION STARS

Aim
To practise vocabulary and participle clauses.

Before class
Make enough copies for each student to have one.

In class
A Begin the activity by drawing a five-sided star on the board and brainstorm vocabulary from the reading, e.g. words related to bullfighting. (Put the topic in the middle of the star and write the words students give you at the tips of the star.) Tell students they are going to have one minute to write as many words as they can around each star. Then handout the photocopies.

B After two minutes stop them and put them in pairs to compare ideas, then tell them to match each sentence to the correct star and write one sentence for the missing topic. Tell them compare this with another pair.

Answers
The weather = 3
The environment = 1
Plants = 2
Animals = not used

8A WHAT COULD HAVE HAPPENED?

Aim
To give practice in forming opinions and using speculative language (modals).

Before class
Make one set for each group. Cut out the cards and put each set in an envelope.

In class
A Explain the activity to students by writing the following information on the board:
The owner of the house, a young woman is sitting on the stairs crying. The burglar is lying on the floor in front of her with blood all around him. A policeman is standing in the doorway.

B Put students in small groups and give out the cards in the envelopes.

C Tell students they must decide what they think happened by picking a card and forming an opinion about it. Encourage them to use modals and model the activity. Write an example phrase on the board, e.g. *The burglar must have gone in through the window.*

D Extend the activity by comparing versions of the story in open class.

8B PREPOSITIONAL CASINO

Aim
To revise nouns and prepositions.

Before class
Make enough copies so each group of three has one.

In class
A Begin the activity by explaining the meaning of *place a bet* and ask students if they have ever been to casino.

B Put students in groups of three. Hand out the photocopies, then go through the instructions. Allocate 100 points to each group.

C Tell them to read the first sentence, decide if it's right or wrong and then place a bet on it. Once you see they have understood the game tell them to do the same with the rest of the sentences.

D Go through each answer one at a time and tell each group to either subtract or add points each time.

E The winning group is the one with the most points.

Answers

1 of	3 with	5 in	7 in
2 on	4 for	6 on	

9A TODAY'S LESSON – A QUICK QUIZ

Aim
To provide further practice of conditional (with present tense) and revise language and vocabulary.

Before class
Make one copy for each pair of students.

In class
A Ask students to close their books and in groups write down all the grammar and vocabulary they remember from the lesson. Tell them they have two minutes.
B Board their answers quickly and answer any questions.
C Tell students they are going to do a quiz on the day's lesson. They have three minutes.
D Hand out the quiz face-down and say 'start!'.
E Stop the activity and check the answers in open class. Ask them how many they got.

> **Answers**
> 1 What do you see yourself doing in the future? Can you see yourself moving to a different firm?
> 2 don't, give
> 3 You **will / You'll** be running the company in a few years if things carry on like this.
> 4 95% sure
> 5 b
> 6 who, what
> 7 answers will vary

9B HENRY'S STORY

Aim
To provide further practice of the third conditional.

Before class
Make one copy for each pair of students.

In class
A Put students in pairs and hand out the photocopy. Explain that Henry had been a very successful businessman before but his life changed because of the things he did.
B Tell students they're going to use the information about his past to write sentences using the third conditional.
C Model the activity. Write, He began arriving late for work on the board and ask students to re-express the sentence with *If he ......* plus possible endings, e.g.
If he hadn't begun arriving late for work, he wouldn't have had problems with his colleagues.

D Ask students to write five sentences about how he ended up as a tramp.
E Extend the activity be getting pairs to compare their statements.

10A MY PREDICTIONS

Aim
To provide further practice of the future perfect.

Before class
Make enough copies so that students have either an A or a B.

In class
A Write two questions on the board: *What will the world be like in 30 years? What will you have done by the end of today?* Write up a couple of their answers and point out the form.
B Tell students they are going to complete a questionnaire about their future. First they write about themselves and then they interview their partner. Monitor and help as necessary.
C Feed back by asking each student to tell the group one thing they learnt about their partner.

10B TAG SNAP

Aim
To practise question tags.

Before class
Make enough copies so each group of three has one.

In class
A Explain how to play the game by demonstrating if necessary.
B Put students into groups of three and tell them to put the questions cards face down on the table. Then, they shuffle the tag cards and divide them between the players. They place these face down in front of them. They take turns to turn over a question card in the middle, then one at a time each player turns over their tag questions – when any player sees one that matches grammatically they shout 'snap!'. That player then gets to keep the question.
C Put two pairs together and tell them to check each other's grammar.
D The player with the most correct questions at the end wins.

11A A DISASTROUS TRIP

Aim
To give further practice of uncountable nouns.

Before class
Make enough copies so that students have either an A, B or C.

In class
A Write *disastrous business trip* on the board. Tell students they have to work out what happened on the business trip by miming to their group their corresponding sentences about the trip.

B Put students in threes and hand out the phrases..

C Tell them to take turns miming the phrases. Remind them that each one contains an uncountable noun.

D Extend the activity by asking the groups to create their own sentences to continue the story. Get them to mime them for the class to guess.

11B THINGS THAT MAKE ME ...

Aim
To practise expressing feelings and opinions with extra emphasis.

Before class
Make one copy for each student.

In class
A Tell students that you are going to do an activity to help them express their emotions better in English. First, they will read some useful phrases to express feelings. Then they will look at some sentences and decide how they feel about each idea.

B Hand out the worksheets and ask students to discuss the phrases in pairs. Answer any questions.

C Get students to read the situations individually and to pick three they would like to talk about.

D Put students in pairs and tell them to tell each other how they feel about the ideas. Encourage them to develop their ideas into a conversation.

E If time, ask pairs to tell the class briefly what they discussed.

12A I'M SUPPOSED TO ......

Aim
To give further practice of the vocabulary in the unit and the language structures (*supposed to be -ing*).

Before class
Make one copy for each pair of students. Cut the handout in half.

In class
A Put students in pairs and hand out the photocopy. Tell them they have to take turns to read part of their sentence and then mine the rest. Their partner must guess the rest of their sentence. Tell them they can choose any of the sentence endings with each sentence starter and that there is not one correct answer for each sentence.

B If time, extend the activity by asking students to write similar sentences in pairs and miming them for another pair to guess.

12B HAPPINESS AND DOLPHINS

Aim
To give practice in using determiners and vocabulary related to health.

Before class
Make one copy for each pair of students, then cut in half and give each pair either an A or a B..

In class
A Tell students they are going to read an article about alternative ways to make people feel better. Later on they will tell another classmate about what they read.

B Put students in pairs. They are either an A or a B. Tell the pairs they should read their article, discuss it together and write down a maximum of eight key words that sum up the text. Then they should practise telling each other about the article using the key words.

C Hand out one article to each pair.

D When the pairs have practised re-telling their article to each other, put them into new AB pairs. Then they take turns telling and listening to the stories.

E If time, ask them if they believe what they read and if they know of any alternative ways to make people better.

13A LIFE STORY

Aim
To give further practice of using past perfect.

Before class
Make enough copies for each student to have one.

In class
A Tell students they are going to read about Aida and her life.
B Hand out the photocopies and tell students to individually match the sentences.
C When they have finished put students in AB pairs and tell them to read their stories to each other and to listen carefully to find the three differences between them.
D Check briefly as a class.

Answers
Correct order:

| 1 B | 3 F | 5 D | 7 A |
| 2 E | 4 C | 6 G | |

Differences:
A: Housewife and mum, B: Housewife and part-time cleaner
A: on her 60th birthday, B: 57th birthday
A: three children, B: four children

13B *I wish you would ...*

Aim
To give further practice of *be always -ing / wish* and *would*.

Before class
Make one copy for each pair.

In class
A Introduce the activity by writing on the board: Your mum is always telling you to tidy your room. Tell students to give you replies using I wish ...
B Put student in pairs. Tell them to match the sentences and the replies.
C When they are finished tell them to choose an *I wish ...* sentence, but not tell their partner. They then have a conversation and they have to try and naturally slip their sentence in. The first person to do this wins. You might like to give them a scenario to start them off, e.g. It's Monday morning and you've run in to your classmate on the street. They can play as many times as they wish.

Answers
Set A

| 1 C | 2 A | 3 D | 4 B |

Set B

| 1 B | 2 D | 3 A | 4 B |

14A VOCABULARY BOXES

Aim
To consolidate vocabulary related to money and extend the activity to incorporate passive structures.

Before class
Make enough copies so that each student has an A, B or C.

In class
A To introduce the activity brainstorm words related to money. Encourage them to use passive structures whenever possible e.g. *It's something that has been signed instead of money* (a cheque).
B Tell them they are going to explain the meanings of each of their words and their partner(s) must guess the word. (You could take in some dictionaries to help them find the meanings.) Let them read through their card and ask you quietly if they have any questions. If you have a few weaker students in the class they should be As.
C Extend the activity by writing questions on the board: Has money ever been withdrawn from your account without your permission? Has your bank ever decided to refuse you something? Keep students in the same group to discuss.

14B WISHES

Aim
To give further practice of the uses of *wish* to express present and past regret.

Before class
Make one copy for each student.

In class
A Introduce the activity by telling students about two things you'd like to change about your life now (using *wish* related to present situations) and two things you wish you'd done (regrets).
B Hand out the photocopy and tell students to look at the sentences and find the ones that relate to their life, then to form sentences. Monitor to make sure they are forming correct sentences.
C When they are ready put them in pairs to tell each other about their wishes (past and present).
D When finished, ask students to share some of their 'wishes' with the class.

15A CROSSWORD

Aim
To consolidate vocabulary related to food and cooking and incorporate some linking words into definitions.

Before class
Make one copy for each pair of students.

In class
A To introduce the activity briefly brainstorm words related to food and cooking, or what they can cook.
B Hand out the photocopy and tell them to do the crossword in pairs.
C Get fast finishers to help other students.
D Extend the activity by telling students to write four definitions of food from the unit and giving them to their partners to guess the answer.

> **Answers**
> Across 4 mixture, 5 stock, 8 peach, 9 stir
> Down 1 chickpeas, 2 squash, 3 flesh, 6 melt, 7 onion, 10 non-stick

15B UNUSUAL NEWS

Aim
To provide further practice of reporting verbs.

Before class
Make enough copies of set A for half the class and enough copies of set B for the other half.

In class
1 Tell students that they're going to read some interesting news stories, decide on the correct title and then complete the gaps with the correct reporting verb.
2 Hand out the photocopies so that each student has an A or a B.
3 When they've finished briefly check the answers – without going into details.
4 Put them in AB pairs and ask them to choose the funniest story they read and tell their partner about it.16A Categories

> **Answers**
> | 1 arrested | 3 alerted | 5 demanded |
> | 2 complained | 4 urged | 6 arrested |

16A CATEGORIES

Aim
To consolidate vocabulary and phrases related to business and provide practice of future continuous.

Before class
Make one copy of the game and remember to cut up the questions – these are to put on your desk so they are separate – and remove the answers.

In class
A Put students into small groups and tell them they are going to play a game to help them revise and remember words and language related to the unit. Give them two minutes to look at pp. 110–113 before they start. Ask them to choose a 'runner' from each group.
B Explain the rules: the runner comes to the teacher's desk and reads the two tasks on the card, then returns to the group to tell them what the tasks are. The group then writes down their answers. The runner then goes back to remember the next question, etc. The first group to finish says 'stop!'
C The first group to finish tells the class their answers, if anyone thinks the answers are incorrect, they say 'challenge'. If the challenge is correct, the challenger's group (or all groups) continue. The group with the most questions answered correctly wins.

16B HOW TO MAKE A PROFIT!

Aim
To provide practice of necessity and ability.

Before class
Make one copy for each student.

In class
A Introduce the activity by asking students what they look for in a good school.
B Tell students they are going to do a problem-solving activity. They have to imagine that they are business consultants who have been called in to save an English language school. In groups they read the situation, check they understand and tell them to read the brief and to think about solutions.
C Put students into small groups, tell them to read the situation and give them five minutes to come up with solutions.
D After five minutes have a group discussion and come up with a plan to save the school.

> **Suggested answers**
> (Use these as prompts if necessary.)
> 1 opening hours, range and types of classes, e.g. business English, levels
> 2 talk to the teacher's, increase salary based on results, offer additional benefits e.g extra holidays, in-house teacher training
> 3 library, computers, fresh coat of paint, new desks
> 4 reduce staff, increase fees, put restrictions on staff use of telephone

Role card 1

Information: You live in a block of flats. During the night some graffiti artists painted a large mural on the outside wall of the block. Some of the neighbours' have called a meeting to see what people think about it and what should be done.

Your opinion: You don't mind it, in fact you think it helps to make the old building look better because it's really atmospheric as it appears to be based around life in the neighbourhood. Unfortunately not everyone agrees with you. Give the other neighbours your opinion and try to persuade them that it's a positive and not a negative for the neighbourhood. Be polite so no-one gets angry! You have 10 minutes to make a collective decision.

Role card 2

Information: You live in a block of flats. During the night some graffiti artists painted a large mural on the outside wall of the block. Some of the neighbours' have called a meeting to see what people think about it and what should be done.

Your opinion: You don't really have a strong opinion about it being there – the walls were really dirty before! You think the mural is a bit dull and depressing and it's not in the least bit inspiring, especially when you have to walk past it at night. You also think it's probably not the kind of thing that some of your neighbours would want on the walls outside. Give the other neighbours your opinion and try to keep the peace by being as polite as possible! You have 10 minutes to make a collective decision.

Role card 3

Information: You live in a block of flats. During the night some graffiti artists painted a large mural on the outside wall of the block. Some of the neighbours' have called a meeting to see what people think about it and what should be done.

Your opinion: You're really keen on free expression. The idea that you have a graffiti artist is the neighbourhood is really appealing. You don't understand why some people are complaining. Try to change your neighbours opinions by telling them about the positive points of having a mural and a graffiti artist in the neighbourhood! Be as polite as possible. You have 10 minutes to make a collective decision.

Role card 4

Information: You live in a block of flats. During the night some graffiti artists painted a large mural on the outside wall of the block. Some of the neighbours' have called a meeting to see what people think about it and what should be done.

Your opinion: You really feel strongly about not allowing graffiti artists to paint wherever and whatever they want. You also feel it's important to give your opinion to the rest of the neighbours in the meeting because you know a couple of the neighbours don't have the same opinion as you. However, you really like your neighbours so you're determined to be as polite a possible. You have 10 minutes to make a collective decision.

1B GUESS THE WORD

Student A

1 an adjective which means *frightening*

2 describes something that is so interesting that it holds your attention completely

3 impossible or difficult to believe

4 the opposite of fortunately

5 an adverb which means *sadly*, often involving suffering

a unfortunately

b tragically

c scary

d gripping

e incredible

Student B

1 tune or phrase that grabs your attention and is difficult to forget

2 very funny

3 another word for *boring*

4 open to interpretation

5 something that causes strong feelings of sadness or sympathy

a dull

b ambiguous

c moving

d catchy

e hilarious

Student A

1 DEPRIVED NEIGHBOURHOOD

a It's a place that isn't very pleasant to live, where living conditions are difficult.

b It's the name of a place that is being renovated, where lots of young people live.

c It's a place that has fashionable shops, most of which belong to famous people.

2 KNOCK DOWN

a To knock down, which is a phrasal verb, means to repeatedly hit something, which makes a noise, like a door outside a house.

b To knock down, which is a phrasal verb, means to destroy a building, often when it's dangerous.

c To knock down, which isn't a phrasal verb, means to remove something from your house.

3 TRENDY

a Trendy, which is similar in meaning to old fashioned, is a word to describe something or someone unfashionable.

b Trendy, which is the opposite of grand, is used to describe people or places that are hideous.

c This word means modern, when people are influenced by the most recent fashions or ideas, it can also refer to a place.

Student B

1 TO BE RUN DOWN

a Run down, which is a phrasal verb, is used when we want to avoid dealing with a problem or difficult situation.

b Run down, which isn't a phrasal verb, means in need of repair, for example a house or neighbourhood can be run down.

c Run down, which isn't a phrasal verb, is a house where rich people live, in an up-and-coming area.

2 AN AFFLUENT NEIGHBOURHOOD

a An area where wealthy people live, most of whom have important jobs, and where there are lots of nice houses.

b An area, which is often dirty, that has hideous buildings.

C An area, whose residents are rich, that has lots of derelict houses.

3 A HIDEOUS BUILDING

a A house, which is usually old, that is attractive and impressive.

b A house, whose owner is ugly, that is grand.

c An extremely ugly house, where most people wouldn't want to live, that no-one likes.

Rio de Janiero Carnival in Brazil

Carnival is Rio's biggest event of the year. Every summer (February in this part of the world) thousands of people from all corners of the world come to join in the four-day celebration. There are hundred of parties that take place before, during and after Carnival all night and all day, with plenty of dancing and singing. And don't miss the highlight of the carnival, the famous Samba Parade. You can be sure it's something you'll never forget!

Taiwan Lantern Festival

The Taipei Lantern Festival is a stunning, colourful festival where the whole city is lit up with glittering lights. There are dragon and lion street dances, acrobatic acts and enormous, magical lantern installations in the middle of the streets. You can visit the markets to buy traditional handicrafts, or even learn how to make your own, with stalls offering fan painting, lantern making, or paper cutting. If you like oriental food you'll be in paradise because the streets are full of delicious sweets and snacks.

Glastonbury Music and Peforming Arts Festival in England

The Festival takes place in a beautiful location – 900 acres in the Vale of Avalon. It's where they say King Arthur was buried. Glastonbury Festival is the largest music and performing arts festival in the world. You'll meet all kinds of people, of all ages, backgrounds, nationalities, lifestyles and musical tastes. Each area of the Festival has its own character and there are always exciting things to do and see.

Bull running in the San Fermin Festival

Would you like to run with the bulls? Every year in July thousands pack into Pamplona to start Spain's most famous bull-running fiesta, San Fermin. Fighting bulls are let out onto the streets and run for about half a mile towards a bull ring. The runners dash along in front of the bulls – getting as close as possible – and trying to avoid getting injured by their sharp horns at the same time! Are you brave enough to run with the bulls?

3A WORD SEARCH

1 Definitions

1   It's a thing you use to hang up your clothes to dry, it's usually small and made of wood or plastic ___

2   It's a bit like blue chewing gum! You can use this if you want to stick something on the wall ___

3   If you want to see better in the dark you should use this, but you'll need some batteries ___

4   You can use this to temporarily mend a rip in your clothes. It's made of metal ___

5   It's a place you visit if you want to buy some wire ___

6   You put water in this so you can wash the floor ___

7   It's a thing you use to open a bottle of wine with ___

8   You need these if you want to keep your papers together ___

9   If you rip your shirt or dress, you use this with a needle to mend your clothes ___

2 Find the words

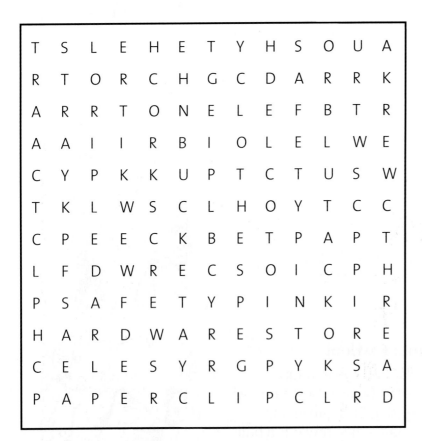

T	S	L	E	H	E	T	Y	H	S	O	U	A
R	T	O	R	C	H	G	C	D	A	R	R	K
A	R	R	T	O	N	E	L	E	F	B	T	R
A	A	I	I	R	B	I	O	L	E	L	W	E
C	Y	P	K	K	U	P	T	C	T	U	S	W
T	K	L	W	S	C	L	H	O	Y	T	C	C
C	P	E	E	C	K	B	E	T	P	A	P	T
L	F	D	W	R	E	C	S	O	I	C	P	H
P	S	A	F	E	T	Y	P	I	N	K	I	R
H	A	R	D	W	A	R	E	S	T	O	R	E
C	E	L	E	S	Y	R	G	P	Y	K	S	A
P	A	P	E	R	C	L	I	P	C	L	R	D

Activity 1

C: _____

SA: Yes, of course. What can I do for you?

C: _____

SA: Yes, lots. What size were you looking for?

C: _____

SA: No, I'm afraid not. The biggest one we have is 16 gig.

C: _____

C: I need one with a lot of memory. Would you happen to know if you have a 32 Gigabyte one?

C: Excuse me. I wonder if you could help me.

C: Do you happen to have any memory cards for a camera?

C: Oh, ok. I'll take a 16 gig one.

> **Glossary:** a Gigabyte is a unit for measuring memory in electronic goods. It is usually written as GB and informally called a *gig*.

Role cards

Student A

Customer You want to buy:	Shop Assistant You only have:
Blu Tack: medium packet	You don't stock rubbers – this is an electronics store!
A spindle of 25 recordable CDs 	 Flash drives: 2, 4, 8, and 16 GB 
Corkscrew	Picture frames: Wooden and metal White: small, medium, large Black: small and medium. 

Student B

Customer You want to buy:	Shop Assistant You only have:
A 10 GB flash drive	All your recordable CDs are 80 minutes long. You have spindles of 50 and 100.
A large, black picture frame 	You don't sell corkscrews! This isn't a kitchen shop.
A rubber – any size will do. 	Blu tack in large packets

1 _____

voting has been so dangerous that .... haven't passed the new law yet .... will lay the seeds of educational reform .... Parliament has decided to .... Democracy is dead! .... prices have gone up so much that some families ....

2 _____

in such a deep recession .... 250 businesses went bankrupt in .... headlines reveal massive bonuses paid out to .... inflation fell by 2% last .... so much money is being printed .... the leader of the party was so corrupt ....

3 _____

such an excellent harvest this year .... water pollution so bad that drinking .... such a shortage of land, they had to move ....

4 _____

government has passed a new green law .... new air freshener is so good that .... coal-fired power stations present such a threat ....

	AGREE	NOT SURE	DISAGREE
1 The more we spend on helping the unemployed, the better the economy will be.			
2 The more technology improves the worse the world will be.			
3 If people talked less about the environment the world would be a better place.			
4 The more languages you speak, the better you understand other cultures.			
5 The harder we work, the happier we will be.			
6 The faster the pace of life, the unhealthier we become.			

✂ -

	AGREE	NOT SURE	DISAGREE
1 The more we spend on helping the unemployed, the better the economy will be.			
2 The more technology improves the worse the world will be.			
3 If people talked less about the environment the world would be a better place.			
4 The more languages you speak, the better you understand other cultures.			
5 The harder we work, the happier we will be.			
6 The faster the pace of life, the unhealthier we become.			

Part A   Abel's background

Abel was a very good half-marathon runner, but he'd never yet run a full marathon. He knew that at 70 he was getting too old for such a hard race, so he decided that he would run a full marathon and it would be his last. He really wanted to try and win it and trained for five hours everyday for six months to get into shape. He also helped his best friend Marta to train for it. She surprised him by saying she wanted to keep him company and encourage him during the race. In fact, he probably dedicated too much time to her because he taught her the route, how to save energy and he even created a nutrition programme for her.

Part B   Marta's background

Marta really liked being a winner. She hated losing in anything and she wanted to be famous so she decided to run the marathon and win it any way she could. First she convinced Abel to help her because she knew he was probably one of the best marathon runners and if she learned his techniques she could win the race. She realised she would have to cheat too because Abel was so good, but that didn't matter, she was determined to do anything to win.

Part C   The result

Abel didn't win the race, he came second. Marta won. People were really surprised to see her looking so fresh at the end of the race. The truth was that Marta only ran the start and the finish of the race, the rest of the time she used the underground to cheat and cut across the course. Abel was devastated – in fact, he cried at the end of the race. Especially when he suspected that Marta had won because she'd cheated. He went home, depressed and lonely, turned the gas on and blew himself up! Marta became famous and now works on TV as a sports presenter.

5B Questions about me

1 Is there anything you've been meaning to do this week and haven't done yet? Why not?
2 Is there any sport you've never fancied doing? Why not?
3 Is there anybody you haven't seen or visited this month but should have? Why not?
4 Is there anything you've been meaning to buy? Why do you need it?
5 Is there anything you've been doing recently to keep fit? If not, why not?
6 Is there anybody you've always wanted to meet? Why?

1 Is there anything you've been meaning to do this week and haven't done yet? Why not?
2 Is there any sport you've never fancied doing? Why not?
3 Is there anybody you haven't seen or visited this month but should have? Why not?
4 Is there anything you've been meaning to buy? Why do you need it?
5 Is there anything you've been doing recently to keep fit? If not, why not?
6 Is there anybody you've always wanted to meet? Why?

1 Is there anything you've been meaning to do this week and haven't done yet? Why not?
2 Is there any sport you've never fancied doing? Why not?
3 Is there anybody you haven't seen or visited this month but should have? Why not?
4 Is there anything you've been meaning to buy? Why do you need it?
5 Is there anything you've been doing recently to keep fit? If not, why not?
6 Is there anybody you've always wanted to meet? Why?

1 Is there anything you've been meaning to do this week and haven't done yet? Why not?
2 Is there any sport you've never fancied doing? Why not?
3 Is there anybody you haven't seen or visited this month but should have? Why not?
4 Is there anything you've been meaning to buy? Why do you need it?
5 Is there anything you've been doing recently to keep fit? If not, why not?
6 Is there anybody you've always wanted to meet? Why?

- very comfortable beds
- a quiet, secluded area
- very posh surroundings
- hardly anything to do
- a bit expensive but incredibly good food
- a fairly long way from home
- absolutely loads to do
- lots of interesting places to visit
- really cheap food
- incredibly relaxing
- amazing scenery
- great nightlife
- beautiful beaches
- welcoming hosts
- pretty easy to get to
- spacious rooms
- absolutely no tourists there

- very comfortable beds
- a quiet, secluded area
- very posh surroundings
- hardly anything to do
- a bit expensive but incredibly good food
- a fairly long way from home
- absolutely loads to do
- lots of interesting places to visit
- really cheap food
- incredibly relaxing
- amazing scenery
- great nightlife
- beautiful beaches
- welcoming hosts
- pretty easy to get to
- spacious rooms
- absolutely no tourists there

- very comfortable beds
- a quiet, secluded area
- very posh surroundings
- hardly anything to do
- a bit expensive but incredibly good food
- a fairly long way from home
- absolutely loads to do
- lots of interesting places to visit
- really cheap food
- incredibly relaxing
- amazing scenery
- great nightlife
- beautiful beaches
- welcoming hosts
- pretty easy to get to
- spacious rooms
- absolutely no tourists there

- very comfortable beds
- a quiet, secluded area
- very posh surroundings
- hardly anything to do
- a bit expensive but incredibly good food
- a fairly long way from home
- absolutely loads to do
- lots of interesting places to visit
- really cheap food
- incredibly relaxing
- amazing scenery
- great nightlife
- beautiful beaches
- welcoming hosts
- pretty easy to get to
- spacious rooms
- absolutely no tourists there

You got your hair cut very short yesterday.

- -

You've just had your money stolen.

- -

You had your room painted orange last week.

- -

You've just had your teeth cleaned.

- -

You need to get your car repaired.

- -

You should get your clothes dry-cleaned.

- -

You need to get your eyes tested.

- -

You're going to get your hair dyed pink.

- -

You've just had your computer updated.

- -

You have to make your bed because you haven't made it for a week!

- -

You need to get your mobile fixed because you can't hear it when it rings.

Turkey

While I was on holiday in Turkey there was a heat wave. I decided to get out of the city because the high temperatures were unbearable. I took the ferry to visit one of the small islands around Istanbul, which were usually a bit cooler.

I decided to rent a bike because it was too hot to walk around. I saw an old man sitting next to some so I tried to ask him how much they cost to rent, if I could use one all day and if they were comfortable.

He looked at me very strangely and moved away. Suddenly I saw he had been sitting in front of the public toilets. He'd thought I was a crazy person trying to rent a toilet for the day!

Uruguay

A friend I had in Uruguay gave me an enormous jar of *Dulce de Leche* wrapped in black paper as a present when I left. I didn't tell her that I hated the taste of caramel.

I really didn't want to carry it, but it wouldn't fit in the rubbish bins, so when I arrived at the airport I went to the toilets and left it there in a corner. As I was going through passport control I saw hundreds of police officers running around and alarms soundings. People were coming out of the toilets looking terrified.

The police evacuated the airport and everybody had to stand in the pouring rain for two hours. I was completely soaked! They had thought there was a bomb wrapped in black paper in the toilets!

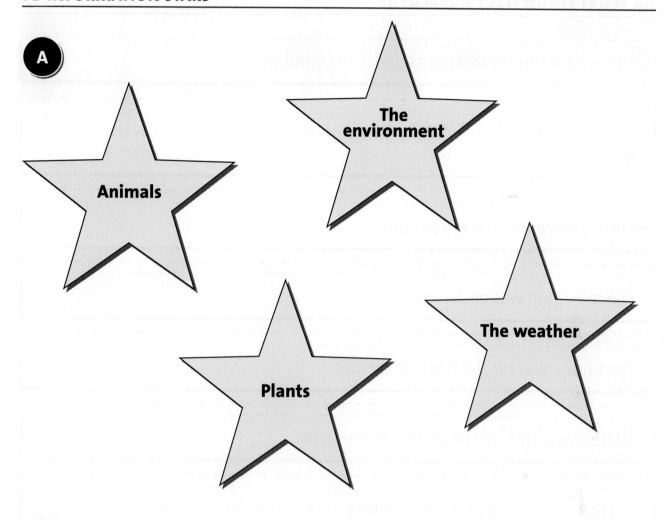

A

Animals

The environment

Plants

The weather

B

1 After several years of research aimed at collecting data about global warming, a group of scientists have presented their findings to the public.

2 Since filming the documentary showing how to make herbal remedies, the TV channel has been receiving calls from the public for further information.

3 The enormous wall intended as a device aimed at protecting the city and its´ inhabitants from tsunamis has been a complete success.

8A WHAT COULD HAVE HAPPENED?

There were muddy footprints under the window.

There were some small drops of blood under the broken window outside the house.

The lights weren't on in the house.

The television was on.

The phone was off the hook on the floor.

There was a knife in the middle of the room.

There was a lot of upturned furniture all over the sitting room.

The owner's dog was limping badly and licking its leg.

There were three large karate competition trophies on a shelf.

There was an old car parked behind some bushes.

The safe was open but nothing had been taken.

The burglar was on the floor bleeding and looking terrified.

8B PREPOSITIONAL CASINO

PREPOSITONAL CASINO

How good is your grammar? Read each sentence, complete it with the correct preposition then place your bet. You have 100 points to start.

If you're right add your bet to your total. If you are wrong subtract the bet. **Remember!** You must bet on every sentence.

1   THE THIEF WAS ACCUSED _____ BURGLARY.
    Bet _____

2   MY UNCLE WAS ARRESTED _____ SUSPICION OF FRAUD.
    Bet _____

3   I'VE NEVER HAD A PROBLEM _____ THE POLICE.
    Bet _____

4   I DON'T THINK THERE'S ANY EXCUSE _____ COMMITTING A CRIME.
    Bet _____

5   THERE'S NO POINT _____ TRYING TO ESCAPE FROM PRISON.
    Bet _____

6   HE HAS ALWAYS FOCUSED _____ HELPING EX-CRIMINALS
    Bet _____

7   PEOPLE DON'T SEEM TO HAVE ANY INTEREST _____ KEEPING UP THE VALUES OF THE PAST.
    Bet _____

- -

PREPOSITONAL CASINO

How good is your grammar? Read each sentence, complete it with the correct preposition then place your bet. You have 100 points to start.

If you're right add your bet to your total. If you are wrong subtract the bet. **Remember!** You must bet on every sentence.

1   THE THIEF WAS ACCUSED _____ BURGLARY.
    Bet _____

2   MY UNCLE WAS ARRESTED _____ SUSPICION OF FRAUD.
    Bet _____

3   I'VE NEVER HAD A PROBLEM _____ THE POLICE.
    Bet _____

4   I DON'T THINK THERE'S ANY EXCUSE _____ COMMITTING A CRIME.
    Bet _____

5   THERE'S NO POINT _____ TRYING TO ESCAPE FROM PRISON.
    Bet _____

6   HE HAS ALWAYS FOCUSED _____ HELPING EX-CRIMINALS
    Bet _____

7   PEOPLE DON'T SEEM TO HAVE ANY INTEREST _____ KEEPING UP THE VALUES OF THE PAST.
    Bet _____

1 Can you put these questions in order from the translation section?
In the future What yourself do you see doing in _____ ?
to a different you see Can yourself moving firm _____ ?

2 Can you remember which words to put in the sentence to complete it?
If things _____ improve with your new job, _____ me a ring.

3 Can you correct the grammatical mistake?
You be running the company in a few years if things carry on like this.

4 Can you remember how sure you are when you use this structure?
You're bound to get lots of offers.
95% sure   50 % sure   30 % sure

5 Can you choose the correct answers to the question?
Do you think you'll ever do a Master's?
a) I doubt b) I doubt it c) I will doubt it

6 Can you finish this statement?
Getting a good job is about _____ you know, not _____ you know.

7 Can you write one of the conditional sentences you used for the role-play about the answer to the question below?
So how're you finding your job? _____

1 Can you put these questions in order from the translation section?
In the future What yourself do you see doing in _____ ?
to a different you see Can yourself moving firm _____ ?

2 Can you remember which words to put in the sentence to complete it?
If things _____ improve with your new job, _____ me a ring.

3 Can you correct the grammatical mistake?
You be running the company in a few years if things carry on like this.

4 Can you remember how sure you are when you use this structure?
You're bound to get lots of offers.
95% sure   50 % sure   30 % sure

5 Can you choose the correct answers to the question?
Do you think you'll ever do a Master's?
a) I doubt b) I doubt it c) I will doubt it

6 Can you finish this statement?
Getting a good job is about _____ you know, not _____ you know.

7 Can you write one of the conditional sentences you used for the role-play about the answer to the question below?
So how're you finding your job? _____

10A My predictions

STUDENT A   What will / won't have you done …?

My future diary	Me	My partner
By the end of the day		
By this time tomorrow		
By next Saturday		
By next month		
In a few weeks' time		
In a few years' time		

STUDENT B   What will / won't have you done …?

My future diary	Me	My partner
By the end of the day		
By this time tomorrow		
By next Saturday		
By next month		
In a few weeks' time		
In a few years' time		

You haven't got any more invitations to the party, ...	didn't I?	didn't I?
You're not from around here, ...	was I?	was I?
You wouldn't happen to know the address, ...	have you?	have you?
You don't remember me, ...	didn't they?	didn't they?
They thrashed them, ...	will she?	will she?
It was so stuffy in there, ...	isn't it?	isn't it?
I really put my foot in it, ...	couldn't you?	couldn't you?
I wasn't supposed to know about it, ...	would you?	would you?
You could have helped me, ...	do you?	do you?
She won't like that, ...	wasn't it?	wasn't it?
You went to the party, ...	could we?	could we?
We couldn't make it some other time, ...	don't you?	don't you?
It's quite an awkward place to get to, ...	have you?	have you?
You haven't got a light, ...	are you?	are you?
You know what time it starts, ...	didn't you?	didn't you?

11A Disastrous trip

Student A

You lost your luggage at the airport.
There was rubbish all over the hotel.
The furniture in the hotel was broken.

Student B

The accommodation was dirty.
You didn't have enough information.
You couldn't stand the food.

Student C

You had to travel on the bus a long way every day.
The equipment didn't work in the office.
You didn't make any progress.

Student A

You lost your luggage at the airport.
There was rubbish all over the hotel.
The furniture in the hotel was broken.

Student B

The accommodation was dirty.
You didn't have enough information.
You couldn't stand the food.

Student C

You had to travel on the bus a long way every day.
The equipment didn't work in the office.
You didn't make any progress.

1 Useful phrases to express feelings

It's really embarrassing when ....

The thing that really infuriates me is when ....

It's quite sad when ....

What I don't like about ....

What annoys me about that is ....

It's so infuriating when ....

The thing I hate is the way that ....

2 Situations

1 You have to introduce someone to another person but you don't remember their name.
2 Buses that always run late.
3 Roadworks all over the city when you're driving and trying to get somewhere fast.
4 People who interrupt you all the time when you're talking.
5 Noisy neighbours at three o'clock in the morning!
6 Fast drivers who zigzag around all the other cars.
7 When you haven't got any change to put in the machine to buy a train or parking ticket and the ticket office is closed.
8 Long queues in shops.
9 People who talk about themselves all the time and never listen.

- -

1 Useful phrases to express feelings

It's really embarrassing when ....

The thing that really infuriates me is when ....

It's quite sad when ....

What I don't like about ....

What annoys me about that is ....

It's so infuriating when ....

The thing I hate is the way that ....

2 Situations

1 You have to introduce someone to another person but you don't remember their name.
2 Buses that always run late.
3 Roadworks all over the city when you're driving and trying to get somewhere fast.
4 People who interrupt you all the time when you're talking.
5 Noisy neighbours at three o'clock in the morning!
6 Fast drivers who zigzag around all the other cars.
7 When you haven't got any change to put in the machine to buy a train or parking ticket and the ticket office is closed.
8 Long queues in shops.
9 People who talk about themselves all the time and never listen.

12A I'M SUPPOSED TO ...

Student A

Say	Mime
1 I'm supposed to be going to a concert with a friend	.... but I've got a rash all over my face.
2 I'm supposed to have an exam this afternoon	.... but I'm short of breath.
3 I'm supposed to be playing football tomorrow	.... but I keep throwing up.
4 I'm supposed to be going away for a few days	.... but I've got a upset stomach

Student B

Say	Mime
A I'm supposed to be seeing a friend this evening	.... but I've got a temperature.
B I'm supposed to go climbing in the weekend	.... but I've got a terrible headache.
C I'm supposed to go back to work soon	.... but my leg is still in plaster.
D I'm supposed to go for a meal with my boss	.... but I've just had an operation.

12B HAPPINESS AND DOLPHINS

Student A

Healthiness – a state of mind?

by our Health Correspondant, Meena Khan.

A growing body of doctors are concerned that the effects of continuous stress are leading to far more serious illnesses than the common cold and flu. This conclusion surprises nobody; the real question is: what can be done about the problem?

A small group of scientists think they may have found the answer. They claim that the scent of a flower, the taste of chocolate or the recollection of a happy memory can help our bodies fight infections. This may seem obvious, but apparently few people realise just how much life's simple pleasures can stimulate the immune system. Furthermore, the positive effects can last for some time.

In fact, researchers believe that these positive experiences could help the body stay healthy for as long as three or even four days. They say the best medicine in the world is positive thinking. People should think about the good things that have happened to them each night before they go to bed. The effect can be dynamic – try it tonight and see for yourself.

Student A

Healthiness – a state of mind?

by our Health Correspondant, Meena Khan.

A growing body of doctors are concerned that the effects of continuous stress are leading to far more serious illnesses than the common cold and flu. This conclusion surprises nobody; the real question is: what can be done about the problem?

A small group of scientists think they may have found the answer. They claim that the scent of a flower, the taste of chocolate or the recollection of a happy memory can help our bodies fight infections. This may seem obvious, but apparently few people realise just how much life's simple pleasures can stimulate the immune system. Furthermore, the positive effects can last for some time.

In fact, researchers believe that these positive experiences could help the body stay healthy for as long as three or even four days. They say the best medicine in the world is positive thinking. People should think about the good things that have happened to them each night before they go to bed. The effect can be dynamic – try it tonight and see for yourself.

Student B

Dolphin Therapy – a new therapy for learning difficulties?

By our Health Correspondent Vera Alfero.

A group of leading scientists have gathered research to suggest that dolphins can have a positive effect on our health. None of them are sure why this is the case, but after studies using a technique called 'dolphin therapy' it seems dolphins can help people suffering from depression or learning difficulties. In one case study a family from England used this with a positive effect on their son. The family sent their nine-year-old, Nikki, for treatment in a dolphin therapy centre. Nikki has always had the physical ability to speak, but he had never learned to use it. Astonishingly, after a few days of swimming with the dolphins the little boy started trying to speak. His family were very happy with the impact this expensive treatment had on the youngster. Nikki's mother is convinced that there is something magical that happens between children and dolphins, something that no doctor or scientist can explain.

Student B

Dolphin Therapy – a new therapy for learning difficulties?

By our Health Correspondent Vera Alfero.

A group of leading scientists have gathered research to suggest that dolphins can have a positive effect on our health. None of them are sure why this is the case, but after studies using a technique called 'dolphin therapy' it seems dolphins can help people suffering from depression or learning difficulties. In one case study a family from England used this with a positive effect on their son. The family sent their nine-year-old, Nikki, for treatment in a dolphin therapy centre. Nikki has always had the physical ability to speak, but he had never learned to use it. Astonishingly, after a few days of swimming with the dolphins the little boy started trying to speak. His family were very happy with the impact this expensive treatment had on the youngster. Nikki's mother is convinced that there is something magical that happens between children and dolphins, something that no doctor or scientist can explain.

13A LIFE STORY

Student A

1	Aida had always wanted to go to university	**A**	.... that said *'if you aren't learning you aren't living.'*
2	She'd always been a housewife and mum to three children	**B**	.... but she'd never had the money or opportunity to go.
3	She'd also dedicated a lot of her time	**C**	.... *'if you aren't learning you aren't living.'*
4	She'd always said to them	**D**	.... and got decent jobs and had fairly happy lives.
5	One by one her children left home	**E**	.... and had spent her life supporting and looking after the kids.
6	On Aida's 60th birthday her children gave her a card with a cheque as her birthday present	**F**	.... to encouraging her children to study so they could have a better life.
7	Her children had written a dedication on the card to her	**G**	.... which contained enough money for her to go to university.

Student B

1	Aida had always wanted to go to university	**A**	.... that said *'if you aren't learning you aren't living.'*
2	She'd always been a housewife and a part-time cleaner	**B**	.... but she'd never had the money or opportunity to go.
3	She'd also dedicated a lot of her time	**C**	.... *'if you aren't learning you aren't living.'*
4	She'd always said to her four children	**D**	.... and got decent jobs and had fairy happy lives.
5	One by one her children left home	**E**	.... and had spent her life supporting and looking after the kids.
6	On Aida's 57th birthday her children gave her a card with a cheque as her birthday present	**F**	.... to encouraging her children to study so they could have a better life.
7	Her children had written a dedication on the card to her	**G**	.... which contained enough money for her to go to university.

Set A

Sentences

1 Your father is always asking you questions.
2 Your brother is constantly complaining about the colour of his bedroom walls.
3 The telephone company is constantly phoning you up.
4 Your sister is always borrowing your stuff without asking.

Replies

A I wish he would go out and buy some paint.
B I wish she would stop doing it!
C I wish he would leave me alone!
D I wish they wouldn't ring so much.

Set B

Sentences

1 Your mum is constantly telling you what to wear.
2 Your friend Tony is constantly on the defensive.
3 Susan is such a bore, she's constantly talking about herself.
4 Your sister's boyfriend is so bad-tempered!

Replies

A I wish she would talk about someone else!
B I wish she wouldn't interfere.
C I wish she would stop seeing him
D I wish he would lighten up a bit.

Set A

Sentences

1 Your father is always asking you questions.
2 Your brother is constantly complaining about the colour of his bedroom walls.
3 The telephone company is constantly phoning you up.
4 Your sister is always borrowing your stuff without asking.

Replies

A I wish he would go out and buy some paint.
B I wish she would stop doing it!
C I wish he would leave me alone!
D I wish they wouldn't ring so much.

Set B

Sentences

1 Your mum is constantly telling you what to wear.
2 Your friend Tony is constantly on the defensive.
3 Susan is such a bore, she's constantly talking about herself.
4 Your sister's boyfriend is so bad-tempered!

Replies

A I wish she would talk about someone else!
B I wish she wouldn't interfere.
C I wish she would stop seeing him
D I wish he would lighten up a bit.

Set A

Sentences

1 Your father is always asking you questions.
2 Your brother is constantly complaining about the colour of his bedroom walls.
3 The telephone company is constantly phoning you up.
4 Your sister is always borrowing your stuff without asking.

Replies

A I wish he would go out and buy some paint.
B I wish she would stop doing it!
C I wish he would leave me alone!
D I wish they wouldn't ring so much.

Set B

Sentences

1 Your mum is constantly telling you what to wear.
2 Your friend Tony is constantly on the defensive.
3 Susan is such a bore, she's constantly talking about herself.
4 Your sister's boyfriend is so bad-tempered!

Replies

A I wish she would talk about someone else!
B I wish she wouldn't interfere.
C I wish she would stop seeing him
D I wish he would lighten up a bit.

Set A

Sentences

1 Your father is always asking you questions.
2 Your brother is constantly complaining about the colour of his bedroom walls.
3 The telephone company is constantly phoning you up.
4 Your sister is always borrowing your stuff without asking.

Replies

A I wish he would go out and buy some paint.
B I wish she would stop doing it!
C I wish he would leave me alone!
D I wish they wouldn't ring so much.

Set B

Sentences

1 Your mum is constantly telling you what to wear.
2 Your friend Tony is constantly on the defensive.
3 Susan is such a bore, she's constantly talking about herself.
4 Your sister's boyfriend is so bad-tempered!

Replies

A I wish she would talk about someone else!
B I wish she wouldn't interfere.
C I wish she would stop seeing him
D I wish he would lighten up a bit.

Student A

account	currency	loan	money
overdraft	debt	credit	cash

✂ -

Student B

to withdraw	to launder	to apply for	to borrow
to lend	to run out of	to withdraw	to pay off

✂ -

Student C

pin number	loan shark	foreign currency	cash point
standing order	cheque	refund	identification

Things I'd like to be different

I wish	I had I was / were I lived I could I wasn't / weren't I didn't	in another country / play the piano stronger / tidier / so careless / so tired solve my money problems / save more a flat of my own / a car / a new TV help my family more / open a bank account win the lottery / buy a house spend so much money / have to work so hard

Regrets I have

I wish	I had I could have I hadn't I had been	studied more / gone to university / listened to my parents more more ambitious / more careful / less greedy visited another country last year / saved more money in the past stayed in my old job / started the new project taken out a big loan / borrowed money from my family

✂ -

Things I'd like to be different

I wish	I had I was / were I lived I could I wasn't / weren't I didn't	in another country / play the piano stronger / tidier / so careless / so tired solve my money problems / save more a flat of my own / a car / a new TV help my family more / open a bank account win the lottery / buy a house spend so much money / have to work so hard

Regrets I have

I wish	I had I could have I hadn't I had been	studied more / gone to university / listened to my parents more more ambitious / more careful / less greedy visited another country last year / saved more money in the past stayed in my old job / started the new project taken out a big loan / borrowed money from my family

15A CROSSWORD

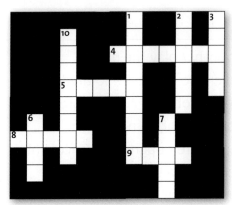

Across ⇨

4 A substance made from a combination of different things.

5 A liquid used to add flavour to food and which is made by boiling meat or fish bones or vegetables in water.

8 This is a fruit with juicy sweet yellow flesh, slightly furry red and yellow skin and a large seed in its centre.

9 To mix a liquid by moving an object, (a spoon for example) in a circular pattern.

Down ⇩

1 Hard pale brown round beans which can be cooked and eaten.

2 To press something very hard so that it is broken or its shape is destroyed.

3 The soft inside part of a fruit or vegetable

6 To turn something solid into something soft or liquid.

7 A brown or red vegetable on the outside and white in the inside, with a strongish smell and flavour, made up of several layers surrounding each other tightly in a round shape.

10 With these pans you can use less oil because your food won't get stuck to the bottom.

Across ⇨

4 A substance made from a combination of different things.

5 A liquid used to add flavour to food and which is made by boiling meat or fish bones or vegetables in water.

8 This is a fruit with juicy sweet yellow flesh, slightly furry red and yellow skin and a large seed in its centre.

9 To mix a liquid by moving an object, (a spoon for example) in a circular pattern.

Down ⇩

1 Hard pale brown round beans which can be cooked and eaten.

2 To press something very hard so that it is broken or its shape is destroyed.

3 The soft inside part of a fruit or vegetable

6 To turn something solid into something soft or liquid.

7 A brown or red vegetable on the outside and white in the inside, with a strongish smell and flavour, made up of several layers surrounding each other tightly in a round shape.

10 With these pans you can use less oil because your food won't get stuck to the bottom.

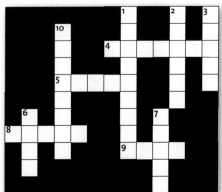

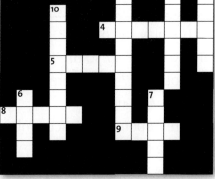

Across ⇨

4 A substance made from a combination of different things.

5 A liquid used to add flavour to food and which is made by boiling meat or fish bones or vegetables in water.

8 This is a fruit with juicy sweet yellow flesh, slightly furry red and yellow skin and a large seed in its centre.

9 To mix a liquid by moving an object, (a spoon for example) in a circular pattern.

Down ⇩

1 Hard pale brown round beans which can be cooked and eaten.

2 To press something very hard so that it is broken or its shape is destroyed.

3 The soft inside part of a fruit or vegetable

6 To turn something solid into something soft or liquid.

7 A brown or red vegetable on the outside and white in the inside, with a strongish smell and flavour, made up of several layers surrounding each other tightly in a round shape.

10 With these pans you can use less oil because your food won't get stuck to the bottom.

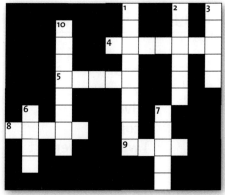

Across ⇨

4 A substance made from a combination of different things.

5 A liquid used to add flavour to food and which is made by boiling meat or fish bones or vegetables in water.

8 This is a fruit with juicy sweet yellow flesh, slightly furry red and yellow skin and a large seed in its centre.

9 To mix a liquid by moving an object, (a spoon for example) in a circular pattern.

Down ⇩

1 Hard pale brown round beans which can be cooked and eaten.

2 To press something very hard so that it is broken or its shape is destroyed.

3 The soft inside part of a fruit or vegetable

6 To turn something solid into something soft or liquid.

7 A brown or red vegetable on the outside and white in the inside, with a strongish smell and flavour, made up of several layers surrounding each other tightly in a round shape.

10 With these pans you can use less oil because your food won't get stuck to the bottom.

Student A

Story 1: A chef from Mexico city was fined for careless bicycle riding. When he was 1 _____ he was riding without his hands on the handlebars reading a newspaper. He told the court, 'this is the only chance I ever get to read a newspaper.'

Story 2: A thief stole a small fridge from a shop in London. When he got home and turned it on, he found that it didn't work. He then took the fridge back to the shop and demanded that it was repaired free of charge. When he couldn't produce a receipt, his request was turned down, so he went round to the police station and 2 _____ During his interview with the police sergeant he was charged with theft – the shop where the theif had stolen the fridge from had reported the theft to the same police station that very morning.

Story 3: A note thrown from a train yesterday landed on a platform in York station. It read, *Mrs White, of 32 Howden Road, Bloxy, Staffordshire, has the oven on with a chicken inside. Please inform the police.'* Luckily, a railway official picked up the note and passed on the message. The Police 3 _____ the fire brigade, and two fire-fighters went to the house and turned off the oven.

■ **The unhappy thief**   ■ **Read and Ride!**   ■ **Don't burn the dinner!**

Story 1: arrested / accused   **Story 2:** claimed / complained   **Story 3:** alerted / urged

Student B

Story 1: A resident of Canterbury, England, bought a tin of Australian peaches. Inside the fruit tin was a bright green and brown insect. The man complained to the Health Department and was told he was a lucky man to find such a rare insect. The officials from the Health Department 4 _____ him to donate the rare insect to the London Museum of Natural History.

Story 2: A guide at Windsor Castle was struggling to make herself heard over the noise of low flying aircraft coming into land at nearby Heathrow Airport. She was interrupted by a tourist who 5 _____ to know what was wrong with the local planning office, and why had they built the castle so close to the airport.

Story 3: A Parisian burglar broke into a house in a suburb of Pairs in 2006. Once inside he began to feel hungry and so went in search of a snack. He went into the kitchen and found his favourite cheese, biscuits and three bottles of champagne. Before he started work he sat down and polished off the lot: the biscuits, cheese and all the champagne. After a while he began to feel sleepy and decided that he would lie down and digest his meal in comfort. He was 6 _____ the next morning fast asleep upstairs in the spare bedroom.

■ **Look before you eat!**   ■ **A dangerous sleep**   ■ **Planes, people and places**

Story 1: complained / urged   **Story 2:** demanded / blamed   **Story 3:** warned / arrested

1 Two example sentences of how to sound more polite by using *would*.	**2** Two possible endings for this phrase: *I'll be taking the seven o'clock plane so ...*	**3** Two characteristics of successful people	**4** Two ways to complete this phrase *a good business person is constantly on the look out for ...*
5 Two ways to say why you're phoning a business colleague.	**6** Two ways Telesnky made his money.	**7** A phrase that means: *money you have earned in a business after paying for everything else.*	**8** A phrasal verb that means to begin a new business.

- -

Suggested answers (for teacher's use)
1 Friday would be good for me, would that suit you? / Would you mind spelling that for me? Would you like .... ?/ Would it be possible .... ?
2 I won't make it home in time for dinner. / I will see you in the office. I should just make the meeting.
3 They're creative / seize opportunities / high achievers / hard workers etc.
4 new opportunities, new business, new ways to make a profit, etc.
5 I'm just phoning / calling to remind you / ask you a favour / pass on a message / to check ...
6 He bought a delicatessen and sold it for a profit, he climbed the corporate ladder and became a UK sales manager, set up a plastic recycling business
7 annual profit
8 set up

Situation:

You are part of a business team of experts asked to save a small language school called 'English Real Quick'. The school was set up about 10 years ago and it used to make a profit. The year before it broke even and last year it made a loss. It offers English classes to local people and translation services as well. Over the past year classes have got smaller. The school needs to improve facilities and looks quite shabby. The school has also lost its family feel, partly because teachers feel overworked and underpaid.

Brief:

The school owner has asked you to provide some advice on how to save the school. Your job is to think about these areas and report back with suggestions on:

1 how to improve services

2 how to improve teaching

3 how to improve facilities

4 how to cut costs

Situation:

You are part of a business team of experts asked to save a small language school called 'English Real Quick'. The school was set up about 10 years ago and it used to make a profit. The year before it broke even and last year it made a loss. It offers English classes to local people and translation services as well. Over the past year classes have got smaller. The school needs to improve facilities and looks quite shabby. The school has also lost its family feel, partly because teachers feel overworked and underpaid.

Brief:

The school owner has asked you to provide some advice on how to save the school. Your job is to think about these areas and report back with suggestions on:

1 how to improve services

2 how to improve teaching

3 how to improve facilities

4 how to cut costs

GRAMMAR REFERENCE

01 ART AND ENTERTAINMENT

Talking about habits

Exercise 1
1 correct
2 I usually go and see films...
3 correct
4 I don't see her as much as I used to, because ...
5 He's always disappearing ...
6 I didn't used to do ...
7 I don't tend to eat out...
8 When I lived in New York, I used to go running ...

Exercise 2
1 As a rule I only listen to classical music.
2 I don't like them as much as I used to.
3 He doesn't tend to do much exercise.
4 We used to fight all the time when we were kids.
5 I'll go to the theatre once in a while, but I don't go every week or anything.
6 They're always watching TV in their house.
7 He was really fit. He would cycle 50km every day.
8 I hardly ever eat any foreign food.

Adjectives and adverbs

Exercise 1
1 frequent
2 occasionally
3 hard
4 later
5 Funnily
6 catchy
7 recent, disturbingly
8 Interestingly, beautifully

Exercise 2
1 I never download films from the Internet.
2 I've hardly seen him all day.
3 He reacted fairly badly to the news.
4 I'm going fishing later in the week.
5 To be honest, I haven't even picked up a book lately.
6 The care was completely destroyed, but amazingly he escaped without a scratch.
7 The special effects are amazing – just incredibly realistic.
8 They got married in 2005, but sadly he died soon after.

Exercise 3
1 e	4 i	7 d
2 j	5 a	8 c
3 b	6 g	9 h

02 SIGHTSEEING

Non-defining relative clauses

Exercise 1
1 who
2 where
3 every single one of which
4 by which time
5 some of which
6 during which time
7 which
8 at which point
9 none of which

Exercise 2
1 We saw Big Ben, Buckingham Palace, Tower Bridge and the London eye, which were all amazing.
2 There were loads of recommendations on the web, most of which were really helpful.
3 We stayed out dancing until two in the morning, by which time I was completely exhausted.
4 We spent a week in Bolivia, during which time the election was on.
5 We spent two days in Bergen, where my girlfriend has family, and then drove down to Stavenger.
6 Chen's grandfather, who is 97, still lives at home with the rest of his family.

The future

Exercise 1
1 A: Shall we get a coffee?
   B: Good idea. You sit here and I'll go and get them.
2 A: I'm meeting Mary later. Do you want to come?
   B: No, I've got an exam tomorrow. I'm going to do some revision.
3 A: I've got to go I'm late for class. It starts in ten minutes.
   B: OK Hey, where is it? I'll give you a lift.
4 A: That was my dad. He's locked himself out of the house. He wants me to go and let him in. Sorry, we'll have to chat another time.
   B: I'll walk with you. I've got to go that way anyway.

5 A: We're going to Gardaland tomorrow.
  B: But what will you do if the weather's bad? The forecast said it might rain.
  A: I don't know. I haven't asked the others yet. We are probably still going to go. I think there are quite a few rides that are covered over.
  B: I'm sure you're bound to enjoy yourselves anyway.

03 THINGS YOU NEED

if, so and *to* for describing purpose

Exercise 1

1 so	4 if	7 so
2 to	5 to	8 so
3 if	6 if	9 to

Exercise 2

1 We need some matches or something to light the stove.
2 Maybe you should wrap some tape round where there's a crack so it doesn't leak.
3 You'll need wire cutters if you want to cut that – not scissors.
4 Have you got something I can stand on so I can change this light bulb?
5 Can't you just use some string to tie it together and make a handle to carry it?

Indirect questions

Exercise 1

1 think
2 idea
3 sure
4 idea
5 happen
6 who
7 what
8 if / whether

Exercise 2

1 wonder if
2 I could have a
3 if they open on
4 correct
5 do you know when they stopped selling
6 correct
7 toilets are on
8 where the best restaurant is.

04 SOCIETY

So / Such

Exercise 1

1 A: 1 so 2 such 3 so 4 so 5 such 6 So 7 such 8 so
2 B: 1 f 2 h 3 d 4 a 5 g 6 e 7 b 8 c

Exercise 2

1 much
2 few
3 many
4 many
5 little

The..., The... +Comparatives

Exercise 1

1 fatter
2 less
3 stronger
4 fewer
5 greater
6 faster
7 stronger
8 more

05 SPORTS AND INTERESTS

Should(n't) have, could(n't) have, would(n't) have

Exercise 1

1 should've
2 shouldn't have
3 should've, wouldn't have
4 underestimated, should've
5 should've, he might not have
6 might've been, could've

Exercise 2

1 would've got
2 would've like
3 wouldn't have minded
4 wouldn't have invited
5 could've broken
6 could've hurt
7 could've had
8 could've done

Present perfect continious/present perfect simple

Exercise 1

1 for
2 all
3 since
4 never
5 yet
6 already
7 always, since

Exercise 2

1 A: Have you managed,
  B: I've been calling,
2 A: Have you seen,
  B: I've been meaning, I just haven't had,

3 A: has Wayne decided,
  B: he's been thinking, He's been looking for, has found,
4 A: she's only played,
  B: She's always been

06 ACCOMMODATION

Modifiers

Exercise
1 This coffee is not very strong,
2 It was absolutely boiling in the tent,
3 There was hardly anyone on the beach,
4 Personally, I thought it was a bit too loud.
5 It was quite expensive,
6 It wasn't particularly warm / hot at night,
7 I don't know the area very well

Have / get something done

Exercise
1 I'm thinking of getting it straightened
2 You should get that photo framed
3 I'm going to have to have the tooth taken out
4 they had all their money and passports stolen
5 we should have had it checked

07 NATURE

Narrative tenses

Exercise
1 couldn't get to sleep,
2 I had forgotten,
3 I got caught,
4 It had got so dark,
5 the snow had melted,
6 I got back,
7 came down,
8 the campsite still hadn't dried out

Participle clauses

Exercise
1 caused
2 affected
3 imported
4 taking, doing
5 damaged
6 funded
7 freed
8 leading, opposing

08 LAW AND ORDER

Present and past infinitives

Exercise 1
1 can't be
2 must be
3 can't be
4 must be
5 must be
6 can't be
7 can't have looked
8 must have taken
9 must have hurt
10 can't have been
11 can't have done
12 must have escaped

Exercise 2
1 B: You must have been,
  A: I might, B: You should,
2 A: He can't be,
  B: He might be,
3 B: she should've done,
  A: It can't have been,
4 A: I might have done,
  B: We should go, I should have reminded

Nouns and prepositions

Exercise 1
1 involvement in
2 addiction to
3 ban on
4 access to
5 damage to
6 anger at
7 recipe for
8 decrease over the last few years in
9 awareness of

Exercise 2
1 a in b for
2 a to b of
3 a against b of
4 a with b about
5 a with, about b among, towards

09 CAREERS AND STUDYING

Conditionals with present tenses

Exercise 1

1 d	3 f	5 b	7 h
2 c	4 g	6 a	8 e

Conditionals with past tenses

Exercise 1
1 been
2 not
3 went
4 stayed
5 would
6 Would
7 have
8 would
9 had
10 be
11 hadn't

10 SOCIALISING

Future perfect

Exercise 1
1 I'm going
2 I'll have lived
3 ease off
4 will probably have started
5 I'm helping, we should've finished
6 you will've spent
7 won't have
8 should've

Question tags

Exercise 1
1 A: You'd like a coffee, wouldn't you?
2 A: You knew him quite well, didn't you?
3 correct
4 A: You weren't at the last class, were you?
5 correct
6 A: You haven't heard of Shakira, have you? / You've heard of Shakira, haven't you?

Exercise 2
1 haven't you?
2 isn't it?
3 don't you?
4 aren't we?
5 should he?
6 can they?

11 TRANSPORT AND TRAVEL

Uncountable nouns

Exercise 1
1 a coffee
2 understanding
3 a really lovely dinner
4 a very happy marriage
5 an understanding
6 dinner
7 coffee
8 Marriage

Exercise 2
1 My **hair** is getting really long. I need a haircut
2 There **is a lot** of accommodation in the town
3 correct
4 There weren't that many **people** in class today
5 The news this week **is** so depressing
6 Sorry, I'm late. I had some **trouble** with my car
7 The tourist board gave me some really useful **advice**
8 correct

Emphatic structures

Exercise 1
1 it + when
2 the thing + lack
3 it + sitting
4 what + amount
5 what + going
6 what + number
7 it + finding
8 the thing + lack
9 what + fact

12 HEALTH AND MEDICINE

Supposed to be –ing and should

Exercise 1
1 should
2 going
3 shouldn't
4 is probably going to
5 supposed to be having
6 shouldn't have
7 I doubt anyone will be
8 supposed to be playing

Determiners

Exercise 1
1 I didn't like **either** of the two treatments, personally
2 They said they had **no** record of my appointment
3 Half **of** the class have **the** flu and most of the other students soon will have
4 Each **of** the three operations lasted about five hours
5 So many **people** make themselves ill through stress
6 **Neither** of my brothers **ever** go for check-ups
7 Every **doctor** I saw failed to diagnose me properly
8 The **whole** hospital was absolutely spotless
9 It's just good to know what all the options **are**
10 They just haven't invested **enough money**

13 LIFE EVENTS

Be always / constantly + -ing / i wish + would

Exercise 1
1 I wish he **would** tidy up sometimes. He's so messy!
2 He's so stubborn. **He never admits** he's wrong!
3 He's so manipulative. **He's** always trying to make me feel guilty.
4 correct
5 I wish he **were / was** more assertive and that he'd defend himself a bit more.
6 She's so cheerful. **She's always** smiling and laughing.
7 correct
8 I really wish **she wouldn't** go on about her boyfriend all the time. It just gets very boring.

Exercise 2
1 He constantly interrupts her when she's talking.
2 I wish she would turn her music down while I'm studying.
3 I wish he wouldn't speak to me as if I were a child.
4 I really wish he weren't so mean and that he wouldn't buy the cheapest thing all the time.
5 They are always joking and messing around.

Past perfect simple and continuous

Exercise 1
1 had won
2 had been stealing
3 had forgotten
4 had been suffering, hadn't told
5 had missed, had been going
6 had been managing, had refused

14 BANKS AND MONEY

Passives

Exercise 1
1 1 had been cloned 2 go through, 3 was asked, 4 had been blocked
2 1 had run up, 2 went, 3 were made, 4 was repossessed, 5 was left
3 1 being involved, 2 had transferred, 3 was arrested, 4 be sentenced, 5 denies / has denied

Wish

Exercise 1
1 didn't have to
2 had thought
3 would cut
4 had booked
5 could've come

15 FOOD

Linking ideas
and, after, once, until, then, afterwards

Exercise
1 as, once
2 despite, then
3 in case, so
4 for, otherwise
5 provided / if, until

Reporting verbs

Exercise
1 correct
2 My grandmother always insists **on** making her...
3 ...and my dad demanded **he put**...
4 ...suggested **that I** start keeping...
5 ...the waiter informed **us / told us** that...
6 ...he just totally **refuses to** eat anything...
7 ...the waiter offered **to give** us...
8 correct

16 BUSINESS

Future continuous

Exercise
1 c	3 a	5 g	7 d
2 e	4 f	6 h	8 b

Expressing necessity and ability

Exercise
1 has enabled us to step up
2 lets you monitor
3 we won't be able to
4 were forced to
5 hadn't made me tell